Nottingham Trent University
CLIFTON LIBRARY
www.ntu.ac.uk/llr

Enquiries: 0115 848 2175

Narratives of Place in Literature and Film

Narratives of place link people and geographic location with a cultural imaginary through literature and visual narration. Contemporary literature and film often frame narratives with specific geographic locations, which saturate the narrative with cultural meanings in relation to natural and man-made landscapes. This interdisciplinary collection seeks to interrogate such connections to probe how place is narrativized in literature and film. Utilizing close readings of specific filmic and literary texts, all chapters serve to tease out cultural and historical meanings in respect of human engagement with landscapes. Always mindful of national, cultural, and topographical specificity, the book is structured around five core themes: Contested Histories of Place; Environmental Landscapes; City-scapes; The Social Construction of Place; and Landscapes of Belonging.

Steven Allen is Senior Lecturer in Film Studies at the University of Winchester, UK, where he is also the Program Leader. He has published widely on Australian cinema, animation, representations of landscapes, and cultural memory. He is a co-editor of *Framing Film: Cinema and the Visual Arts* and the author of *Cinema, Pain and Pleasure: Consent and the Controlled Body*. Recent research has centered on Australian cinema including "The Undead Down Under" (in *The Zombie Renaissance in Popular Culture* (Palgrave Macmillan)) and "Australian Animation: Landscape, Isolation and Connections" (in *Animated Landscapes: History, Form and Function* (Bloomsbury)). He is currently writing a monograph entitled *Decentring the Outback in Australian Cinema* (Palgrave Macmillan) and is a judge for the Australian Teachers of Media awards.

Kirsten Møllegaard is a Professor of English at the University of Hawai'i at Hilo. She teaches courses in comics and graphic novels, gender and women's studies, film, literature, myth and folklore, and rhetoric. Her research interests focus on the dynamics of places, people, and stories past and present. Her research articles and book reviews have appeared in *International Journal of Comic Art, Journal of American Culture, Journal of Popular Culture, Supernatural Studies, Western American Literature*, and *Folklore*. Her most recent book chapters appear in *The Absent Mother in the Cultural Imagination* (2017); *Toy Stories: The Toy as Hero in Literature, Comics, and Film* (2017); *Folk Belief and Traditions of the Supernatural* (2016); and *Unsettling Assumptions: Tradition, Gender, Drag* (2014). She serves on the board of directors of the Hawai'i Council for the Humanities and enthusiastically supports public humanities events on Hawai'i Island.

Routledge Research in Cultural and Media Studies

For more information about this series, please visit: https://www.routledge.com

Narratives of Place in Literature and Film

Edited by Steven Allen and
Kirsten Møllegaard

Routledge
Taylor & Francis Group

NEW YORK AND LONDON

First published 2019
by Routledge
52 Vanderbilt Avenue, New York, NY 10017

and by Routledge
2 Park Square, Milton Park, Abingdon, Oxon OX14 4RN

*Routledge is an imprint of the Taylor & Francis Group, an
informa business*

© 2019 Taylor & Francis

Library of Congress Cataloging-in-Publication Data
CIP data has been applied for.

ISBN: 978-1-138-49992-8 (hbk)
ISBN: 978-1-351-01383-3 (ebk)

Typeset in Sabon
by codeMantra

For Sarah, as always, and in loving memory of P.K.A. (Trish) Reynolds (1933–2018).

For John.

Contents

List of Contributors

Steven Allen is a Senior Lecturer in Film Studies at the University of Winchester, UK, where he is also the Program Leader. He has published widely on Australian cinema, animation, representations of landscapes, and cultural memory. He is a co-editor of *Framing Film: Cinema and the Visual Arts* and the author of *Cinema, Pain and Pleasure: Consent and the Controlled Body*. Recent research has centered on Australian cinema including "The Undead Down Under" (in *The Zombie Renaissance in Popular Culture* (Palgrave Macmillan)) and "Australian Animation: Landscape, Isolation and Connections" (in *Animated Landscapes: History, Form and Function* (Bloomsbury)). He is currently writing a monograph entitled *Decentring the Outback in Australian Cinema* (Palgrave Macmillan) and is a judge for the Australian Teachers of Media awards.

Daniel Andersson is an Associate Professor in Scandinavian Languages at Umeå University in Northern Sweden. Recently, he has studied the social and linguistic construction of nature and place in written representations of the colonization of Lapland, a project from which his chapter in this collection has emanated. A monograph (in Swedish) on this theme is also currently under publication. Another recent project deals with the contemporary efforts to make Sami place names visible on road signs in Northern Sweden, and what these processes tell about the significance of indigenous place names in postcolonial societies. A case study of the efforts made to get the Ume Sami name *Ubmeje* approved as an official name for the city of Umeå is to be published in the journal *Scandinavian Studies*.

Sarah Casey Benyahia is a film and media studies teacher and is completing a PhD at the University of Essex. The focus of her research is memory, time, and history in contemporary art house cinema, identifying the emergence of the temporal gateway film, a form of cinema which explores the effects of traumatic national events through the experience of temporality. She is the author of several film studies textbooks as well as the author of "Salander in Cyberspace" in Peacock, S. (ed) *Stieg Larsson's Millennium Trilogy* (Palgrave, 2012), co-author of

Doing Film Studies (Routledge, 2012), *Crime* (Routledge, 2011), and has contributed essays on *Caché* and *Todo Sobre Mi Madre* to *The Routledge Encyclopedia of Films* (2014).

Pat Brereton is a Professor in the School of Communications at Dublin City University, Ireland. His books include *Hollywood Utopia: Ecology in Contemporary American Cinema* (2005), *Continuum Guide to Media Education* (2001), the *Historical Dictionary of Irish Cinema* (2007) with Roderick Flynn, *Smart Cinema: DVD Add-ons and New Audience Pleasures* (2012), and *Environmental Ethics and Film* (2016). Together with numerous journal articles and book chapters, he is currently working on a study entitled *Environmental Literacy: Digital Media Audiences*, which is due for publication by Routledge in 2019. He is committed to a wide range of interdisciplinary studies and research, focused around Ireland, Environmental Communications and New Media studies.

Stuti Govil is currently pursuing a PhD at the Department of Geography, Rutgers University. She graduated with a Master's degree in Critical Media and Cultural Studies from School of Oriental and African Studies (SOAS), University of London, and pursued a Bachelor's degree in Journalism from Kamala Nehru College, University of Delhi. Her primary research interests lie in the intersection of critical theory and urban studies and the ways in which they are demarcated across various fault lines. She hopes to successfully document one day in the life of a city. She has gained experience working in media, development, and education sectors. She managed academics and helped design the curriculum at the Vedica Scholars Programme for Women – a management and liberal arts course dedicated to building a cadre of women professionals in India. She also worked as a Consultant with the World Bank, South Asia Poverty Reduction Group, advising on privacy and open governance laws.

Kylo-Patrick R. Hart (PhD, University of Michigan) is Chair of the Department of Film, Television and Digital Media at Texas Christian University, where he teaches courses in film and television history, theory, and criticism, film screenwriting, and queer media studies. He is the author or editor of several books about media, including *The AIDS Movie: Representing a Pandemic in Film and Television*, *Film and Sexual Politics*, *Film and Television Stardom*, *Images for a Generation Doomed: The Films and Career of Gregg Araki*, *Living in the Limelight: Dynamics of the Celebrity Experience*, *Queer Males in Contemporary Cinema: Becoming Visible*, and *Queer TV in the 21st Century: Essays on Broadcasting from Taboo to Acceptance*.

Matthew Kerry's research interests are in film representations of landscape and national identity. His monograph *The Holiday and British*

Film (2012) looks at representations of the holiday in British film, from the sublime to the raucous. In particular, he analyzes the relationship between places of leisure and the construction of national identity. Kerry's chapter in *Filmurbia, Screening the Suburbs* (2017) examines representations of postwar suburbia by the Children's Film Foundation and the ways in which children form identities by consuming the streets. He has also written several articles on home movies and amateur film, and is the co-author of *Introducing Media Practice: The Essential Guide* (2018), a core textbook for undergraduate students of media practice. Kerry lectures in media at Nottingham Trent University, UK.

C. Yamini Krishna is a PhD scholar from the Department of Film Studies, The English and Foreign Languages University, Hyderabad. Her work is on the history of cinema in Hyderabad. She studies the history of cinema as a part of the sociocultural history of the city. Her other areas of interest are urban studies, princely states, cultural history, and digital cultures. She has received the Centre for Study of Developing Societies fellowship in 2015–2016 and Charles Wallace Trust Fellowship in 2017. She has presented her work at several international conferences.

Danica Sterud Miller (Puyallup Tribe of Indians) is an Assistant Professor of American Indian Studies at the University of Washington Tacoma. She grew up on one of the last unceded lands of Puyallup Territory, which is necessarily reflected throughout her academic work. She has written extensively on American Indian literature, though now her research focuses on her twinned obsessions of Puyallup sovereignty and Lushootseed language revitalization.

Michael P. Moreno is an Associate Professor of English and Diversity Studies at Green River College in the state of Washington. He earned his PhD from the University of California, Riverside, in 2007 in English with disciplinary concentrations in Latinx literature and culture, twentieth/twenty-first century American literature, and spatial theory. Publications include *Term Paper Resource Guide to Latino History*; anthological chapters in *Strange Phenomena: Time, the City and the Literary Imagination*; *We Wear the Mask: Paul Lawrence Dunbar and the Representation of Black Identity*; *Speaking desde las heridas: Cibertestimonios Transfronterizos/Transborder (September 11, 2001–March 11, 2007)*; *Reel Histories: Studies in American Film*; and journal articles in *Reconstruction: Studies in Contemporary Culture*; *Iowa Journal of Cultural Studies*; *Journal X: A Journal in Culture & Criticism*; and *British Association for American Studies Journal*.

Kirsten Møllegaard is a Professor of English at the University of Hawai'i at Hilo. She teaches courses in comics and graphic novels, gender and women's studies, film, literature, myth and folklore, and rhetoric. Her research interests focus on the dynamics of places, people, and stories past and present. Her research articles and book reviews have appeared in *International Journal of Comic Art, Journal of American Culture, Journal of Popular Culture, Supernatural Studies, Western American Literature,* and *Folklore.* Her most recent book chapters appear in *The Absent Mother in the Cultural Imagination* (2017); *Toy Stories: The Toy as Hero in Literature, Comics, and Film* (2017); *Folk Belief and Traditions of the Supernatural* (2016); and *Unsettling Assumptions: Tradition, Gender, Drag* (2014). She serves on the board of directors of the Hawai'i Council for the Humanities and enthusiastically supports public humanities events on Hawai'i Island.

Addamms Songe Mututa is a German Academic Exchange Service (DAAD) researcher, studying dual PhD in film and cities at Eberhard Karls Universität Tübingen and the University of the Witwatersrand. Broadly, he is engaged in literary cultures of the Global South, with interest in African cinema theory and practice, cultural and literary studies, and cities and citizenship. Previously, he graduated from Kenyatta University, Nairobi, with a Master of Art degree in Theater Arts and Film Technology. He holds a Bachelor of Creative Arts degree from Moi University, Eldoret. He is skilled in video production technologies and graphics design, with extensive experience in multimedia management and production.

Aparajita Nanda is a recipient of a Visiting Associate Professorship to the departments of English and African American Studies, University of California, Berkeley, and a Fulbright faculty teaching scholarship, and now teaches at the University of California, Berkeley, and Santa Clara University. Her recent book publications include *Black California, The Strangled Cry, Romancing the Strange,* and *Ethnic Literatures and Transnationalism: Critical Imaginaries for a Global World.* She has published more than twelve book chapters, including her latest ones on California literature with Cambridge University Press, and Octavia Butler in the Modern Language Association publication, *Approaches to Teaching Octavia E. Butler in the Academy.* She has published several articles in peer-reviewed journals as well as academic treatises (by invitation) for *Oxford African American Studies* edited by Henry Louis Gates, Jr.

David M. Robinson is the Distinguished Professor Emeritus of American Literature and the Director Emeritus of the Center for the Humanities at Oregon State University. He has held fellowships from the National Endowment for the Humanities and the American Council of Learned Societies and served as Fulbright Professor at the University of Heidelberg, Germany. In 2010 he was elected a Fellow of the

Massachusetts Historical Society. He authored the chapter "Emerson, Thoreau, Fuller and Transcendentalism" for the Duke University Press Annual, *American Literary Scholarship*, from 1988 to 2008. His publications include *Natural Life: Thoreau's Worldly Transcendentalism* (Cornell); *Emerson and the Conduct of Life* (Cambridge); *World of Relations: The Achievement of Peter Taylor* (Kentucky); *The Unitarians and the Universalists* (Greenwood); "Margaret Fuller and the Transcendental Ethos," *PMLA* 1982; and *Apostle of Culture: Emerson as Preacher and Lecturer* (Penn). He has also edited the collections *The Spiritual Emerson* and *The Political Emerson* (Beacon Press). His current projects include studies of Margaret Fuller's Political Identity; Stanley Cavell and Transcendentalism; and Thoreau's Sacred Places.

Joanna Wilson-Scott obtained an MSc in Social Anthropology and an MA in Comparative Literature from University College London, before completing a PhD in 2017 at the University of Leicester that focused on contemporary American literature and narratives of causality. Since then she has taught at the University of Gloucestershire and is a 2019 Visiting Research Fellow at the Rothermere American Institute at the University of Oxford, working on the domestic effects of the Anthropocene in climate fiction. Her research interests are informed by her interdisciplinary background, and include the home, violence, water, liminality, and narratives of inclement weather. Alongside her research, she is the editor of *The New Luciad*, an annual creative anthology of poetry, prose, and visual arts.

General Introduction

Steven Allen and Kirsten Møllegaard

Narratives of place link people and geographical location with cultural imaginaries through folktales, literature, film, song, and popular culture. The social and cultural spatialities of place have ancient roots, yet continue to morph and transform over time and under the influences of fluctuations in human migration and settlement. From the very beginnings of civilization, humans have connected to geographical places close and afar by telling stories about them, memorizing pathways and seasonal changes, observing the presence or absence of animals, resources, and other humans, and by naming land and sea formations. Some place names tell of ancient battles between mythological beings or trace the migratory paths of animal herds from winter to summer. Other place names anthropomorphize the living landscape in analogy to the human body and suggest that rivers have arms and that mountains have faces, or that the landscape has gender. Yet other places have changed names several times, sometimes because newcomers or new regimes have wanted to imprint the landscape with names in their own language to reinforce their control of it, and at other times taxonomies have been replaced to erase uncomfortable histories. The world map is full of names of places, each one named or renamed by humans, and hence connected to the way humans relate to the physical landscape and to social relationships outlined by borders, territories, nations, homelands, and imagined communities of political, social, and economic alliances. The politics of space and spatiality is intrinsically linked to historical, cultural, and social contexts and to the way narratives connect people to places.

Narratives of Place in Literature and Film is an interdisciplinary collection of essays that interrogate such connections in order to probe how place is narrativized in literature and film. Utilizing close readings of specific filmic and literary texts, all chapters serve to tease out cultural and historical meanings in respect of human engagement with landscapes. Throughout this book, the notion of place is treated as a process, not simply as a static location. Place is conceived of as mutable in respect of human conceptualization, remembrance, and usage, and this book seeks to interpret how such fluidity is represented in cinematic and written texts.

This collection brings together considerations of place in respect of Africa, Asia, Australasia, mainland and offshore Europe, and North America. These regional narratives, and the migrations occurring between them, invite readers to explore how locally grounded narratives reflect global concerns, as well as how globally impactful events touch local imaginaries. This book's global perspective addresses an area not often explored in the existing literature. It is "glocal" in the sense of exploring local narratives of place within a global context. In this regard, all the chapters operate within the larger framework of the ongoing effects of colonialism, the industrial revolution, and human migrations between nations and between country and city that began in the late 1700s and continue unabated today. A primary aim of this book is therefore to provide an interdisciplinary exploration of narratives of place to highlight connections across academic fields engaged with landscape. Consequently, it contains not only scholarship emerging from studies of literature and film but also the research of academics working in American Indian Studies, Language Studies, Queer Studies, and Urban Studies. Through its interdisciplinary approach, this volume brings a distinct environmental humanities lens to bear on depictions of place and hence on the growing global awareness of the power of narratives of place in cultural imaginaries.

With a central starting point in the cinematic and literary representation of geographical places, this book aims to explore thematically how land-, sea-, and cityscapes appear in narratives about place. The perception of place is influenced by historical, cultural, economic, and gendered discourses. This book has two main objectives: one, to put narratives of place into a global perspective via a representative range of analytical essays on cinematic and literary texts from various parts of the world; two, to provide an interdisciplinary platform for exploring the concepts associated with place, such as space, spatiality, landscape, nature, and anthropocenic impact, by way of specific literary and cinematic examples.

Always mindful of national, cultural, and topographical specificity, the book's variety of topics achieves an assured focus on narratives of place through analyses revolving around five core themes, which structure the organization of the chapters: Contested Histories of Place; Environmental Landscapes; Cityscapes; The Social Construction of Place; and Landscapes of Belonging. Each thematic section is prefaced by a detailed introduction that outlines the key arguments and lists the central films and works of literature analyzed in each chapter. This organizational structure allows readers to identify specific texts and see how the themes connect meaningfully to the book's overall frame of narratives of place.

One of the clichés associated with globalization is the loss of the local and the erasure of place-based specificity. However, as this volume demonstrates, contemporary literature and film often situate narratives in specific geographic locations, which saturate the narrative with cultural meanings in relation to natural and man-made landscapes. From the labyrinthine streets of big cities to landmarks in open landscapes, place provides rich visual settings and literary subtexts. Place may be man-made or natural, but is always-already imbued with meaning and cultural significance. In *Landscape and Memory*, Simon Schama comments, "landscapes are culture before they are nature" (1995, 61). In cultural production, place is associated with human identity and ideologically with the formation of nations, borders, indigeneity, and perceptions of selfhood and otherness. The cinematic and literary texts explored in this book are probed to reveal how landscapes are defined, used, and imagined, so that humans are placed within and in relationship to their locales. Bringing together a unique perspective on how places are narrated allows readers to compare and contrast various critical positions on the production of place.

Work Cited

Schama, Simon. 1995. *Landscape and Memory*. New York: Knopf.

Part I

Contested Histories of Place: Colonialism, Indigeneity, and Marginalization

Introduction

Steven Allen and Kirsten Møllegaard

Colonialism and postcolonialism are important discourses in considering how indigeneity is defined and performed historically and in contemporary societies. In a Eurocentric worldview, cultural identity and political sovereignty are often assumed to be directly associated with territorial occupancy. Permanent human settlement is a key concept in a Eurocentric understanding of territorial sovereignty to the effect that the absence of permanent settlement gives rise to the concept of *terra nullius*, or empty land. However, nomadic peoples experience landscapes from other perspectives, and their perceptions of the land's resources have historically led to clashes with settlers and challenges to the concept of individual landownership. In the case of vast global empires like the British, the local history of one ethnic group's colonization of another group may be subsumed, or silenced, under the cloak of colonial administration. Part I includes three examples of how colonial displacement leads to altered perceptions of land and place, including the renaming of geographical locations.

In the settler colonization of North America, American Indian peoples were forced to give up their traditional territories. In many cases, tribes were already decimated by introduced diseases. There was loss of access to resources, and due to military campaigns tribes ended up on reservations without the natural resources to sustain their cultural practices. Danica Sterud Miller's chapter "Constructing Sovereignties in Leslie Marmon Silko's *Ceremony* and Sherman Alexie's *The Absolutely True Diary of a Part-Time Indian*" compares the ways that two award-winning Native American authors portray Indianness in the context of reservation life. Miller's analysis reveals important perspectives on the perception of place in two distinct Native American cultures. Miller, a Puyallup tribal member, situates her analysis in relation to the formulations of colonialism, which are at the heart of tribal status in the United States. Given the challenges in defining American Indian sovereignty outside of a federal rubric and the difficulties in articulating self-determination as an assertion of contemporary and future cultural practices, her chapter illustrates how Alexie and Silko reconfigure sovereignty within their unique tribal forms, and position distinct land-based relationships. Miller explores how tribal homelands and displacement to Indian reservations may simultaneously interrupt and perpetuate American Indians' ancestral, spiritual relationship to places and lead to cultural annihilation due to the continual trauma of contemporary and historical colonialism.

Also on the topic of settler colonialism, Daniel Andersson's chapter "Colonial and Indigenous Movements Towards and Through the Landscapes of Swedish Lapland in the Journals of Petrus Læstadius" focuses on internal settler colonization in the western parts of Northern Sweden. Between 1750 and 1873, the national government encouraged citizens from other parts of Sweden to establish small-scale agricultural settlements on the land that the indigenous Sami used for hunting, fishing, and reindeer herding. Lapland, or Sápmi, stretches from the Arctic regions of Norway, Sweden, and Finland across to the Kola Peninsula in Russia. The Sami people, who are indigenous to this vast area, have historically been pressured further and further away from territories they claim as their ancestral homelands. Through a critical reading of two journals written by the young missionary priest of local Sami origin, Petrus Læstadius, and published in 1828 and 1833, Andersson examines how colonization changed the demographics of the area and gradually led to the loss of land rights for the Sami people. In colonial narratives, place is always a sociopolitical construction that typically perceives of nature as the opposite of culture, and hence posits the people living in "nature" as less civilized and less deserving of territorial rights in comparison to the settler colonizers who cultivate the soil and believe in a Christian world order. Andersson discusses how ideas about place, nature, and culture are embedded in Læstadius' journals. Significantly, Andersson demonstrates how Læstadius, despite his Christian devotion and absorption in the ideological discourses of his time, straddled two cultures and often vacillated between indigenous and scientific epistemologies. Andersson explores these ambiguities, which he identifies as perpetuated in contemporary discourses surrounding placemaking processes in Northern Sweden.

In India, the ghosts of British colonialism continue to haunt lived experience as well as the literary imagination. Aparajita Nanda's chapter "Geographies of Marginalization and Identity Politics in Kiran Desai's *The Inheritance of Loss*" analyzes how the colonial landscape leaves its mark on human identity. Desai's 2006 novel chronicles the tension between settler and native culture and the resulting cultural schizophrenia. In her analysis, Nanda foregrounds ways of seeing as ways of remembering because memories are embedded in landscapes, place names, and personal histories within the overall frame of the nation-state. Nanda argues that Desai takes the "scape" (view) of India as a psychological map built upon the country's colonial history of loss and fracture, with the novel's protagonist losing his sense of belonging and having only memories of "inherited loss" as suggested in the novel's title. Nanda situates her analysis with the greater colonial geopolitics of space, specifically by tracing the effects of the 1947 Indian partition in the multi-ethnic area of Darjeeling, a district situated in the Himalayan foothills, and connects the partition's aftereffects to the Gorkha National Liberation Front movement of the 1980s, which sought to establish an autonomous Nepali-speaking Ghorkaland. Nanda examines the contributions to memory, marginalization, and sense of loss in relation to features of the geographic environment, local myths, and colonial history. In this analysis, she discusses how "space" creates social exclusion of colonized people that cuts across class, age, even generational divides. As an example of postcolonial literature, Desai's novel traces how cultural meanings animate and agitate the production of space, create social difference, and fuel nationalist rhetoric.

This section on contested histories of place offers indigenous and settler perspectives on local histories and memories of place that ultimately connect to global historical experiences: colonialism and the loss of land and cultural sovereignty to Euro-American powers.

1 Constructing Sovereignties in Leslie Marmon Silko's *Ceremony* and Sherman Alexie's *The Absolutely True Diary of a Part-Time Indian*

Danica Sterud Miller (Puyallup Tribe of Indians)

American Indian tribal communities and their relationship to place are traditionally a spiritual practice, but under the auspices of settler colonialism, literal and figurative place becomes sites of trauma.[1] How to negotiate these seemingly contradictory, yet coexisting experiences – ancestral devotion to place concurrent with displacement to reservations – preoccupies two of the most well-read American Indian novels, Leslie Marmon Silko's (Laguna)[2] *Ceremony* (1977) and Sherman Alexie's (Spokane/Coeur d'Alene)[3] *The Absolutely True Diary of a Part-Time Indian* (2007).[4] Despite the popularity of both *Ceremony* and *Absolutely True Diary*, surprisingly no critical work has compared the two texts; however, they have enough overt similarities that a close reading between the two novels suggests not only that *Absolutely True Diary* is inspired by *Ceremony* but also that *Absolutely True Diary* participates within a similar self-determination dialogue that *Ceremony* supports. Silko's novel suggests that indigenous communities have spiritual strength resulting from their connection to ancestral place, but the consequences of that insularity, Alexie argues, are indigenous annihilation. *Ceremony* extends a historical definition of indigeneity by a return to a land-based epistemology; *Absolutely True Diary*, conversely, redefines indigeneity as inherently nomadic. Using formulations of settler colonialism and tribal status, defining sovereignty outside of a United States federal rubric, and asserting self-determination as an indigenous practice, I will illustrate how Alexie and Silko construct sovereignty within their unique indigenous communities. *Ceremony* argues that an ancestral land-based epistemology is inherent to indigenous identity. Despite Alexie's respectful debt to Silko's work, he radically departs from her assessment by redefining indigeneity as the freedom to have relationships with multiple land locations. In *Absolutely True Diary*, to be indigenous is to be sovereign of the land, as opposed to practicing sovereignty only within a designated place. Place, then, in Alexie's work, becomes a spiritual relation to indigenous sovereignty outside the constructs of settler colonial land commodification.

Both novels interrogate what it means to be American Indian in relation to place and community. Much like *Ceremony* is about a half-blood Laguna Indian struggling to understand his relationship to his people, *Absolutely True Diary* concerns a young Spokane Indian, Arnold "Junior" Spirit, regarded by his tribal community, as the title suggests, as a "part-time Indian" because he attends an entirely white, off-reservation school. The novel is a fictionalized account of Alexie's own upbringing on the Spokane reservation, an isolated place Junior describes as "located approximately one million miles north of Important and two billion miles west of Happy" (30). Junior, who is atypically ambitious, switches to an off-reservation school, Rearden, where true to Alexie's own biography, the only other Indian at the school is the mascot.[5] By his own admission, Alexie's esthetic is heavily influenced by Silko's work. On the jacket copy of the thirtieth anniversary edition of *Ceremony* (2006), the back page is blank except for this comment from Alexie:

> *Ceremony* is the greatest novel in Native American literature. It is one of the greatest novels of any time and place. I have read this book so many times that I probably have it memorized. I teach it and I learn it and I am continually in awe of its power, beauty, rage, and vision, and violence.
>
> (Silko 2006)

Silko's influence becomes even more apparent when Alexie's *Absolutely True Diary* is read alongside Silko's *Ceremony* and evaluated as a response to and a debate of the polemic *Ceremony* articulates in terms of indigenous sovereignty.

Indigeneity, Sovereignty, and Place

For the purposes of this chapter, I am interested in how the authors use their characters to destabilize the settler colonial project, specifically Westernized commodification of place, by constructing indigeneity (and by extension sovereignty) according to the standards of their indigenous communities outside of a settler colonial framework. A brief history, then, of the settler colonialism via the reservation system is necessary. According to William Canby:

> Reservations were originally intended to keep distance and peace between Indians and non-Indians, but they came to be viewed also

as instruments for "civilizing" the Indians. Each reservation was placed in charge of an Indian agent whose mission was to supervise the Indian's adaptation to non-Indian ways...... when reservation schools were first set up in 1865, they too were directed by religious organizations with a goal of "Christianizing" the Indians.

(1998, 19)

After the initial federal reservation system was enacted, it was quickly followed by the General Allotment Act of 1887 (more popularly known as the Dawes Act), which attempted to destroy indigenous American transhistorical communities by dividing tribal reservation land into individually owned allotments. The federal government "believed that if individual Indians were given plots of land to cultivate, they would prosper and become assimilated into the mainstream of American culture as middle-class farmers" (21). The government also believed that private ownership – as opposed to communal land holdings which indigenous Americans traditionally practiced – would encourage tribes to develop into multiple nuclear familial units, and not as the strong, interdependent peoples they were at the time: "The tribes, which were viewed as obstacles to the cultural and economic development of the Indians, would quickly wither away" (21). The reservation system manipulated indigenous sacred land relationships into a commodity to be owned and sold; a commodity, in addition, controlled by the paternalistic federal government.

Indigenous communities are based in a land-and-kinship solidarity with a clearly articulated sense of place. According to Yi-Fu Tuan, space is a physical location, but space "becomes place as we get to know it better and endow it with meaning" (1977, 6). From an indigenous lens, place is central to indigenous belief systems. Kathryn. W. Shanley explains,

> For Indigenous peoples – people vitally connected to geographical locations – place means both an imagined home and a vibrantly interactive space inhabited by many sentient beings, what Western thinking might call a "metaphysical" space. Place means kinship in its broadest terms
>
> (2015, 6)

But place within a settler colonial framework becomes space as a distinct commodity to be controlled, manipulated, and exploited, and further, indigenous peoples themselves become commodities to be controlled, manipulated, and exploited (Hoxie 2008, 1163). Even with the disastrous consequences of settler colonialism for American Indian communities, American Indians continue to adhere to their specific constructions of indigeneity, either as a response to settler colonialism, or as a concurrent continuation of ancestral traditions.

Both *Ceremony* and *Absolutely True Diary* decolonize Westernized constructions of space by using an indigenous lens to understand the indigenous relationship to literal and figurative place. *Ceremony* enacts this decolonization through a continuation of ancestral Laguna physical place innately collapsed within Laguna figurative place. For the Laguna (and indeed, many indigenous peoples), a distinction between physical place and an indigenous epistemology is nonexistent because place cannot be commodified into space outside of an indigenous belief system. In *Ceremony*, a mixed-blood Laguna Indian, Tayo, returns to the Laguna reservation from World War II suffering from post-traumatic stress disorder. When he is finally released from the Veterans' Hospital, he is still far from well, and his grandmother arranges a ceremony with the Laguna medicine man, Ku'oosh.[6] Despite his doctor's strict orders to avoid "Indian medicine" and his Auntie's warnings that "Old Ku'oosh will bring his bag of weeds and dust. The doctor won't like it," Ku'oosh visits Tayo just the same (Silko 1977, 31). Ku'oosh, however, cannot perform a ceremony for Tayo because there is no ceremony for this new kind of warfare. Many Laguna veterans, Ku'oosh adds, are suffering like Tayo. Tayo visits another medicine man, Betonie, also a mixed-blood American Indian, who helps him understand that his pain and suffering are not only the result of the war, but they are also the result of the abuse Western colonization has committed against the Laguna and the earth. Tayo's ceremony ends at a Laguna uranium mine, where he witnesses fellow Laguna veteran Emo torturing their mutual friend, Harley. Emo hopes to provoke Tayo into participating in the violence, but by not killing Emo, Tayo arrests (for now) the settler colonial violence that plagues the Laguna people.

As the last step in Tayo's ceremony occurs at a uranium mine – uranium mined here resulted in the creation of the first atomic bombs – Tayo finally understands and acknowledges the violence that settler colonialism has wreaked upon the earth. Tayo's ceremony fundamentally intertwines with the physical earth of his indigenous community and Tayo's journey of healing unearths his relationship with Laguna land. In the end, Tayo realizes that to be Laguna has little to do with the literal Laguna blood he claims from his mother; instead, to be Laguna is to live in a symbiotic relationship with Laguna land. Indigenous sovereignty, Silko stresses in *Ceremony*, can only be reached through a place-based indigeneity. This reading of *Ceremony* notably does not suggest reclaiming land from United States colonization. Indeed, the Laguna were not removed to reservations – their ancestral land is also their federal reservation land – so decolonizing place becomes less a physical act and more of an epistemological one. While the Laguna were not removed to reservations other than their ancestral homeland, they did lose much of their land to Western colonization, settlement, and contamination from uranium mining. Decolonization then, in *Ceremony*, means reclaiming the epistemologies inherent in their (reservation) land.

Indigenous Imaginings Outside of the Settler State

Through various federal acts and policies – namely the previously mentioned Dawes Act, the Marshall Trilogy (Johnson v. M'Intosh, Cherokee v. Georgia, and Cherokee v. Worcester), and blood quantum guidelines – citizenship in federally recognized American Indian tribes is largely under the standards of the United States federal government and not under the standards of the indigenous nations themselves. One of the ways the United States regulates (and thus, controls) indigenous sovereignty is by limiting tribal enrollment to one tribe per person. Prior to settler colonialism, most indigenous communities allowed people to be members of multiple tribes; indeed, for many indigenous communities, this was encouraged as a sign of prestige. To force an indigenous person to choose which tribe to enroll into causes trauma by alienating crucial, ancestral parts of the indigenous self. *Ceremony* and *Absolutely True Diary* both attempt to decolonize federal control over tribal citizenship by redefining tribal affiliation outside the federal colonial narrative. For example, in *Ceremony*, while fighting in World War II, Tayo refuses to kill a Japanese soldier because he believes the soldier to be his Uncle Josiah. Tayo does not understand the connection his subconscious makes, but Betonie clarifies for Tayo: "The Japanese... It isn't surprising you saw him with them. You saw who they were. Thirty thousand years ago they were not strangers" (115). To be a member of an ancestral tribal community, Betonie implies, transcends Western national borders. The United States may have been at war with Japan, but communities exist outside these imposed borders.

Working within the same constructions of indigeneity that Silko uses, Alexie (2007) imagines indigenous communities outside the rubric of settler colonial space. Junior understands that he belongs to multiple tribes: "I realized that, sure, I was a Spokane Indian. I belonged to that tribe. But I also belonged to the tribe of American immigrants. And to the tribe of basketball players. And to the tribe of bookworms" (217). Junior, a full-blood Spokane, claims to be an American immigrant. Much like Tayo recognized the similarities between himself and the Japanese soldier despite the international war and United States' anti-Japanese propaganda, Junior also recognizes that as a citizen of the Spokane tribe, he does not identify as American by birth, but as American by choice. Even though all American Indians are United States citizens by the Indian Citizenship Act of 1924, he identifies as a member of the tribe of American immigrants, a community both of America and foreign to it. Outside of the novel, Alexie has vocally supported this view, "Ever since 9/11, I have worked hard to be very public about my multi-tribal identity. I think fundamentalism is the mistaken belief that one belongs to only one tribe; I am the opposite of that" (Davis and Stevenson 2009, 187). Once Junior identifies himself as a tribal member(s) outside of the federal rubric, he realizes, "I knew that

I was going to be okay" (Alexie 2007, 217). Scholar and activist Andrea Smith echoes this sentiment, "Many people in Native studies believe alternative forms of governance can be developed that are not based on nation-states. We can work towards 'transcendent change' by not presuming it will happen within the confines of the US state" (2010).

Another way the federal government controls indigenous sovereignty is by using indigenous blood quantum as a qualifier for tribal enrollment. Eric Cheyfitz notes that,

> The emergence of the idea of race as a scientific category in the first half of the nineteenth century in the United States was simultaneous with the emergence of biology as a category of knowledge and scientific racism as a mode of justifying both the enslavement of African Americans and the genocide of American Indians.
>
> (2004, 59)

Races were not merely different categories of peoples, but, "race itself became the chief explanation for observed human differences" (Tallbear 2013, 33). Blood as a signifier of nationality and culture, both a scientifically debunked hypothesis and a thoroughly racist one, is nonetheless the major standard for enrollment into federally recognized American Indian tribes. The federal government tracks the blood quantum of American Indians and the percentage of the individual's tribally affiliated blood largely determines whether the person will be eligible for tribal enrollment. Both *Ceremony* and *Absolutely True Diary* decolonize blood quantum as an indicator of indigeneity. Silko repeatedly shows that Rocky is not a real Laguna despite his full-blood quantum because he supports settler colonial epistemologies of land and community alienation:

> [Rocky] was already thinking of the years ahead and the new places and people that were waiting for him in the future he had lived for since he first began to believe in the word "someday" the way white people do
>
> (Silko 1977, 67)

Rocky's sense of self is constructed within Western individualism outside of Laguna understandings of place-based indigeneity. In contrast, Tayo feels ostracized from his Laguna community because of his obvious mixed-blood. He is mocked for his hazel eyes and unknown father. While blood as a measure of Laguna belonging was an unknown concept until settler colonialism, Silko shows how the Laguna adopted this concept and colonized their own people through this practice. Through Tayo, Silko decolonizes the settler colonial mythology of blood quantum and racial purity by showing that Tayo is truly Laguna because of his deep kinship with Laguna place. Tayo, when he completes his ceremony, says to himself, "we came out of this land and we are hers" (236). To be indigenous is to practice a land-based epistemology, and in the case of the Laguna, an epistemology to a specific land base. Tayo's indigeneity, by the end of the novel, is based on his symbiotic (and literal) land relationship, and not defined by the federally imposed blood quantum laws.

Alexie pointedly refutes Silko's construction of indigeneity with his character Rowdy. Rowdy is tied to his indigenous land base and is a full-blood Spokane, neither of which offers him any community solace. In direct contrast to the indigenous construct that *Ceremony* suggests, Rowdy's firm connection to his reservation land base does not indicate an indigenous identity, but indicates his imprisonment by the federal reservation system. When in kindergarten, Rowdy got into a fight with three older kids and hit the teacher who tried to break up the fight. The teacher asked him what was wrong, to which Rowdy replied, "Everything!" (Alexie 2007, 18). Rowdy's parents are alcoholics, and his father physically and verbally abuses Rowdy and his mother. The novel implies, though never states explicitly, that Rowdy's extremely violent outbursts are not only environmental, but also the biological effects of Fetal Alcohol Spectrum Disorders (FASD). The novel itself begins with several mentions of the inadequate, even traumatic, health care provided by Indian Health Service. Junior has ten teeth pulled in one day, and because the dentist believes Indians do not feel pain, he only uses half the recommended anesthesia dosage (2). There are several references to Rowdy's violent emotions and Attention Deficit Hyperactivity Disorder, both of which are signs of FASD. However, because of the substandard health care provided by the reservation system, Rowdy receives no medical care or diagnosis. Living on the reservation makes Rowdy statistically more likely to both have FASD and, as the novel makes clear, receive no medical treatment if he is (Kuerschner 2001, 7). Rowdy's relationship to his Spokane land base does not make him more Spokane, but it makes him more trapped by the dictates of settler colonialism. Rowdy is tied to the Spokane reservation not because of the indigenous strength the land provides, but because the reservation system has created a federal prison where indigenous tradition has been replaced by a tradition of poverty, violence, and alcoholism. Junior's description of his family lacks any mention of his Spokane indigeneity: "My parents came from poor people who came from poor people who came from poor people, all the way back to the very first poor people" (Alexie 2007, 11). His ancestral tradition is one of poverty, not of culture, community, and land. Reservation land itself is to be blamed for this cyclical legacy: "But we reservation Indians don't get to realize our dreams. We don't get those chances. Or choices. We're just poor. That's all we are" (13). According to the lessons reservation life has taught Junior, Indianness, the reservation, and poverty are intrinsic to each other. In *Absolutely True Diary*, indigenous devotion to ancestral place has become less an epistemological act and more a tool of settler colonial control.

Alexie's Radical (Re)Construction of Indigenous Sovereignty

As suggested by the title, *The Absolutely True Diary of a Part-Time Indian*, Junior identifies as Indian only part of the time because when he transfers to the Rearden school, he is no longer on the reservation. Although Junior still lives at home and spends the majority of his time on the reservation, he considers himself (and believes himself to be considered by other Spokane) as Indian only when he physically resides on the reservation. His indigenous self is tied to a literal place. As Silko argues throughout *Ceremony*, to be Laguna is to practice a literal place-based epistemology. Alexie, however, shows that the literal place of reservations – due to federal control – makes indigeneity and indigenous survival impossible. In *Absolutely True Diary*, reservations, according to Junior, are prisons and death camps. Junior explains, "Reservations were meant to be prisons, you know? Indians were supposed to move onto reservations and die. We were supposed to disappear. But somehow or another, Indians have forgotten that reservations were meant to be death camps" (217). According to Junior's geometry teacher, Mr Peabody, the smartest kid he ever taught is Junior's older sister, Mary, who, he further informs Junior, wanted to be a romance writer. This surprises Junior because after graduation, Mary lives in the family's basement, with no job or goals. When Junior starts commuting twenty-two miles to his new high school – which he sometimes has to walk because he has no reliable form of transportation – Mary, inspired by his enthusiasm, elopes with a Flathead Indian and moves to Montana. She seems to be living her own romance novel: "This reservation had tried to suffocate her, had kept her trapped in a basement, and now she was out roaming the huge grassy fields of Montana" (91). Months later, Mary, drunk and unconscious, burns to death in a party fire. Mary moved out of her parents' basement and attempted to do something with her life, but because she moves to another reservation, Alexie implies, she still resides in the same figurative basement where all reservation Indians live. American Indians, Alexie's text warns, have privileged the physical space over the spiritual place. In *Absolutely True Diary*, the reservation, an American Indian place as dictated by the United States, cannot give the spiritual relationship that indigenous place has historically offered American Indian communities because settler colonialism has destroyed the innate indigeneity of land. Alexie has reiterated this view in various other texts[7] and interviews: "One of the things we forget as natives and non-natives is that reservations were created as concentration camps. They were created so Indians would be shipped there and die. I really think that's still their purpose: to kill" (Weich 2009, 171). To be a member of an indigenous nation is then to recognize the colonial control of the United States, and to live on the reservation is to submit to that control. As Alexie makes clear throughout *Absolutely True Diary*, reservation life means Indian death.

While federal policies no longer practice the overt genocidal practices of previous centuries, according to Alexie's polemic, federal control over Indian reservations kills Indians through substandard health care, rampant alcoholism, cyclical poverty, substandard education, and lack of environmental regulation.

For many indigenous communities, including the Laguna of *Ceremony*, a land-based epistemology is the fundamental paradigm of their tribe. Betonie describes this feeling as "comfortable":

> "We know these hills, and we are comfortable here." There was something about the way the old man said the word "comfortable." It had a different meaning – not the comfort of big houses or rich food or even clean streets, but the comfort of belonging with the land, and the peace of being with these hills.
>
> (Silko 1977, 108)

However, most indigenous communities were removed to reservations and their reservation land is not their ancestral land. Karen Piper (1997) further adds the following:

> While reservations have been technically granted "sovereignty," it is sovereignty only under the umbrella of U.S. protectionism. So even where Indians have occupied the same land, the mental mapping of cultural patterns that established the perception of the landscape have been reorganized.
>
> (487)

An indigenous belief system based on specific land cannot exist as it has traditionally existed because settler colonialism has fundamentally altered that relationship: "Under settler colonialism the right to live on the ancestral land has been so compromised, either by changes to the land itself or by interventions in cultural and ceremonial practices, as to estrange many Indigenous people from it" (Coleman 2016, 62). While Silko argues that such a relationship can still exist outside of the dictates of colonialism, for many indigenous peoples, the pressure to live in an active state of decolonization is difficult, and often traumatic.

Alexie further suggests that not only do reservations trap Indians via federal control, but the reservation land itself harms Indians because federal control has created an environmental deregulated dystopia. Near the end of *Absolutely True Diary*, we learn of Junior's fear of Turtle Lake, which is located on the Spokane reservation. The "crazy deep" lake is, according to legend, bottomless (Alexie 2007, 222). Scientists attempted to find the lake's depth, but the expedition was called off because, "the nearby uranium mine made their radar/sonar go nuts" (222).

One time the lake caught fire and another time the lake kept a dead horse from decomposing. Junior's fear of the lake is not because of the lake's vicinity to the uranium mine. Junior makes no connection between these seemingly freakish occurrences and the possibility that the lake is contaminated with uranium. For Junior, the normalization of the uranium mine as part of the reservation masks the horrific possibilities that uranium mines contain. The uranium mine is a passing reference for Junior, but a disturbing one for the reader. Unlike in *Ceremony* where Tayo heals the earth and himself from the violence of settler colonialism as exemplified by the uranium mine in which his ceremony ends, there is no such healing in *Absolutely True Diary*. The uranium mine lurks in the background of the text and reminds the reader that federal policies enable uranium mining on Indian reservations. Rowdy and Junior, like all Spokane kids, spend their hot summers swimming in Turtle Lake. Alexie hints that the lake is contaminated with uranium, but there is no confirmation of contamination. Just as Alexie hints that Rowdy is a victim of undiagnosed FASD, he also hints that Junior's birth defects (hydrocephalus, epilepsy, stuttering, and hyperdontia[8]) are possible results from unregulated uranium mining.

How then to articulate indigenous sovereignty outside of the thoroughly racist colonial criteria? Joanne Barker (2011) explains that articulation occurs when indigenous communities,

> assert traditions as the cultural beliefs and practices that they understand as uniquely their own, not as a yardstick of conformity to an authentic past but as what binds them together in relationship and responsibility to one another in the present and future
>
> (21)

Both novels explicitly redefine tribal identity by removing the settler colonial impositions and using an indigenous lens instead. They differ, however: in *Ceremony*, indigenous community is defined as physically place-specific, whereas in *Absolutely True Diary*, to adhere to a place-specific land-base is yet another method of settler colonial control. Indigeneity, by the end of *Absolutely True Diary*, is nomadism. Despite Alexie's clear respect for Silko's work, he departs from her construction of indigenous sovereignty when he constructs indigeneity as the ability to be of places, not of a specific place. By the end of *Absolutely True Diary*, Junior and Rowdy are friends again, despite Rowdy's feeling of betrayal after Junior left to go to the off-reservation school. Importantly, Rowdy, who is most trapped by the dictates of federal reservation colonialism, redefines indigeneity for Junior:

> I was reading this book about old-time Indians, about how we used to be nomadic... so I looked up nomadic in the dictionary, and it

means people who move around, who keep moving, in search of
food and water and grazing land... Hardly anybody on this rez is
nomadic. Except for you. You're the nomadic one

(229)

For Rowdy, to be an authentic Indian – to be Spokane in the most traditional sense – means not to be of a literal place, but the ability to embody
place and places. Like most Salish peoples, the Spokane had winter and
summer homes, with extensive traveling between and during seasonal
migrations. Rowdy's directive emphasizes both a return to traditional
Spokane practices and a construction of indigeneity without the barriers
that colonialism erects. Indigenous place, for Alexie, is to construct a
land relationship outside of colonialism. To decolonize reservation land
is to re/construct indigenous place.

American Indian sovereignty, as defined by the United States, is largely
a Westernized construct used to justify religious and economic settler
colonialism. While the United States defines the limits of American Indian sovereignty within a Westernized legal framework, indigenous constructions of sovereignty continued and continue to exist concurrently
with settler colonial ones. In other words, as Taiaiake Alfred (Mohawk)
(2005)[9] states,

> The discourse of sovereignty upon which the current post facto
> justification rests is an exclusively European discourse. That is,
> European assertions in both a legal and political sense were made
> strictly vis-a-vis other European powers, and did not impinge upon
> or necessarily even affect in law or politics the rights and status of
> indigenous nations. It is only from our distant historical vantage
> point, and standing upon a counterfactual rock, that we are able
> to see European usurpations of indigenous sovereignty as justified.
>
> (34)

The United States definition of American Indian sovereignty is a construction of settler colonialism that has had little to no input from
the indigenous sovereignties it was and is supposedly regulating.
"Sovereignty – and its related histories, perspectives, and identities –
is embedded within the specific social relations in which it is invoked
and given meaning" (Barker 2005, 21). To decolonize indigeneity
and sovereignty out of settler colonialism is to reconstruct indigenous sovereignty within its own historical processes. *Ceremony* and
Absolutely True Diary do just that; however, it is these indigenous
constructions, initially along similar lines, that, in terms of Alexie's
work, radically and pointedly, reconfigure place. *Ceremony* decolonizes settler colonialism by reconstructing the Laguna out of a federally imposed framework, which Alexie also does for the Spokane

in *Absolutely True Diary*. Place, however, for Silko, is a physical relationship that denotes the Laguna; for Alexie, place is a metaphoric representation of ancestral Spokane traditions and decolonized contemporary indigeneity.

Notes

1 In order to foreground the continual state of settler colonialism of indigenous peoples in the now United States, I choose to use the term American Indian, which is the United States federal term for an indigenous person within United States borders. I choose not to use Native American, which implies a democratic inclusion within the United States, an inclusion I find impossible within the contemporary colonial settler state. However, I strive to be as Indigenous community specific as possible when applicable.
2 Leslie Marmon Silko identifies as Laguna Pueblo, though she is also of Anglo American and Mexican descent. The Laguna Pueblo are a federally recognized American Indian tribe located in western New Mexico. Silko was raised on the edges of the Laguna Pueblo reservation, but her mixed ancestry meant she was not allowed to participate in many Laguna ceremonies.
3 Sherman Alexie identifies as Spokane Indian (from his mother) and Coeur d'Alene Indian (from his father). The Spokane Tribe is an American Indian plateau tribe with a reservation located in eastern Washington. The Coeur d'Alene Tribe of Indians' reservation is located in nearby Idaho.
4 For the sake of brevity, I will refer to *The Absolutely True Diary of a Part-Time Indian* as *Absolutely True Diary*.
5 Like Junior, Alexie had a very successful high school basketball career; however, after he missed a free throw in the last minute of the deciding state championship game, the local paper ran the headline: "Alexie Misses Free Throw, Indians Lose Again" (Egan 1998, 16).
6 Indian Health Services (IHS) is notoriously underfunded and understaffed, and until the 1990s, IHS was also endemically and systematically racist, though there are attempts to fix this at present. Tayo is dismissed from the hospital, despite his visible sickness, for all of these reasons.
7 In his semiautobiographical film, *The Business of Fancydancing* (2002), he also refers to the Spokane reservation as a "prison."
8 Junior, like Alexie, is born with these medical problems, several of which have environmental causes.
9 The Mohawk Tribe historically resided in what is present-day upstate New York. They are part of the Haudenosaunee (Iroquois Confederacy).

Works Cited

Alexie, Sherman. 2007. *The Absolutely True Story of a Part-Time Indian*. New York: Little Brown and Company.
———— Director. 2002. *The Business of Fancydancing*. Film. Seattle, WA: Fallsapart Productions.
Alfred, Taiaiake. 2005. "Sovereignty." In *Sovereignty Matters: Locations of Contestation and Possibility in Indigenous Struggles for Self-Determination*, 33–50. Lincoln, NE: University of Nebraska.
Barker, Joanne. 2011. *Native Acts: Law, Recognition, and Cultural Authenticity*. Durham, NC: Duke University Press.

———— 2005. "For Whom Sovereignty Matters." In *Sovereignty Matters: Locations of Contestation and Possibility in Indigenous Struggles for Self-Determination*, 1–31. Lincoln, NE: University of Nebraska.

Canby, William C. 1998. *American Indian Law in a Nutshell*. 4th ed. St. Paul: West Group.

Cheyfitz, Eric. 2004. "'What is an Indian?': Identity Politics in the United States Federal Indian Law and American Indian Literatures." *Ariel* 35 (1/2): 59–80.

Coleman, Daniel. 2016. "Indigenous Place and Diaspora Space: Of Literalism and Abstraction." *Settler Colonial Studies* 6 (1): 61–76.

Davis, Tanita, and Sarah Stevenson. 2009. "Sherman Alexie." In *Conversations with Sherman Alexie*, edited by Nancy J. Peterson, 187–97. Oxford, MI: University of Mississippi.

Egan, Timothy. 1998. "An Indian without Reservations." *New York Times Magazine*, January 18, 1998: 191.

Hoxie, Frederick E. 2008. "Retrieving the Red Continent: Settler Colonialism and the History of American Indians in the US." *Ethnic and Racial Studies* 31 (1): 153–67.

Kuerschner, Suzanne L.B. 2001. *Beyond the Gloom and Doom: Tools for Help and Hope with Native People Affected by Fetal Alcohol Syndrome and Related Neuro-Development Disorders*. Portland: National Indian Child Welfare Association.

Piper, Karen. 1997. "Police Zones: Territory and Identity in Leslie Marmon Silko's Ceremony." *American Indian Quarterly* 21 (3) (Summer): 483–97.

Shanley, Kathryn W. 2015. "'Mapping' Indigenous Presence: The Declaration on the Rights of Indigenous Peoples at Rhetorical Turns and Tipping Points." In *Mapping Indigenous Presence: North Scandinavian and North American Perspectives*, edited by Kathryn W. Shanley and Bjørg Evjen, 5–26. Tucson, AZ: University of Arizona Press.

Silko, Leslie Marmon. 1977. *Ceremony*. New York: Penguin.

———— (1977) 2006. *Ceremony*. New York: Penguin.

Smith, Andrea. 2010. "Indigeneity, Settler Colonialism, White Supremacy." *Global Dialogue*, 12 (2). https://web.archive.org/web/20160313102901/http://worlddialogue.org/content.php?id=488.

Tallbear, Kim. 2013. *Native American DNA: Tribal Belonging and the False Promise of Genetic Science*. Minneapolis, MN: University of Minneapolis Press.

Tuan, Yi-Fu. 1977. *Space and Place: The Perspective of Experience*. Minneapolis, MN, University of Minnesota Press.

Weich, David. 2009. "Revising Sherman Alexie." In *Conversations with Sherman Alexie*, edited by Nancy J. Peterson, 169–79. Oxford, MI: University of Mississippi.

Filmography

The Business of Fancydancing. Dir. Sherman Alexie, USA, 2002.

2 Colonial and Indigenous Movements toward and through the Landscapes of Swedish Lapland in the Journals of Petrus Læstadius

Daniel Andersson

Introduction

In this chapter, I argue that movement – the way individuals and groups are imagined to move toward and through the landscape – can be used to understand and problematize the colonization of Lapland[1] in the 1700s and 1800s.[2] The discussion is based on analysis of texts from the early 1800s by the young missionary priest Petrus Læstadius (1802–1841). Drawing on works within postcolonial studies, I explore how different movements in the texts create a paradoxical place of desolate, wild, and dangerous nature that at the same time is inhabited by the indigenous Sami. Some aspects of how the Sami move through the landscape signal a way of being in Lapland that differs from Læstadius himself and the Swedish settlers. This, together with the paradox of desolate nature and Sami presence, points to a possible "indigenous dimension" that allows the Sami to be there, but not play any real role in the development of place and society. When taking into account the movements of the colonization itself in the texts, a hierarchical view of culture is revealed as foundational to Læstadius' understanding and justification of the colonization.

Petrus Læstadius and the Journals

Born in 1802 in Arvidsjaur in Northern Sweden, Petrus Læstadius, together with his brother Lars Levi,[3] grew up in Kvikkjokk, in the household of their oldest brother Carl Erik.[4] His family was in part of Sami origin and he spoke Lule Sami.[5] He was ordained in 1825 and two year later he entered the service as a missionary in Swedish Lapland.[6] This position involved overseeing the Sami catechists who traveled with the nomadic Sami, teaching the children knowledge of Christianity. His time as a missionary – 1827 to 1832 – is the theme of his books.

Læstadius took up subscriptions for an upcoming travel narrative based on his work in Lapland in 1828 and the first book was published in 1831 under the title *Journal af Petrus Læstadius för första året af hans tjenstgöring såsom missionaire i Lappmarken* [Journal by Petrus

Læstadius of the first year of his service as missionary in Lapland]. The book received good reviews and Læstadius was even awarded a prize for the book by the Swedish Academy. His writing has been praised for its authenticity and unpretentious narrative zest, for example, by the literary critic Fredrik Böök (1918, 269).

The first book constitutes an adventurous narrative of Læstadius traveling in Lapland, meeting people and facing dangers, in the context of the Swedish colonization. It also contains ethnographic descriptions of the way of life of the Sami and the settlers. His style is characterized by an abundance of quotes and allusions, often without clear references, to the Bible, classical authors, and contemporary Swedish literature – particularly Esaias Tegnér and Vitalis.[7] Sometimes these intertextual connections add a level of significance to the places of Lapland, for instance, when two headlands in Rossne are said to be "the Pillars of Hercules"[8] of Lake Hornavan.

Two years after the first book, Læstadius published the sequel: *Fortsättning af Journalen öfver missions-resor i Lappmarken, innefattande åren 1828–1832* [Continuation of the Journal of missionary travels in Lapland, Comprising the Years 1828–1832]. Being more descriptive and investigative, this book contains relatively few narrative parts and it failed to reach the success of the first book. After the missionary service, in 1836, Petrus Læstadius became a vicar and died in 1841, only thirty-nine years old.

Læstadius' books influenced the Swedish public's understanding of Lapland at the time and are still today highly valued as sources about the older Sami way of life. The researcher Erik Bylund, for example, writes that, in Læstadius' writings, one finds an "invaluable source of knowledge about the earliest settler period" (1956, 28). They are generally referred to as Læstadius' *journals*, an epithet that will be used in the rest of this chapter.

The Colonization of Lapland

The political and historical context of Læstadius' writings is the colonization of Lapland. Although different in many regards from the European overseas colonization that most often is associated with the notion of colonialism, the colonization of Lapland shares several key features, for instance, the establishment of settlements in distant areas (Said 1993, 8) and "the conquest and control of other people's lands and goods" (Loomba 2015, 20).

The Swedish state's relationship with Lapland and its Sami inhabitants was originally based on taxation (Bergman and Edlund 2016), and since the end of the 1600s, an old land division system, which the state also used for taxation purposes, and which divided land and water resources between the Sami families (Lundmark 2010, 36).[9] Eventually, in order to expand its territory, the Swedish state began to support permanent settlements in Lapland (Bylund 1956). Regulations issued toward the end of the 1600s offered settlers tax exemptions and freedom from military service in exchange for the clearing of land, building of houses, etc. (Kvist 1992, 66) and after new regulations in 1749, the so-called *Lappmarksreglementet,* the colonization picked up speed. Nils Arell (1979, 12) connects the Swedish state's renewed interest in colonizing Lapland to contemporary mercantilist ideas. The new regulations allowed the Sami to become settlers and limited the settlers' hunting and fishing rights, something that was supposed to reduce the grounds for conflict between the settlers and the Sami. The basis for the latter assumption was the so-called parallel theory, that is, the idea that the Sami and the settlers could coexist through different ways of utilizing nature (Mörner 1982, 250–51). In the parishes of Arvidsjaur and Arjeplog, which are part of the geographical area in Læstadius' narratives, 32 percent of the new settlements between 1776 and 1867 were taken up by the Sami. Many forest Sami[10] applied to become settlers on their own Sami Tax Lands, in order to stop other settlers from claiming the area (Lundmark 2010, 68). One of the consequences of the colonization of Lapland was that Sami land rights and hunting and fishing rights were gradually eroded (Lundmark 2010, 91).

The colonization of Lapland involved dramatic changes with regard to demography and land ownership. The understandings of this period, created and spread by depictions such as Læstadius' journals, are important as such understandings influenced the colonial creation of place for a very long time.

Place and Movement

A central concept in this chapter is movement – or rather conceptions, including images, of movements – as integral to the creation of place. The notion of *place*, to begin with, is here understood as a location in space, with a certain material composition that has been provided with meaning (cf. Cresswell 2009, 176). Yi-Fu Tuan (1977, 6) writes: "What begins as undifferentiated space becomes place as we get to know it better and endow it with value." Widely disseminated written representations, like the texts studied here, are influential in creating place, by defining geographical areas and forming and spreading conceptions about them.

The cultural geographer John Agnew (2011) points to three dimensions that recur in the theoretical discussion of *place*: place as a certain geographical position with relations to other locations through interaction and movement, place as settings where everyday life activities take place, and place as *sense of place*. In this chapter, I am looking at place through the lens of movement, thus drawing from the first of these three place dimensions.

Agnew's own examples of this dimension are cities and settlements, which he argues are usually understood as systems of places, whose relationships are characterized by mobility (2011, 326). When applying these theoretical positions to colonial contexts, certain characteristics need to be kept in mind. Nature often plays an important role as the setting for the colonizing activities and for meetings between indigenous peoples and colonizers, but also the fact that colonization often entails a radical transformation of how people in a certain area interact with nature. Looking at depictions of colonization through the lens of *movement* means asking who or what is moving, what characterizes movements and what this means for the creation of place. I focus on the movements of Læstadius himself through the landscapes of Lapland, the movement of his fiancée from the south of Sweden to Lapland, the movements of the indigenous Sami, and finally, on the movement of the colonization process in itself, and some of the characteristics and directions given by Læstadius.

Drown, Starve, or Freeze to Death?

The most salient movements in the journals are Petrus Læstadius' own travels in Lapland, often in the company of his horse Slompen. Characteristic of these travels are the long distances and poor traveling conditions. His travels take place "in Lapland's desolate forests"[11] (Læstadius 1831, 317) and are associated with hardship and grave danger. In several narrative episodes, he describes how he risks his own and Slompen's life on stormy lakes, thin ice and snow-covered paths. He concludes as follows:

> A missionary has three main inconveniences to fear: drown, starve to death or freeze to death. Sometimes during the summer, he shall wade over rapid streams: if one slips on one single step, one is lost, if not the wonderful hand of providence still comes to the rescue, as proof of its presence. Sometimes one has to travel by boat on the great lakes and look death in the eye among the roaring waves, sometimes walk on thin ice, with the fear of getting a cold bath at the bottom of the lake. In the wide forests and on the desolate mountains one sometimes walks in darkness and fog, without knowing where. When the provisions run out, where will one get bread? Or if one, during winter, gets lost, and does not encounter people, but has to spend the nights outside during minus 40 degrees [Celsius] what shall one cover oneself with?
>
> (Læstadius 1831, 180)

Læstadius' narratives exemplify a common trope regarding Northern Sweden: through time it has been the region's wilderness, extreme weather and various dangers that have excited people's imaginations and encouraged travelers and explorers. The long distances traveled by Læstadius paint a picture of a vast and uninhabited wilderness, an image often present in colonial discourses around the world: empty, wild nature is the *terra nullius* that is needed in order for colonization to proceed and for the colonizers to be able to "tame" and claim the land (Lines 1992). This emptiness is also paradoxical in Læstadius' journals, since it clashes with the long Sami presence in Lapland – described at length in the journals – and the many Sami living there. It was after all Læstadius' job as a missionary to travel to the Sami communities and oversee the Christian catechists. I will return to this paradox below.

Læstadius looks at Lapland from different perspectives. He is from the area, and in that he differs from many writers who have depicted Northern Sweden strictly from an outside perspective, even though he also looks at the landscape from an outsider's point of view. He has his intended readers on the subscription list, and he is especially proud to have gotten the famous Swedish author Esaias Tegnér as the first subscriber (Læstadius 1833, 135). Læstadius' way of looking through outsiders' eyes at his own homelands never becomes more apparent than when he describes another movement in the first journal, namely the moving of his fiancée Carolina Fredrika Hagberg, from her home in Raspo in Uppland in the south of Sweden to Lapland. Petrus travels to her, to take her home with him, and when he describes how she experiences it all, the reader is given a view of Lapland from her perspective – as he imagines it:

> Engaged to a man, whose wandering life, like a storm bird, hovered in storms and bad weather among the wild mountains and forests of Lapland, these, the homes of the Rimthussar, what thoughts must not rise in her soul. And when this man, after a year has gone by, comes to take her with him, must it not look something like when Alonzo came and snatched his bride with him to the kingdom of shadows, where horrible ghosts would dance around them? How would not her surroundings' conceptions about the never sun-glazed lands of the North attack her soul! Who wonders then at the tears, which her heart sometimes sheds?
>
> (Læstadius 1833, 97–98)

Besides Carolina's conceptions of her husband to be and his wandering life, it is the place, Lapland, that is the focus of the outsiders' gaze: it has stormy and bad weather, the forests are wild and contain the homes of Rimthussar, which are the frost giants of the Edda poetry (Nordberg 1977, 73). The place Carolina is heading to is eternally dark, it is the "never sun-glazed land" and by likening Petrus and Carolina to Alonzo and his bride Imogene, Lapland even becomes a kingdom of Death.[12]

Carolina's movement from the south of Sweden paints a picture of Lapland as Thule, the exotic land beyond the north wind, where storms, darkness, and horrid creatures threaten. These depictions are filled with emotions, and this view of Lapland, attributed to Carolina and her surroundings, is a reasonable explanation for the young fiancée's tears, according to Læstadius. His own movements through the wild and dangerous nature, as well as the outsiders' exotic gaze, create a place with little human presence and activity; as will be illustrated in the next section, this image is challenged in the texts by the indigenous Sami's presence.

Sami Movements

While on the one hand characterized by wild nature, Lapland is also the home of the Sami, who through Læstadius' texts have a clear presence in the area. The Sami also get a solid historical anchoring in Lapland. The Swedish settlers, Læstadius claims, arrived in Lapland in the last half of the 1600s, but, in order to locate the first appearance of the Sami, one might "need to go back to the 1600s before the birth of Christ, and one might still not find it" (Læstadius 1833, 451). In the following section, I will focus on the Sami movements in the texts, in pursuit of an explanation to this seemingly paradoxical way of depicting Lapland as empty and wild, and at the same time inhabited by the Sami.

Læstadius describes the nomadic indigenous Sami in his journals as mainly migrating from east to west and back. The nomadic way of herding reindeer means moving with the seasons, from the mountain regions in the summer, often all the way out to the coast in the winter. Notably, these travels lack precise depictions in the journals: the direction is clear, but never described in great detail when it comes to specific places for pasture, temporary camps, river crossings, and so forth. Although the lack of detail creates a vagueness regarding the Sami reindeer-herding movements through the Lapland landscapes, the nomadic lifestyle in itself makes the Sami elusive to Læstadius: their summer and winter camps are hard for him to find, and several times when he arrives at his destination, it turns out that the Sami have already moved on. This vagueness, both regarding the details of the Sami movements, and the one created by the nomadic lifestyle, adds to the colonial conception of Sami presence in Lapland as elusive.

Indigenous people in colonial texts are often not present in the same way as the colonizers. Mary Louise Pratt (2008, 48ff.) analyzes how the indigenous Khoikhoi are portrayed in various colonial narratives. In the post-Linnean texts of Anders Sparrman (*Voyage to the Cape of Good Hope*, 1783) and William Paterson (*Narrative of Four Voyages in the Land of the Hottentots and the Kaffirs*, 1789), Pratt highlights how the Khoikhoi servants "move in and out of the edges of the story" without being distinguished from each other and without having their own identity. Pratt calls their presence in the texts "ghostly" because while they become objects for detailed ethnographic description, they are deprived of their own culture and history and their voices are never heard. The Sami in Læstadius' texts are not ghostly in the same way. As mentioned earlier, the Sami are in fact the whole reason for Læstadius' travels to begin with. At the same time, there is something inherently different about the Sami's way of being in the landscape in comparison to the settlers, or Læstadius himself. One may wonder, for example, how the Sami seem to be able to live and move about in Lapland without much trouble, while Læstadius ends up in life-threatening situations wherever he goes, and when the land is so desolate and inhospitable for the settlers?

The following episode captures the conception of the Sami as hard to find, as well as another characteristic of the Sami movements in the landscapes, namely that they find their way more efficiently than the Swedes. Læstadius recounts how he used a description given by a Swedish man called Benjamin to find a Sami named Unnas at Lake Madtaure. Læstadius begins his travels, but the directions he receives are not detailed enough and instead of reaching Unnas, he ends up wandering around in the forest, eventually making his way up on a mountain in order to get a good view. He writes,

> I went away, but soon found that Swedes do not describe the country and the path as firmly and clearly to the unfamiliar hiking man as the Sami do. Based on the description by Sami I have many times gone where I have never been before, but quite well found the way I wanted. They describe mountains, lakes, bogs etc. so well that you easily recognize them [...].
>
> (Læstadius 1831, 430)

Standing on the mountain, Læstadius hears from a distance a "human voice that yoiked"[13] (432) and he shouts a response without being heard. He concludes that the voice belongs to a herdsman with reindeer or someone hunting, but he dares not follow the voice "into the dark limitless forest" (432). Instead he works his way back to the path and eventually finds his way to Unnas' camp. He continues,

> Then I came to Unnas' residence, which I sought; but no human was there. It is apparently so that also fishing Sami have camps, where they stay, and it is in no way certain for the unfamiliar where to seek them. I did not know where to turn in this, for me, unknown wasteland, to find any human.
>
> (Læstadius 1831, 432–33)

Læstadius sets up camp and starts planning where to go next. He hesitates, trying to find a sign of the Sami soon returning, and when he is about to give up and leave, a young Sami named Lars Larsson, arrives at the camp. He too, it turns out, seeks the Sami Unnas, and when he starts to look around for signs, he notices a stick in the ground, pointing toward the northwest. Lars Larsson concludes that Unnas has traveled to a campsite in that direction, and they go together and soon find Unnas. Læstadius concludes,

> For me as an outsider it would have been impossible to find my way. The stick at the beach that showed the direction was put there on purpose just for this objective, but I could not draw any conclusion from it, being unaccustomed to these kinds of signs.
>
> (Læstadius 1831, 436)

Compared to the sedentary settlers, the nomadic lifestyle in Lapland is elusive, almost mysterious. Being Swedish versus Sami in Lapland almost involves inhabiting different dimensions. The Sami can move through the landscapes in ways not accessible to Swedes; their way of being – and especially moving – is both evasive and in a way, ghostly. There is an echo of the parallel theory in this dimensional separation, that is, the idea that the Sami and settlers could coexist due to different ways of utilizing nature.

Going West: Colonization as Movement

The third type of movement in Læstadius' journal has to do with the colonization itself. On the ground, the dominant movement of colonization is that of the non-Sami settlers who come to Lapland and start building permanent settlements. For Læstadius, however, the main movement of the colonization of Lapland is the introduction of *culture*. This is a process repeatedly described using the metaphor of war and conquest, for example, as in the following passage:

> The one that sets out to conquer a hostile land usually fails in his doings, if he moves forward too rapidly and too far from his reserves, so that communication is interrupted. The same happens to the one that wants to make an even more glorious conquest, namely to use culture to take the possession of a desolate land.
>
> (Læstadius 1831, 11)

What is it that is being conquered in this metaphor? The weapon is the culture process, the prize is ownership of the transformed lands, but who is the enemy? This conquest is not described as the settlers conquering the Sami, or interestingly since Læstadius is a Christian missionary, Sami religion. Instead a possible answer is that the enemy to be conquered is the absence of higher culture, symbolized by nature in its "purest" form. That would be in line with a characteristic way of approaching nature from a colonial project's point of view, namely to either *tame* or *civilize* a wild and primitive nature (see Lines 1992), or to reshape nature to better serve human needs (Adams 2003). An important part of Læstadius' higher culture is, of course, Christianity, but it is striking that so much of his discourse centers around more practical socioeconomic issues.

A similar use of language is employed several times, for example, in the second journal when Læstadius elaborates on the colonization process dedicating large parts of the text to the topic. He believes that the progression of culture is the most important part of a country's history, and he returns to the war metaphor:

> After reading everywhere how conquerors have stricken down armies and devastated kingdoms, one can for the sake of change be amused by seeing how settlers clear forests and dig ditches.
> (Læstadius 1833, 170)

Although the settler activities are used as a contrasting example – and surely with a hint of humor – this and similar examples continue to strengthen the analogy between the hard work of the settler and the "glorious" wars fought by kings and their armies. As noted earlier, Læstadius represents the nature of Lapland in terms of long distances that are hard to travel, a harsh climate, barren soil, dangerous ice and rapids, darkness, and fog, thus suggesting that nature constitutes an obstacle to the introduction of culture. The cultivation of Lapland, which Læstadius himself is a part of through his missionary travels, becomes a great achievement precisely because of these obstacles: the glorious conquest would not be as glorious if it were easy.

Looking more closely at the concept of *culture* in the journals, two characteristics emerge: first, that it exists in different degrees – from lower to higher – and, second, that there is a natural or at least preferred direction of development, from lower to higher culture. The idea of cultural development is very old and still exists today as we imagine that societies are constantly evolving. Still today many regard societal development as hierarchical, where, for example, industrialist societies are regarded as on a "higher" level of development than agricultural ones.

Lennart Lundmark (2002, 11–12) refers to Mike Hawkins (1997) and highlights three thinkers whose ideas inspired these thought models: first, Charles-Louis Montesquieu (1689–1755) who described the development of societies as going from barbaric to civilized governance; second, Claude-Adrien Helvétius (1715–1771) who, particularly in his posthumous book *De l'homme* (1773), focused on population growth which he believed led groups of hunters to develop into nomads with domestic animals and finally to sedentary farmers; and third, Jacques Turgot (1727–1781) who believed that all people first were hunters, then nomads and finally reached the highest level, namely agriculturalists. With Turgot, there was also a clear valuation: the different levels were described as "higher" and "lower."

When Læstadius wrote and published his journals in the beginning of the 1830s, such a hierarchical culture mindset was commonplace in the social debates in Sweden. In the latter part of the nineteenth century in Sweden, these ideas about cultural hierarchies fused with racial thinking: those at a "lower" cultural level were also understood as belonging to a "lower standing" race (Lundmark 2002, 12). Although models of cultural hierarchies leave a theoretical opportunity to move "upward" – unlike purely racist ideologies – they build on and convey preconceived opinions and stereotypes about groups of people who not only lack objective validity, but also lead to injustices, unequal power relations, and racism.

The idea that culture exists at different levels is shown, for example, when Læstadius discusses the Finns in the writings of Tacitus,[14] and characterizes them as "purely a hunting nation, on the lowest degree of culture, living only for the day" (Læstadius 1833, 470). He continues, "A nomadic people undeniably stand at a higher degree than a hunting nation" (470). When Læstadius describes the Sami he makes a clear distinction between the forest Sami and the mountain Sami. About the former, he writes "they also are at a better level of culture than the rest so that they among Sami undisputedly are the best" (Læstadius 1831, 225). He values the forest Sami highly and romanticizes their way of living, while the mountain Sami in several passages are described as uncivilized and rough. Finally, at the top of this cultural hierarchy are the farming people. In a discussion of the knowledge about Christianity among the mountain Sami, with references to comparable contexts around the world, Læstadius concludes that a nomadic people never have reached the degree of culture of a farming people (Læstadius 1831, 184).

Læstadius argues that the cultivation of land, and not animal husbandry, should be the priority of the people in the north, for example, when he describes the years of famine at the beginning of the 1800s in the second journal. He supports this opinion using the idea of a preferred path of cultural development:

> To revert from cultivation to animal husbandry is a step back on the path of culture, which no civilized people should take. Tilled land, transformed to pasture, shall always be looked upon by the humanitarian with dissatisfaction and a certain sad feeling.
>
> (Læstadius 1833, 421)[15]

One way of understanding Læstadius' construction of Lapland as inhabited by the Sami, and at the same time as a sort of "pure nature," is with regard to the sharp dichotomy between nature and culture, where the Sami are closer to nature than the "higher" farming culture that the colonizers encourage. Similar examples of colonial discourse from Australia are discussed by Bruce Buchan and Mary Heath (2006), who argue that colonial discourse about indigenous peoples' social structures and relationships with the lands – inspired by John Locke's ideas about the state of nature – created a logic within which the continent of Australia could be defined as *terra nullius*.

A certain geography pertains to these cultural stages and to the colonizing movement in Læstadius' writings. The mountain Sami, representing the lowest degree of culture, are found in the western mountain regions, and the forest Sami, whom Læstadius sees as the "best" among Sami, are found in the forest areas further to the east. By the coast, even further to the east, there are towns and farming communities, that is, representatives of the highest cultural level. This "cultural geography" entails that movement through landscapes in Lapland also means movement through these cultural stages.

In a study with many parallels to the present, Bruce Willems-Braun (1997) looks at the writings of the amateur ethnologist George Dawson, who traveled with the Geological Survey of Canada during the 1870s and 1880s. He finds that indigenous people are not made invisible in Dawson's text, on the contrary, they are described in great detail, but they are disconnected from the landscape and fixed within certain geographical areas, such as villages. Outside of these villages there is empty nature that indigenous peoples only travel across, without leaving either traces or demand for ownership. According to Willems-Braun, this colonial discourse divides the area into primitive parts inhabited by the indigenous peoples, and modern and dynamic parts where the emerging Canadian nation is (1997, 12). Læstadius' Lapland can be viewed as a cultural continuum going from east to west: the crude mountain Sami at one end, followed by the forest Sami and eventually by the culturally advanced farming settlements. The separation in the journals between indigenous and primitive, on the one hand, and dynamic farming culture, on the other hand, is not primarily geographical. Rather, they exist side by side: the Sami travel through the landscape close to nature, elusive, and almost ghostly to the outsider's gaze. The settlers, on the other hand, are manifest, sedentary, and "conquerors" of nature through farming activities.

In Læstadius' journals, Sami culture even becomes a sort of precursor to the colonizers' agrarian society in Lapland, which is perceived to be more advanced. This representation illustrates not only the idea of cultural hierarchies, but also the way in which the different cultural levels are seen as stages in an ongoing development. He even suggests that

Sami culture is a prerequisite for colonization, without which "the whole of Lapland would most likely still be a complete wasteland" (Læstadius 1833, 27).

As the colonization of Lapland allowed the Sami to become settlers, one can ask to what degree Læstadius includes the Sami in the ideological movement taking place in Lapland – from lower to higher culture. As seen in the following quote, Læstadius dismisses an interpretation of cultural levels based on biology and allows the Sami to take part in the development, however, not as Sami, but as acculturated Swedes:

> When the Sami becomes a settler, he becomes completely Swedish, and cannot in a later generation be distinguished from Swedes: that proves that it is not the nature he is born with, but circumstances that stops him from becoming more cultivated than he is.
>
> (Læstadius 1833, 480)

Læstadius sees a future for Northern Sweden based on farming. He does not include the Sami in this vision in any other way than that they abandon their culture and become farmers.

Concluding Remarks

It is hard not to connect the way the Sami inhabits Lapland in Læstadius' journals to "the parallel theory," the idea that settlers and the Sami utilized nature in different ways and therefore could coexist. This ideology was an important part of the Swedish politics of colonization, and is easily distinguished in the governing regulations, for example, *Lappmarksreglementet* from 1749. In a way, through this ideology, the Sami are conveniently removed from the stage of the colonization and assigned to a parallel "indigenous dimension."

The tendency to both romanticize the Sami for living close to nature, and at the same time dismiss them in a way that excludes them from the continuing development of Northern Sweden seems to pave the way for the indigenous politics in Sweden that developed during the end of the nineteenth century, called the *Lapp shall Remain Lapp* policy. This was an ideology of segregation, where the reindeer-herding Sami were to be protected from outside influences, while the non-reindeer-herding Sami were to be assimilated (Lantto 2012, 14ff.). The idea was based on the positioning of Sami culture early in the cultural hierarchy, as weak and threatened by the stronger Swedish culture and therefore in need of protection. Various policies were implemented that were supposed to "shield" the Sami culture from the stronger Swedish one, for example, special nomadic schools for the Sami children, so that they could maintain their connection to reindeer herding (Lindmark 2013, 144).

As I hope to have illustrated in this chapter, the way different groups are described as moving toward and through the landscape in colonial texts is a fruitful way of examining the ideology and mechanics of colonialism. Sami movements are especially interesting given the importance of nomadism in popular as well as official views of what it means to be Sami in Sweden and when discussing land rights. A call to pay more attention to movements when writing Sami history has also been put forward by Anna Lydia Svalastog (2015). She criticizes maps of Sápmi – of the traditional Sami lands – because they rely on an "implicit ethnocentric understanding of settlement as norm" and fail to capture the dynamics of Sami geography (44). By including movements, for example, the Sami people could be understood not as isolated – living far away from other people – but more correctly as partakers in a dynamic geographical context (17). One concrete example of how maps of Sápmi incorrectly depict Sami presence in Sweden is that Sápmi in all older maps – and many new ones too – stops short many miles before reaching the coastal area. This means that traditional Sami winter pastures along the coast are completely hidden in these maps. The parallels to written descriptions of the Sami are many. Although the Sami in Læstadius' writings are constantly moving, in contrast to the static maps of Sápmi, when these movements become inaccessible to the reader Sami presence becomes fleeting – and ghostly.

By looking more closely at the movements in Petrus Læstadius' two journals, we have been given a glimpse into the ideological creation of Northern Sweden during the time of the colonization and also into the implementation and development of Swedish Sami policy.

Notes

1 At the time of the colonization and when Læstadius wrote his journals, the area in question was called *Lappmarken* (Eng. Lapland). Today, *Lappland* is the Swedish name of an administrative area. When the word *Lapland* is used in this chapter, it refers to the older *Lappmarken*.

2 I would like to thank Berit Åström, Lars-Erik Edlund and the participants of the higher seminar at Vaartoe – Center for Sami Research at Umeå University for many insightful comments on earlier drafts of this manuscript.

3 Lars Levi Læstadius was to become a famous religious leader, author, and botanist.

4 This short description of Petrus' life is built upon the detailed biography by Arne Nordberg (1974).

5 There are several Sami languages in Sápmi. In Sweden, South Sami, Ume Sami, Lule Sami, Pite Sami, and North Sami are spoken (Scheller and Vinka 2016).

6 More specifically Piteå Lappmark.

7 Esaias Tegnér (1782–1846) was a famous Swedish professor, bishop, and writer whose bibliography includes the national romantic epic *Frithjof's Saga*. Vitalis was the pseudonym of the Swedish poet Erik Sjöberg (1794–1828).

8 A term used during antiquity for the promontories that flank the entrance to the strait of Gibraltar.
9 This system of Sami Tax Lands (Sw. *lappskatteland*) was abolished in 1928.
10 The name *forest Sami* (Sw. *skogssamer;* older *skogslappar* or *granlappar*) refers to those Sami living in the woods all year round, in distinction to the mountain Sami (Sw. *fjällsamer,* older *fjällappar*), who move with the reindeer up to the fells during summer. This distinction is still in use today, for example, when categorizing the different Sami villages in either *skogssamebyar* or *fjällsamebyar*.
11 All translations of Læstadius' texts are by the author of this chapter.
12 Læstadius refers to the ghost ballad Alonzo the Brave and the Fair Imogene (Nordberg 1977, 73).
13 Yoiking is a traditional Sami way of singing.
14 Tacitus' "Fenni" mentioned in *Germania* 98 AD has been suggested to refer to the Sami people.
15 In a footnote to this passage, Læstadius adds a quote from Vergil: "Impious hæc tam culta novalia miles habebit, Barbarus has segetes" (Læstadius 1833, 421), that is, "Shall the impious soldier possess these so well cultivated fields? a Barbarian these lands?" (Martyn 1820, 26).

Works Cited

Adams, William M. 2003. "Nature and the Colonial Mind." In *Decolonizing Nature: Strategies for Conservation in a Post-Colonial Era*, edited by William M. Adams and Martin Mulligan, 16–50. London, Sterling, VA: Earthscan Publications.
Agnew, John A. 2011. "Space and Place." In *The Sage Handbook of Geographical Knowledge*, edited by John A. Agnew and David N. Livingstone, 316–30. Los Angeles, CA: Sage.
Arell, Nils. 1979. *Kolonisationen i lappmarken. Några näringsgeografiska aspekter.* Stockholm: Esselte studium.
Bergman, Ingela and Lars-Erik Edlund. 2016. "Birkarlar and Sámi – Inter-Cultural Contacts Beyond State Control: Reconsidering the Standing of External Tradesmen (birkarlar) in Medieval Sámi Societies." *Acta Borealia: A Nordic Journal of Circumpolar Societies* 33 (1): 52–80.
Böök, Fredrik. 1918. *Den romantiska tidsåldern i svensk litteratur.* Stockholm: P. A. Norstedt och söners förlag.
Buchan, Bruce and Mary Heath. 2006. "Savagery and Civilization: From Terra Nullius to the 'Tide of History'." *Ethnicities* 6 (1): 5–26.
Bylund, Erik. 1956. *Koloniseringen av Pite lappmark t.o.m. år 1867.* Uppsala: Almqvist and Wiksells boktryckeri AB.
Cresswell, Tim. 2009. "Place." In *International Encyclopedia of Human Geography*, 169–77. Amsterdam: Elsevier.
Hawkins, Mike. 1997. *Social Darwinism in European and American Thought.* Cambridge: Cambridge University Press.
Kvist, Roger. 1992. "Swedish Saami Policy, 1550–1990." In *Readings in Saami History, Culture and Language III*, edited by Roger Kvist, 63–77. Umeå: Center for Arctic Cultural Research.
Lantto, Patrik. 2012. *Lappväsendet. Tillämpningen av svensk samepolitik 1885–1971.* Umeå: Vaartoe. Centrum för samisk forskning. Umeå universitet.

Læstadius, Petrus. 1831. *Journal af Petrus Læstadius för första året af hans tjenstgöring såsom missionaire i Lappmarken.* Stockholm: Hæggström.

——— 1833. *Fortsättning af Journalen öfver missions-resor i Lappmarken, innefattande åren 1828–1832.* Stockholm: Nordström.

Lindmark, Daniel. 2013. "Colonial Encounter in Early Modern Sápmi." In *Scandinavian Colonialism and the Rise of Modernity: Small Time Agents in a Global Arena*, edited by Magdalena Naum and Jonas M. Nordin, 131–46. New York: Springer.

Lines, William J. 1992. *Taming the Great South Land: A History of the Conquest of Nature in Australia.* Sydney, NSW: Allen and Unwin.

Loomba, Ania. 2015. *Colonialism/Postcolonialism.* 3rd ed. Milton Park, Abingdon: Routledge.

Lundmark, Lennart. 2002. *"Lappen är ombytlig, ostadig och obekväm." Svenska statens samepolitik i rasismens tidevarv.* Umeå: Norrlands universitetsförlag.

——— 2010. *Stulet land: Svensk makt på samisk mark.* Stockholm: Ordfront.

Martyn, John. 1820. *P. Virgilii Maronis Bucolicorum Eclogæ Decem: The Bucolicks of Virgil, with an English Translation and Notes.* Oxford: Printed by W. Baxter for G. and W.B. Whittaker, London.

Mörner, Magnus. 1982. "The Colonization of Norrland by Settlers during the Nineteenth Century in a Broader Perspective." *Scandinavian Journal of History* 7 (1–4): 315–37.

Nordberg, Arne. 1974. *Petrus Læstadius. Upplysare och upprorsman.* Luleå: Norrbottens Museum.

——— 1977. "Kommentar till Journalen och Fortsättning af journalen." In *Petrus Læestadius journaler. Faksimiletext och kommentar. 3. Kommentar och ordförklaringar samt person- och ortsregister,* published by Arne Nordberg, 30–102. Umeå: Skytteanska samfundet.

Pratt, Mary Louise. 2008. *Imperial Eyes: Travel Writing and Transculturation.* 2nd ed. London and New York: Routledge.

Said, Edward. 1993. *Culture and Imperialism.* London: Chatto and Windus.

Scheller, Elisabeth and Mikael Vinka. 2016. "The Saami Languages." In *Encyclopedia of the Barents Region. Vol. 2. N-Y,* edited by Max Olov Olsson, 265–70. Oslo: Pax.

Svalastog, Anna Lydia. 2015. "Mapping Sami Life and Culture." *Visions of Sápmi,* edited by Gunlög Fur and Anna Lydia Svalastog, 17–45. Röros: Arthub Publisher.

Tuan, Yi-Fu. 1977. *Space and Place: The Perspective of Experience.* Minneapolis, MN: University of Minnesota Press.

Willems-Braun, Bruce. 1997. "Buried Epistemologies: The Politics of Nature in (Post)colonial British Columbia." *Annals of the Association of American Geographers* 87 (1): 3–31.

3 Geographies of Marginalization and Identity Politics in Kiran Desai's *The Inheritance of Loss*

Aparajita Nanda

[M]emory is a sort of anti-museum: it is not localizable. Fragments of it come out in legends. Objects and words also have hollow places in which a past sleeps ... It is striking here that places people live in are like the presences of diverse absences. What can be seen designates what is no longer there ... [I]t is the very definition of a place, in fact, that it is composed by these series of displacements and effects among the fragmented strata that form it and that it plays on these moving layers ... Places are fragmentary and inward-turning histories ... accumulated times that can be unfolded.

(de Certeau 1984, 108)

Memory, as Michel de Certeau defines it, not only goes back in time, but is about silenced time; it is about muted histories, myths, and legends that remain encysted in individual and collective memories of a social group. Collective memory, as Maurice Halbwachs (1992) points out, is a shared pool of knowledge that is reconstructed by one generation and another, which in the process often garners auxiliary facts. It is this memory that makes a place a palimpsest,[1] with the hauntings of "partially erased" writing (read: memory) that remains as a trace of origin myths and tales and often constitutes history. An inhabitant of the place is already connected to an "absence that structures it as existence and makes it 'be there' – that is recognized only in spatial interpretations of the place" (109). As Valentin Mudimbe (1991, 169) clarifies, "[t]he object of an anthropological curiosity (a culture, its institutions, rituals, or mythical narratives) constitutes a place with its proper rules that the anthropologist's activity and interpretation transform into a new space. This new product is a 'practiced place.'" This act of interpretation embodies the placeness. And naturally the exploration of the concept of space provides an insight essential to the comprehension of reality that leaves an indelible mark on the resident's identity. Space plays a multi-dimensional role in one's life; the tripartite division of space by Henri Lefebvre (1991) into perceived, conceptualized, and lived space goes on to suggest that space is an interactive discourse that affects humans and is defined or altered by humans who occupy a particular place. Thus, not only are the present and the past of any place significant, but also the "diverse absences" or traces of mythical memory that, as de Certeau says, "culturally orders and geographically borders places" (Hrasnica 2014, 15).

This discourse of place and space becomes exponentially complicated in Kiran Desai's *The Inheritance of Loss* (2006) as the narrative alternates between Kalimpong in India and Cambridge in England. It tracks the lives of an expatriate judge, Jemubhai Patel, who in colonial times goes to Cambridge for higher education only to return to India; and Gyan, tutor to the Judge's granddaughter, who never leaves India. The British colonization of India had established a dualistic and binary model of thinking that emphasized white empowerment and virility against native infirmity and impotence. Jemubhai and Gyan are trapped by this history, imprisoned by the places to which they belong or desire to belong. This chapter looks at how the characters, given their situations, often seek to read the places they inhabit as spaces of liberation and empowerment. On deeper analysis, however, the reader understands that these spaces are neither freeing nor empowering; they are ambiguous and contradictory and confound both Jemubhai and Gyan by permanently branding them as inheritors of loss[2], the emasculated others of colonization, the roots of which may be traced back to a palimpsestic memory.

Desai's novel pays close attention to geographical place. Situated in the foothills of the Himalayas, Kalimpong is located in the western part of the district of Darjeeling. Darjeeling is the headquarters of the Sadar district, which is located at an elevation of 6,700 feet. It is an area of frequent landslides and earthquakes where the potential of sudden natural disasters creates a sustained sense of subterranean instability. The disruptive violence in the geographical/geological environment and the havoc wreaked by humans on mother earth degrade place to mere space and destabilize the residents' impression of security and "placeness" (Ferguson 2009). Historically, the place has also been a hotbed of warfare, colonial occupation, chaos, and discrimination. Until the intervention of the British East India Company in the early nineteenth century, the area suffered intermittent conflict between Sikkim and Nepal; this temporarily ended in the defeat of the Gorkhas by the British and the signing of the Sugauli Treaty in 1815. Later, however, continued friction between the East India Company and the Sikkimese authority led to another spree of warfare and the British annexation of the entire district of Darjeeling in 1865. Under British rule, the Darjeeling area was declared a backward tract (Borbora 2003), where socioeconomic problems were rife. With the independence of India in 1947, Darjeeling was merged with the state of West Bengal. However, ethnic demands of the Nepali population in Darjeeling escalated in the 1950s and 1960s and by the 1980s had snowballed into violent agitations for a separate state of Gorkhaland, which formed the crux of the Gorkha National Liberation Front (GNLF) movement. In complete contradiction to its topography and history is the toponymy of Darjeeling. The name of the place evolved from the Sanskrit "Durjaya Linga," referring to the invincible prowess of Lord Shiva, the ruling Hindu deity of the Himalayas. The name Darjeeling can also be traced back to the Tibetan words *dorje*, the thunderbolt scepter of the Hindu deity Indra, and *ling*, a place or land (Samanta 2000, 66). Kalimpong means Land of Kings. These toponymic suggestions fortify a sense of protective stability endorsed by deific strength. The historical memory, the geographical place, and the mythic resonance in the place name contribute radically to a sense of confusion that incapacitates both Jemubhai and Gyan forever.

It can be argued that the narratives of the Judge and Gyan show that the lives they live and the lives they desire to live emanate from the geopolitics of space, which are permanently defined by what Marianne Hirsch (2012) calls a sense of "postmemory," the painful inheritance of trauma through generations. *The Inheritance of Loss* analyzes how geographic environments contribute to the traumatic process of marginalization and creation of identity, and how space socially excludes colonized people across class, age, even generational divides. Ruvani Ranasinha (2016, 65) highlights a passage that "signals the artificiality of shifting national borders" that left the natives as mere pawns in a game of colonial power:

> Here, where India blurred into Bhutan and Sikkim ... it had always been a messy map ... A great amount of warring, betraying, bartering had occurred; between Nepal, England, Tibet, India ... Darjeeling stolen from here, Kalimpong plucked from there – despite the mist charging down like a dragon, dissolving, undoing, making ridiculous the drawing of borders.
>
> (Desai 2006, 10)

The artificiality refers to how borders and claims on the land had been arbitrarily decided by the colonizers and changed at will. The impact of this on the displaced native population had been devastating with significant loss of lives and property. The most horrifying example of this colonial tactic was, of course, the division of India in 1947 into two contending nations, India and Pakistan. In the same way that Indian independence in 1947 separated people who had lived in harmony for hundreds if not thousands of years, the establishment of a Gorkha state promised again to disrupt the peace in which places like Kalimpong had existed for all this time. In an ironic replay of the 1947 Indian partition, Desai's novel describes the thwarted GNLF movement of the 1980s in Darjeeling.[3] Place, once again, stands witness to a history of loss. The play of history, as a recursive device, and the role of the geographic environment along with the toponymical underpinnings create a space that satirizes and rewrites the lives of the inhabitants. Space here works both as a physical living being and as an imaginary cultural construct that leaves behind psychologically maimed individuals, insecure in being, emasculated in psyche. The inherent ambiguity and sense of indecision at the heart of these debilitated characters, the Judge and Gyan, which originate in the geographic environment and the mythic memory of the place, owe a lot to colonization, and combine to create an empty machismo that mocks their perceptions of manhood by exposing their flawed cores.

Trapped in a delusional sense of power, a self-damning sense of inferiority, and a horrifying sense of aggression that overwhelm the Judge's convoluted psyche, Jemubhai remains a figure of dark humor – a ridiculous monstrosity. Jemubhai Popatlal Patel, whose middle name denotes a popular comic sidekick to Bollywood heroes, is referred to as "the Judge" in most of the narrative. The Judge's story, revealed through flashbacks, puts together his birth in the peasant caste and his parents' single-minded endeavor to see him succeed academically and thus buy a ticket out of poverty. This brings a chance to study law at Cambridge University and finally to pass the Indian Civil Service Examination and return to India as a judge. Jemubhai, however, never takes his parents seriously, and it is only when he sees a picture of Queen Victoria that he begins to take school seriously: "He found her froggy expression compelling and felt deeply impressed that a woman so plain could also have been so powerful. The more he pondered this oddity, the more his respect for her and the English grew" (Desai 2006, 66). Herein begins his fascination with white supremacy, the attitudes and ideologies associated with European dominance over "colored" native populations, which imbue his psyche with delusional visions of power. Ironically, this attitude also marks his psyche with a deep sense of inferiority that goes back to his ethnicity and place of birth. Subsequent behavioral anomalies of the Judge all emanate from this devastating contradiction between commonness and power that for the Judge translates into gross, aggressive, and abusive behavior directed toward his parents, his wife, and even his granddaughter's tutor, in all of whom he sees a reflection of himself. Contained in a space of allocated colonial power, Jemubhai becomes a victim of the notion of hegemony as proposed by Antonio Gramsci (1971), which defines domination as a paradoxical relationship of consent maintained through political and ideological discourses. David Turnbull (1993, 7–9) points out that often the purposeful distortions of colonial maps were to convey to the natives the power of a distant center and how the colonies should perceive that center of power; the metaphorical implication of the picture similarly projects the imperial power of the Queen and her control over her subjects from a distance.

Jemubhai's admiration for this space (read: the greatness of the Empire) psychologically nurtures his desire to emigrate and buy into a superior status and belittle his native cultural values. Thus, as he leaves the shores of India for England, he looks at his father with pity and shame, for the man was "barely educated" (Desai 2006, 42). Jemubhai loathes the food his mother had prepared with love and care, throwing it away as the product of "undignified love, Indian love, stinking, unaesthetic love – the monsters of the ocean could have what she had so bravely packed getting up in her predawn mush" (43). The physical and metaphysical journey of Jemubhai Patel had begun: "Never again would he know love of a human being that wasn't adulterated by another contradictory emotion" (42). "Contradictory emotion" leaves him in the throes of a deeply desired "English" power and strength and the obvious weakness of his victimized position of being born a native. This discrepancy seems to be strengthened by the geographical seascape with its empowering promises of "travel around [the] globe" (42). And yet the feeling is fleeting as it ultimately weakens Jemubhai, for

> when [he] had first learned that the ocean traveled around a globe, he had felt strengthened by this fact, but now when he stood on the confetti-strewn deck of the ship, looking out at the sea flexing its endless muscles, he felt this knowledge weaken him.
>
> (42)

Clearly the space of the high seas, which recalls imperial ventures of colonizing the world (represented by the very masculine "flexing [of] endless muscles"), at this instance overpowers Jemubhai until his own inadequacy is revealed.

Jemubhai's academic sojourn in Britain furthers this sense of confusion and alienation as he internalizes the Cantabrigian cityscape of ostracization, racism, and marginalization. His stay in Cambridge brings to the fore the discrepancies between his actual life and his desired fantasy life as part of his investment in the Empire. He becomes the target of vicious racial stereotyping: from people refusing to rent him a room to elderly ladies who move away from him "when he [sits] next to them in the bus ... [G]irls [hold] their noses and giggle ... 'Phew, he stinks of curry!'" (45). Food is often linked to notions of home, comfort, and nostalgia particularly in a foreign land. It is interesting to note how the Indian curry becomes a brutal signifier of racism here. But even more interesting is how the hateful rhetoric makes Jemubhai more a "stranger to himself than he was to those around him, [as he] found his own skin odd-colored, his own accent peculiar" (45). He develops a sense of self-hatred wherein "[h]e envie[s] the English [and] loathe[s] the Indians" (131). A typical example of what Homi Bhabha calls "a reformed, recognizable Other ... *as a subject of difference that is almost the same, but not quite*" (1994, 86, emphasis in the original), Jemubhai slowly becomes a recluse "despised by absolutely everyone, English and Indians" (Desai 2006, 131). The discriminatory politics of the foreign place permanently instills a deep-rooted sense of insecurity in Jemubhai who, even when he returns to India, remains branded by the misconstrued social status he had hankered for in England. He expects his family "would have the good taste to be impressed and even a little awed by what he had become, but instead they were laughing" (184). Insulted by their reaction, he lashes out at his wife, seeking perhaps his own distorted redemption in a bid to cleanse his own Indianness. He hates her "typically Indian bum" and physically abuses her when he discovers footprints on the toilet seat, by taking "her head and [pushing] it into the toilet bowl" (189, 190). He quips in a delirious chant: "She was squatting on it, she was squatting on it!" (190). Despite his intense loathing of her, he indulges in constant and consistent sex with her, all the while reminding himself, "[h]e would teach her the same lessons of loneliness and shame he had learned himself" (186). All in all, his perverse treatment of his parents and his wife seems to recycle the treatment that had been meted out to him in England. By internalizing the racial hatred, Jemubhai once again proves his victimized status as he remains stuck in a psychological space defined by colonialism. Moreover, his gullibility regarding everything British exposes his naivete as he defects from Indian to British culture.

Disgusted with his circumstances, the Judge retires early in an attempt to isolate himself from the lesser Indian mortals; in actuality, this is his defense mechanism to deal with his out-of-place-ness, "a foreigner in his own country" (32). He buys a house, Cho Oyu in Kalimpong, Darjeeling – the elevated location in the hills possibly feeding his power-hungry ego, for as Bill Ashcroft (2001, 172) points out, "to inhabit place is, in a variety of ways, to inhabit power." The swashbuckling entry, reminiscent of a medieval knight, as he rides "up on horseback, push[ing] open the door into that space lit with a monastic light, the quality of which altered with the sunlight outside," naturally helps him to feel that "he was entering a sensibility rather than a house" (Desai 2006, 32). The physical details of the house and the artifacts it contains script another narrative, though. When the Gorkha boys steal from the Judge's home, they find "a dusty row of" guns and bottles of "Grand Marnier, amontillado sherry, and Talishker" – the contents had "evaporated completely and some had turned to vinegar" (6, 8). The glamor of yesteryear was dead as the Judge had retired and his house had fallen into decay: "It was cold, but inside the house, it was still colder, the dark, the freeze, contained by stone walls several feet deep ... The walls were singed and sodden ... thickets of soot clumped batlike upon the ceiling" (1, 2). Ranasinha (2016, 68) notes that "the state of the house reflects the judge's 'downfall from wealth' and current genteel poverty gleefully noted by his less-well-off visitors" – the Gorkha insurgents who humiliate the Judge to no end, making him repeat at one point, "I am a fool" (Desai 2006, 8). The Judge's cringing acquiescence makes him out as a coward bereft of any masculine retaliation. Also, after the incident, none of his neighbors come to sympathize with him. The Judge had removed himself from everybody and was shunned by all and sundry. Clearly the life he lives in Kalimpong remains as an extension of the memory and hangover of his English sojourn. Cho Oyu, in its resplendent seclusion, has been recognized by Margaret Scanlan (2010, 270) as a "metaphor of colonial decay," its basement infiltrated by water, insects, and mice.[4] The house, a ruin of its former glory, is also undermined by a deep-seated contradiction that dooms its core foundation. And this paradox draws on the geopolitics of the place, both Kalimpong and Darjeeling – undermined not only by geological disasters but also by the toponymic assurances that inject a note of mockery in the region's claim to glory. The tragedy of the Judge is that he lives on as "a parody of an Englishman, devoted to his dog Mutt and the nursery treats of pre-war Britain" (Desai 2006, 271); the pathos of this tragedy, I feel, is further enhanced by the ridiculous denial of the Judge refusing to recognize the collective memory of the place. Subconsciously crippled by a deep-seated confusion that draws on colonial hauntings and the deific powers ensconced in the name of the house as well (*Cho Oyu* in Tibetan means "turquoise goddess"), the Judge lives on as a travesty to be mocked and disrespected by everyone.

The Judge's deep-rooted insecurity drives him to despise and embarrass others as he sees his native self reflected in them. In one instance, he feels compelled to humiliate Gyan, his granddaughter's tutor. To exonerate himself from the insults he had been forced to endure in England when he had been asked to recite a poem from memory, Jemubhai asks Gyan to recite a poem and keeps mocking him by laughing "in a cheerless and horrible manner" (120). As pathetic as the Judge is, so is Gyan who suffers from the same delusional confusions and contradictions as his employer. However, there is a marked difference between the two. Gyan's contradictions have far more complex roots as he sees himself (and by extension his people) as doubly colonized by the British Empire and Indian nationalism. He struggles against his marginalized status that is further undermined by the paradoxical oscillation he must feel, being a native son of the foothills of the Himalayas, between deific stability and assurance, on the one hand, and chaos and turmoil, on the other, never to be rid of either.

By virtue of the double colonization, Gyan remains a victim of the socioeconomic space that defines him. Gyan's sense of worthlessness is evident from very early on and expanded throughout the book; even his introduction insinuates his dual marginality. He enters the story when the Judge's granddaughter, a Westernized Indian orphan named Sai, requires a tutor. Sai's grandfather hires Gyan to take over tutoring in science and mathematics but only after Sai's other tutor, Noni, exhausts her abilities to teach in these subjects. Gyan gets the job only as a result of a vacancy, a vacuum in which he is mere filler. Even his name, which in Sanskrit means knowledge, mocks his very existence, as Sai's grandfather does not hire Gyan because he boasts some exceptional pedagogical prowess which places him next in line to tutor Sai; the Judge hires Gyan simply because the principal of the local college recommends him as a promising but out of work student. Essentially, Gyan's economic need, brought to the fore by the dire conditions of the economic crisis of the 1980s, forces him to accept the position. In fact, after Gyan and Sai have a fight, she goes in search of him in an impoverished neighborhood of Kalimpong. Sai's visit to Gyan's home amplifies both the economic and social disparity that divides them. Ironically enough, Sai realizes the deep contradiction that defines Gyan: "[t]he house [doesn't] match Gyan's talk, his English, his looks, his clothes, or his schooling" (280). It portrays how the contradiction, between the place that Gyan inhabits and the enhanced socioeconomic space he lays claim to, plays a seminal role in embarrassing him forever.

Despite his desire, Gyan realizes that any effort to ameliorate his condition needs him to overcome several social barriers. Foremost among them is a deep-seated inferiority complex that gnaws away at Gyan's soul. He repeatedly refers to his mediocrity as compared to the convent educated "splendid" Sai (119); social class and the privileges it brings, even in independent (so-called postcolonial, for a country once colonized is colonized forever) India, are still determined by the colonial legacy, the credo of which is "English is better than Hindi" (33). In fact, at one point, Gyan, more and more aware of his being out-of-place around Sai, has to deal with a guilt that reads as if his plebeian-ness could be contagious, and "it [would be] wrong of him to ... force this ordinariness upon [Sai]" (119). This perception of contagion that cuts across the social divide has very interesting parallels in the history of contagious diseases in the tropics and the European population that in postcolonial India sought refuge in hill stations like Darjeeling. As Nandini Bhattacharya argues, these colonial enclaves became a sanatorium for "medicalized leisure," (2012, 91) a safe enclave that resisted the contagion of diseases and yet whose medical and social exclusivity were threatened by the overcrowding of the Indian masses, what Dane Kennedy calls "the Intrusion of the Other" (as quoted in Bhattacharya 2012, 84).

And yet once inducted into the Patel household, Gyan is driven by dreams of bettering his social standing by inhabiting spaces where he feels he can reinvent his identity. For a moment he seems to lose himself as he recites a poem at the bidding of Sai's grandfather: "Where the head is held high, Where knowledge is free .... Into that heaven of freedom, my Father, let me and my country awake"[5] (120). Gyan's recitation of this poem reflects his newfound drive to seek "that heaven of freedom" that can meet all his expectations, his only liberating space here being love, "intense, tiny pleasures that nevertheless created a feeling of space on all sides" (120, 299). As Gyan becomes more and more comfortable with Sai, his own purpose becomes increasingly apparent to him; he chooses to commit himself to a space of self-discovery defined by beliefs, which seem to extend past what he thought he was capable of.

Gyan's desires, which exceed his realm of possibility, entice him, whether consciously or subconsciously, to cross professional and gender boundaries that transform the place into a transgressional space. Gyan's first encounter with his tutee, which appears to be focused only on academics, is charged with "tremendous anticipation" that leaves both Gyan and Sai gasping for breath (81). The night of the storm, which Gyan spends at Sai's house, provides a place for physical proximity; the raging storm outside is cited as an excuse for "the growing impossibility of speech [that] make[s] other intimacies easier" (127). What begins as adolescent foreplay (for after all, Gyan is twenty and Sai sixteen years of age) quickly transitions from a tentative examination of Sai's body parts ("Collar bones, eyelashes, chin") to a highly charged discourse of sexual consumption, and when Sai "couldn't bear it – she closed her eyes and felt the terrified measure of his lips on hers, trying to match one shape with the other" (137, 138). The personal and the political realities seem to merge here. As Gyan transgresses conservative gender divides (both the tutor/tutee and the unwed male/female boundaries) his landscaped (the body parts are so carefully mapped out here) actions replay the actual and attempted annexation of territory, both of the colonial and the 1980s insurgency. Gyan's actions transform the mapped out body into a transgressive space that he claims as his own. But transgression has its pitfalls too, particularly in the cultural context. And as "rain and wind whooshed and banged, the trees heaved and sighed, and the lightning shamelessly unzipped the sky," Gyan is drowned in a spurt of guilt ironically tinged with a sense of bravado at having touched forbidden territories (132).

Having failed in his self-discovery through love and freedom in his relationship with Sai, Gyan's newfound sense of courage now prompts him to seek release and reinvent himself in the political place of the times. Gyan translates his sudden allegiance to the GNLF cause as a retaliatory space. He lashes out at Sai, calling her a "copycat," who mindlessly conforms to Western culture (180). As a result, Shyam Ji Dubey (2012, 3) points out, Gyan "[retreats] to his own culture" by joining the GNLF. I would hardly call it a retreat; in fact, I think Gyan makes another bid for a space of liberation, a space of progression in his otherwise docile life. At this point, Gyan's mind is ignited by "the stirring stories of when citizens had risen up in their millions and demanded that the British leave" (Desai 2006, 174). He no longer considers Sai's Westernized upbringing as superior to his own, but as an insult to the entire Gorkha struggle. This sudden reversal of attitude toward Sai is an outcome of Gyan's failed venture to discover himself through love. Talking about love, Gyan says, "But so fluid a thing was love. It wasn't firm, he was learning ... it was wobbliness that lent itself to betrayal, taking the mold of whatever he poured it into" (194). This wobbliness is fed also by the ambivalence of the origin memory of the toponymic resonances embedded in the place, the strife for delusional power that easily leads to betrayal, for after all, it is Gyan who sends the Gorkha boys to steal guns from the Judge's house. By extension, Gyan's attempt at achieving power proves equally unreliable as he "trie[s] to be a part of the larger questions, trie[s] to become part of politics and history" (299). Gyan's exposure to the place, the political reality of 1980s Darjeeling, leaves him doubly confused (his foray into politics a mere extension of his failure in love) and his attempt at seeking a sense of liberation in the revolutionary space of the GNLF therefore a ludicrous farce.

Defined by nebulous fluidity and resultant insecurity, Gyan joins the GNLF not for any particular ideological commitment. He is swept away on a landslide of nationalist rhetoric: "Gorkhaland for the Gorkhas" or "Victory to the Gorkha Liberation Army" (8; 172). Gyan gets caught within this perceived rhetorical space as he seeks to validate his manhood through the GNLF. One day when he is buying rice in the market, Gyan encounters "a procession coming panting up Mintri Road led by young men holding their kukris aloft and shouting, 'Jai Gorkha'" (172). Gyan is "gathered up" by this procession, the mobility of the place as it plays into his spatial interpretation makes him "slide" along only because he recognizes the faces of his college friends "Chang, Bhang, Owl, Donkey" (172).[6] He seems to garner validation for his meager, marginalized, and in fact vulnerable status as he seeks "an affirmation he'd never felt before" (173). Gyan remains a pathetic victim of spatial politics, as he draws sustenance from this revolutionary space in an attempt to find a meaning and purpose for his life. At one point, he feels ashamed of his association with Sai, and in a desperate bid to reject the "feminine" space and the juvenile memories associated with it, as a "requirement of his adulthood," he voices "an adamant opinion that the Gorkha movement take the harshest route possible" (177). Gyan continues to believe in the merits of the GNLF in order to justify his own possessive involvement in their nostalgic claim to "a masculine atmosphere" (177). Spending time around his Gorkha brethren *seems* to make Gyan a passionate and vocal member of the insurgency, but in reality he is "[f]ired by alcohol" as he shares the anger of his compatriots (176). The space feeds his desire to fantasize about a power he has never had and will never have; thus his attempt remains a delusional spark – a final bid to access manhood and power only to be denied both, for as the narrative ends, Gyan leaves the GNLF movement with nothing achieved – almost as he had entered it.

David Spielman (2010, 88) points out that both the Judge and Gyan advocate "radical postcolonial sensibility" in the throes of seminal contradictions that emanate from their "lived" experience. I would add that their desired lives evolve not only from the ramifications of a colonial hangover but also from the native cultural meanings that animate this space of memory and its impact on the human psyche. All along the Judge refuses to accept the place to which he belongs – that no matter how much he tries he will always be Indian – and instead chooses to ignore the contradiction and operate as if he were a British man among uncultured freaks. Furthermore, the geographic milieu of his place of retirement, along with the native myths and legends as part of collective memory represented primarily in names, plays a subterranean role in further undermining his psyche. As the Judge stands defined by the place he desires to inhabit, Gyan is ensnared by the place he inhabits; a victim to the ambivalences he feels toward his life, including but not limited to his feelings for Sai, and his joining the GNLF. He constantly thinks about his motivations and questions whether they were justified. Gyan is a son of the soil and his indecisive nature reflects the contribution of geographic environment and mythic culture to his process of marginalization. The multiple marginalizations ultimately leave him in a self-contradictory mode. To re-define their lives, both the characters interpret the places as centered on liberation, but instead are characterized by the inherent contradiction at the heart of this "practiced place" that denies them manhood forever.

Any attempt at self-definition must take into account the multilayered sociopolitical and geographical contexts inherited by the self-definer; however, neither the Judge nor Gyan recognize or accept the palimpsestic nature of the places they inhabit and, consequently, the identities they have inherited. Driven by delusional dreams of achieving a manhood, social status, and power they can never attain, both men attempt to rewrite this historical script of loss; however, they can only reshape – not escape – this narrative, for as a palimpsest, it has already been multiply rescribed, replete with memories both present and absent which, unable to ever be fully erased, can only be affected. Thus, in their desperate, Sisyphean efforts to discard these inherited identities, they resort to acts of violence and aggression. By the novel's end, the Judge remains a horrifying version of eroded manhood, desperately glossing over his own failings by transferring them onto others, and Gyan, a meager shadow of manhood seeking endorsement of his adulthood through his juvenile escapades. Without accounting for the overlaid identities, cultural myths, geopolitical boundaries, and (post-)colonial histories of the places they inhabit, the conflict of their cultural memory bleeds through, and their acts of self-definition become self-destructive.

Notes

1 The *Oxford English Dictionary* defines palimpsest as a "parchment or other writing surface on which the original text has been effaced or partially erased, and then overwritten by another; a manuscript in which later writing has been superimposed on earlier (effaced) writing" (OED).

2 The British ruled India for almost 250 years. When they granted independence to India on August 15, 1947, they split the country into two contending nations, India and Pakistan. India, they claimed, was for Hindus, while Pakistan was for Muslims. This momentous decision led to unprecedented violence, rioting, and loss of life as families desperately tried to cross over the newly instituted borders – the Hindus fleeing to India and Muslims to Pakistan. The aftermath of this partitioning surely counts as one of the most horrifying losses that India (or humanity for that matter) has suffered.

3 Ona Sabo adds: "By satirizing the Nepalis' map-making attempts, the novel suggests that [any] self-definition needs to take into account a larger context, in this case, colonial and regional politics" (2012, 383).

4 See Ferguson (2009) on how nature undermines edifices and Martins (2010) as to how the private space of Cho Oyu is invaded by the GNLF boys and the ravages of nature to leave Jemubhai's existence and his house in jeopardy.

5 Rabindranath Tagore's poem "Where the mind is without fear" articulates the Indian Nobel Laureate's vision of a "modern" postcolonial India, whose citizens can fearlessly strive for social reforms that seek to break rigid, traditional boundaries.

6 The names Chang and Bhang are caricatures of characteristically Indian names.

Works Cited

Ashcroft, Bill. 2001. *Post-Colonial Transformations*. New York: Routledge.

Bhabha, Homi. 1994. *The Location of Culture*. London: Routledge.

Bhattacharya, Nandini. 2012. *Contagion and Enclaves: Tropical Medicine in Colonial India*. Liverpool: Liverpool University Press.

Borbora, Sanjoy. 2003. Experiences on Autonomy in East and North East: A Report on the Third Civil Society Dialogue on Human Resources and Peace. Accessed November 20, 2017. www.mcrg.ac.in/civilsocietydialogue3.htm.

de Certeau, Michel. 1984. *The Practice of Everyday Life*. Translated by Steven F. Rendall. Berkeley: University of California Press.

Desai, Kiran. 2006. *The Inheritance of Loss*. New York: Groove Press.

Dubey, Shyam Ji. 2012. "Identity Crisis in Kiran Desai's *The Inheritance of Loss*." *The Criterion: An International Journal in English* 3 (1): 1–4.

Ferguson, Jesse Patrick. 2009. "Violent Dis-Placements: Natural and Human Violence in Kiran Desai's *The Inheritance of Loss*." *Journal of Commonwealth Literature* 44 (2): 35–49.

Gramsci, Antonio. 1971. *Selections from the Prison Notebooks of Antonio Gramsci*. Translated by Quintin Hoare and Geoffrey Nowell Smith. London: Lawrence and Wishart.

Halbwachs, Maurice. 1992. *On Collective Memory*. Translated by Lewis A. Coser. Chicago: University of Chicago Press.

Hirsch, Marianne. 2012. *The Generation of Postmemory: Writing and Visual Culture after the Holocaust*. New York: Columbia University Press.

Hrasnica, Amela. 2014. "New York City as a Place of Immigrant Experience in Kiran Desai's *Inheritance of Loss*." M.A. thesis, University of Sarajevo.

Lefebvre, Henri. 1991. *The Production of Space*. Translated by Donald Nicholson-Smith. Oxford: Blackwell.

Martins, Margarida. 2010. "Landscape and Identity in Contemporary South Asian Women Writers." *The International Journal of Interdisciplinary Social Sciences* 5 (5): 439–45.

Mudimbe, Valentin. 1991. *Parables and Fables: Exegesis, Textuality, and Politics in Central Africa*. Wisconsin: University of Wisconsin Press.

Oxford English Dictionary, s.v. "Palimpsest," Accessed August 25, 2017. https://en.oxforddictionaries.com/definition/palimpsest.

Ranasinha, Ruvani. 2016. *Contemporary Diasporic South Asian Women's Fiction: Gender, Narration and Globalization*. London: Palgrave Macmillan.

Sabo, Oana. 2012. "Disjunctures and Diaspora in Kiran Desai's *The Inheritance of Loss*." *The Journal of Commonwealth Literature* 47 (3): 375–92.

Samanta, Amiya K. 2000. *Gorkhaland Movement: A Study in Ethnic Separatism*. New Delhi: A.P.H Publishing Corporation.

Scanlan, Margaret. 2010. "Migrating from Terror: The Postcolonial Novel after September 11." *Journal of Postcolonial Writing* 46 (3–4): 266–78.

Spielman, David. 2010. "'Solid Knowledge' and Contradictions in Kiran Desai's *The Inheritance of Loss*." *Critique* 51 (1): 74–89.

Turnbull, David. 1993. *Maps and Territories: Science is an Atlas, A Portfolio of Exhibits*. Chicago: University of Chicago Press.

Part II

Environmental Landscapes: Constructing and Consuming Nature

Introduction

Steven Allen and Kirsten Møllegaard

Place is frequently demarcated by the simple binary of man-made versus natural. Although the comparison emphasizes direct physical intervention, the associated distinction of culture and nature reveals that the dichotomy also operates in terms of ways of seeing, so that what does not fit the culturally accepted view of human-inhabited/marked place is deemed untouched, natural, or, as discussed in Part I, *terra nullius*. Furthermore, as Ross Gibson (1992, 75) has commented, "The very notion of nature is a cultural construct." Part of such a construct embodies humankind's various notions of environmentalism. Prevailing attitudes toward environmentalism tend to weigh concerns for preservation against economic benefits, with place viewed as either an economic resource or a natural haven. That the cultural and the natural might be more intertwined than this suggests is largely eclipsed in mainstream, Western understandings of environmental landscapes, though not necessarily so in other cultures.

Part II focuses on environmental landscapes and examines the various claims made about, and on, "natural" places and how these have been represented in literature and film. The chapters are united by questions of change and nature, including how the cultural impacts the natural environment, and how nature is constructed for human consumption in film, literature, and contemporary folklore.

In the chapter "Tasmania: Australia's Cinematic Landscape of Loss," Steven Allen analyzes three films, *Dying Breed* (Jody Dwyer, 2008), *The Hunter* (Daniel Nettheim, 2012), and *Van Diemen's Land* (Jonathan auf der Heide, 2009), which depict quests for the extinct thylacine (aka the Tasmanian Tiger) and the nineteenth-century escape of cannibal convict Alexander Pearce. Allen argues that these films' visual and aural representation of wilderness serves as a celebration of what has been saved, while the narratives explore a cultural landscape of loss. Tasmania's landscape has been a battleground of competing claims since

British colonization and beyond. The folkloric returns of past traumas, such as the officially extinct status of the thylacine (the last specimen died in captivity in 1936) compounded by reported sightings of the animal up until today, serve as means to process a landscape defined by loss. The films facilitate a hypothetical yearning in conversation with the historical record by exploring folkloric elements in relation to a land apparently screened off from the rest of the world. In this manner, the films process contemporary tensions regarding meanings and values attached to place. Drawing on a cultural and ecocritical understanding of Tasmania, Allen points out that Tasmania more recently has become a popular destination for nature-based tourism and ecotourism because of its pristine isolation, and its cinematic depiction in the past ten years has portrayed a series of (re)discoveries of the primordial landscape as protagonists travel through a land defined by loss and separation.

Within film studies, considerations of place are typically framed around the political axis of national and local identity, rather than through the more universal ecological lens of environmental sustainability and communal interconnectivity. Pat Brereton's chapter "Perceptions of Place in an Irish Energy Landscape on Film" focuses on the rapid growth of an Irish ecological sense of place and how it has been shaped and influenced by the filmic imagination. Recalling Ireland's long-standing antipathy toward invasive energy production and nuclear power – especially protests against dumping radioactive waste from the UK into the Irish Sea, alongside the harvesting of raised peat bogs in the Irish Midlands – Brereton investigates the roots of an Irish environmental sense of place. While the dominant myth visualized within historical Irish cultural narratives has remained a pastoral one, which foregrounds an almost Arcadian evocation of the happy swain close to nature, Brereton explores how this perception has been challenged. He argues that some fiction films, together with documentary activism, can promote a new form of environmental and spatial literacy that draws from a deep-rooted sense of place. He compares the romanticization of place in Irish cinema in *Man of Aran* (Robert Flaherty, 1934) and *The Field* (Jim Sheridan, 1990) to *Eat the Peach* (Peter Ormrod, 1986) to show how Irish film has been preoccupied with a farming ideology of transforming wilderness into a fertile agricultural land.

No discussion of environmentalist narratives can fail to address Henry David Thoreau's impact on our perception of nature, especially in the context of the United States. David M. Robinson's chapter "Walking the Mythical Path: Thoreau's Old Marlboro Road" examines Thoreau's essay "Walking" (1862), one of his lesser discussed works, in which he reflects on walking along the Old Marlborough Road. "Walking" explores unending transformation, depicting Thoreau's daily walks as mythical quests, efforts to know the ever-renewing unknown in nature. Central to these walks is the largely abandoned "old" road from Concord to

Marlborough, whose neglect and seclusion constitute its philosophical strength and ideological appeal. The Old Marlborough Road is the path of the "saunterer," the heroic knight forever in search of new and liberating experience. It is not a road from one place to another, but a Taoist's perpetual way forward that provides the saunterer access to "a subtle magnetism in Nature," and thus to the ever-present "wild" that defines and animates us. Robinson explores the multiple imaginative dimensions that Thoreau invests in the Old Marlborough Road, which encompass the religious pilgrimage in the modern age, and the emerging conception of the wilderness as an ethical and political category. These themes are closely intertwined in the essay, and carry with them examples of Thoreau's post-*Walden* intellectual focus as he evolves from transcendentalist to practicing naturalist.

In all three chapters, we see how place is both physically and symbolically malleable when defined in terms of the cultural and the natural. Each chapter addresses either cinematic or literary texts that shed light on the idealism of environmentalism within the political and philosophical construction of nature.

Work Cited

Gibson, Ross. 1992. *South of the West: Postcolonialism and the Narrative Construction of Australia*. Bloomington: Indiana University Press.

4 Tasmania

Australia's Cinematic Landscape of Loss

Steven Allen

Introduction

Tasmania is Australia's only island state. Separated from the mainland by 150 miles of ocean, Nicholas Shakespeare (2005, 7) declares that "Tasmania is in myth and in history a secret place, a rarely visited place." Its distance, but also its location's colonial past, including British penal colonies, and the institutionalized maltreatment of the island's Aboriginal people, the Palawa, are central to such evasiveness. First named by Europeans in 1642 as Van Diemen's Land, in 1856 it underwent renaming, partially to escape its troubled heritage. Its very isolation has, more recently, brought it visibility, with its remote wilderness attracting big spending ecotourists, and visitor numbers of 1.24 million in 2016 (Tourism Tasmania 2016, 1).

The simultaneous fascination and desire to cast out informs the depictions of the island, and is underpinned by notions of guilt in terms of lost natural and cultural landscapes. This chapter examines three films from the past ten years that are set in Tasmania – *Dying Breed* (Jody Dwyer 2008), *Van Diemen's Land* (Jonathan auf der Heide, 2009) and *The Hunter* (Daniel Nettheim, 2012) – and that are linked by their depiction of recounted tales of loss. *Dying Breed* and *The Hunter* are set in the present and are premised on quests to find the "extinct" thylacine, or Tasmanian tiger; *Van Diemen's Land* is a historical account of Alexander Pearce, the notorious "cannibal convict," a figure whose legacy also features in *Dying Breed*. The intertwining of convictism and the Tasmanian tiger is not without precedent. When colonized, "The first Europeans to set eyes on a thylacine were five escaped English convicts" (Shakespeare 2005, 310); fittingly it tied them in a shared history. Mistakenly testified to be "a large tiger," subsequent accounts of the thylacine would fuse the mythological with the scientific (see Paddle 2000, 26–36). A similar amalgamation operates in the films, as they coalesce observation, testament, mistaken perceptions, and wish fulfillment to examine human and nonhuman absent presences in the landscape.

The thylacine was a large marsupial predator that once roamed both mainland Australia and Tasmania. By the time of colonization, it survived only on the isolated island. Shamefully, the thylacine was deliberately hunted, including being subjected to a bounty scheme between 1888 and 1909. The last wild thylacine was reportedly killed in 1930, and the final captive animal died in Hobart zoo in 1936. Since the thylacine's apparent demise, numerous searches, large bounties, reported sightings, and elaborate plans to clone DNA have failed to produce an authenticated animal. Instead, the thylacine survives through the testimonies of those claiming to have sighted it.

Also reliant upon testimony is the tale of Alexander Pearce, which "has been narrated many times in song, on the stage, in print, and on screen" (Stadler 2012b). Pearce was transported to Van Diemen's Land in 1820 for stealing six pairs of shoes. He would notoriously abscond from Sarah Island, Macquarie Harbour, with seven other convicts, in 1822. Journeying for 49 days, he covered over 125 miles of largely untraveled (by Europeans) terrain. En route, two of his companions fled, and returned to the penal settlement, only to die, while the others were murdered in turn by Pearce's group to feed the remainder. When captured months later, Pearce, the lone survivor, confessed his cannibalism, but the authorities rejected his claims, believing he was covering for his companions, who must still be at large. Like the sightings of the thylacine, it is a story based on doubt. Returned to Macquarie Harbour, Pearce subsequently escaped with another prisoner, Thomas Cox. When again back in custody, Pearce provided two additional documented confessions, including admitting to killing and eating Cox; he was hanged in 1824 (see Hughes 1996, 219–26; Stadler et al. 2016, 104, n.3).

Tying together both sets of narratives across the three films are the themes of loss, testimony, and intrusion on nature. *The Hunter* features Martin David (Willem Dafoe) recruited to track down and kill the last thylacine after renewed sightings. Hired to provide DNA samples for a biotech company, Martin poses as a university scientist, and stays with the family of a missing environmentalist, Jarrah (Marc Watson-Paul), in a community divided between the ecological and economic values of the wilderness; the two perspectives are portrayed as irreconcilable. *Dying Breed* depicts four travelers, including zoology student Nina (Mirrah Foulkes), searching for the thylacine. Dismissed as mere legend, Nina's sister had claimed to have found a Tasmanian tiger's pawprint, before she mysteriously drowned. Both films are journeys by outsiders, "committing eco-cultural trespass" as Catherine Simpson (2010, 51) calls the visitors in *Dying Breed*. Comparably, *Van Diemen's Land* features convict interlopers, and through being set in the past, it asserts a lineage of encroachment on this land.

The trio of films also share encounters with the wilderness that are framed through folkloric tales that blur truth and doubt. Evidently, narratives featuring the thylacine do so as they foreground alleged sightings amidst hope and disbelief. Although present in both *The Hunter* and *Dying Breed,* it is not the thylacine but Alexander Pearce's story, "the stuff of folklore" (Morris 2009) that inspires the latter. The film reimagines Pearce's story, envisaging him having fathered an isolated population of people eaters during his escape, and with his present-day progeny intent on preserving their community's way of life. Unlike the other two films, it highlights cultural heritage amidst the natural, albeit with the cannibals paired with nature, for their culture is also being intruded upon ("you tourists have no tradition"). The combination is defined as dangerous, as the community preys on outsiders. In addition, *Van Diemen's Land* is similarly focused on Pearce, and tells the story of his first escape. Because of its historical setting, it is framed as an authentic illustration of his confessions, with an emphasis on the act of (re)narrating via the use of the protagonist's voice-over.

Through their depiction of outsiders in the Tasmanian landscape, the films explore prevalent anxieties regarding loss and conservation. Ostensibly asserting a dualism of nature and culture, a stance regularly played out across political, ecological, and cultural debates, the application of folklore, as well as undermining empirical certainty, implicitly acknowledges that place cannot be disaggregated via the simplistic binary. Vera Norwood (1996, 334) states "Nature and culture are interactive processes: human culture is affected by the landscape as well as effecting change on it." The films indicate such an intertwining, but nonetheless take an anthropocentric stance whereby "nonhuman nature is defined solely by its relation to the human and the cultural" (Narraway 2012). The landscape is not only read in terms of human experience of loss, but also celebrated via an ecotourist gaze that serves as a testimony to what has been preserved. Just as natural and cultural landscapes are seen to be competing for validity in contemporary Tasmania, so too are they here, but absent presences, such as the thylacine, bring doubt in terms of what has been lost. Although providing temporary hope, the doubt ultimately enables the loss to be continually repeated, thereby privileging cultural contrition over a holistic understanding of the changing wilderness.

Wilderness and the Gothic

Emily Bullock frames the cinematic depictions of the island state through the lens of "Tasmanian Gothic," which brings together the varied but often harsh landscape (dense forests, vast ravines), the unpredictable climate (gloomy, lingering mists), and the omnipresent colonial history into a Gothic fusion of out-of-placeness. She concludes that such cinema articulates "Tasmanian anxieties about its past, its future and its perpetually wracked present" (2011, 78). Undoubtedly valid, such a view can be limiting; temporal intrusion cannot be examined at the expense of multifaceted spatial intrusion. Bullock's exploration of Tasmania's fretfulness is centered on the colonial past of convictism and the treatment of Palawa; therefore, it largely avoids the ecological concerns that run parallel in contemporary debates. Jane Stadler argues for a "move away from the settler-colonial perception of landscape as a villainous adversary" pointing instead for the need to appreciate "an ecological gaze" (2012a). Charting environmental concerns in Tasmanian cinema from 1925 onwards, Stadler argues that, collectively, the films depict an entanglement of two falsely conceived polarities: the landscape as malevolent threat to humans (Gothic) and as an environment threatened by humans (ecological gaze). I argue that the ecological gaze, although present, is consistently reduced to an estheticized landscape that undermines the perils faced by the environment. Moreover, it largely ignores explicit engagement with the ecological complexity of relationships between organisms and their environments, instead using the landscape to buttress a distinction between nature and culture. Offering a strong correlation to contemporaneous debates regarding the treatment of Tasmania's wilderness, the films neglect any form of deep ecology, which would see nature having intrinsic value outside its use as a resource for humans, and instead afford repeated failed attempts to assuage guilt of past losses.

Competition over the land – both its use and its meaning – has underpinned much of Tasmania's history since colonization. The Black Line strategy deployed by Governor Arthur in 1830 attempted "to drive four of the nine Tasmanian Aboriginal nations from their homelands to another part of the island" (Ryan 2013, 3). More recently, battles have existed between conservationists and those seeing nature as a resource, such as hydroelectric corporations and logging companies. Indeed, in 1972, Tasmania was the site of the "first political party [United Tasmania Group] based on an environmental platform to contest elections anywhere in the world" (Rainbow 1992, 327); the 1980s witnessed the popularization of state and federal Green parties, and Australia launched the world's first National Ecotourism Accreditation Program in 1996 (Ecotourism Australia 2017). In part a consequence of such initiatives, the Tasmanian Wilderness World Heritage Area (TWWHA), a UNESCO site, now measures in excess of 1,500,000 hectares, approximately 20 percent of the island's land mass (Parks and Wildlife Services Tasmania 2017).

Jim Russell and Mirjana Jambrecina (2010, 126) note that "'wilderness' is not a component of any of the World Heritage criteria." The term itself, although open to multiple definitions (see Garrard 2012, 66–92), tends to "designate a place apart from, and opposed to, human culture" (67). That the TWWHA contains rural communities makes the definition problematic, with the wilderness status not universally welcomed. Of all the UNESCO sites, the TWWHA has been changed the most, with the Federal Government attempting to remove 74,000 hectares from it only one year after they were added in 2013 (Mathiesen 2014). The forestry agenda was confirmed in 2014 when Prime Minister Tony Abbott declared "We have quite enough national parks, we have quite enough locked-up forests already" (in Milman 2014). Logging has a strong economic and cultural history, and the films reflect this: it is associated with the intrusive penal colony in *Van Diemen's Land,* and forestry and conservation are polarized positions in *The Hunter*; but none of the films center this ecological debate. Rather, they appear to mediate broader questions about the wilderness, and its relevance to contemporary Tasmania.

Embedded within TWWHA are two terms that some Tasmanians see as being at odds: wilderness and heritage.[1] Some argue that meanings attached to places within TWWHA, including the colonial and postcolonial histories, are being sacrificed to construct a perceived pristine nature. This includes the removal of, or decision not to maintain, access roads and other human traces, such as stock routes and huts. We might regard this as artifact-based sites being erased in favor of a wilderness; however, as noted by Russell and Jambrecina (2002, 128), the very notion of wilderness is problematic for Aboriginal people that see the "natural areas as integral with cultural life." Indeed, as Deborah Rose states, definitions of wilderness that "claim that these landscapes are 'natural' miss the whole point of the nourishing Australian terrains" (1996, 18). Furthermore, successive World Heritage Area nominations were applied for, at least in part, on cultural grounds, including occupation by Aboriginal people from 35,000 years ago and nineteenth-century convict history (Russell and Jambrecina 2002, 126). Nonetheless, the polarization remains.

The three films under discussion in this chapter can be read in relation to these tensions, for there is a heightened estheticization of the wilderness, while narratively they draw upon heritage, in the form of folkloric tales of loss and extinction. Before focusing on the latter, some analysis of the representational mode of the films is necessary.

Tasmania's Cinematic Wilderness

The two films set in the present day, *Dying Breed* and *The Hunter,* begin by contrasting modernity and wilderness. Although *Dying Breed* has a historical flashback prior to its title credits, both films feature airport/aircraft scenes to establish their contemporary settings, while they share subsequent scenes depicting outsiders arriving in Tasmania by airplane. All three films begin their showcasing of the natural landscape via a series of traveling shots that snake between the verdant, confining environment. Throughout, shot scales are chosen to infer the dominance of the landscape over the human visitors and to contrast them with an apparently more natural world. Moreover, the land is not known (and perhaps even knowable), with representations unable to express the wilderness. In *The Hunter,* parts of the Highlands are described as not mapped, with a character commenting a "satellite map's all right, but it doesn't mean anyone's been there." *Dying Breed* features a dam that intrudes on the landscape, and at first is not believed to be on the map, while the film's central premise is that an undiscovered community of cannibals exists in the wilderness. And *Van Diemen's Land* depicts meandering convicts, doubling back at dead ends, and exclaiming "this is not Table Mountain." All three stress the experiential quality of nature, which resonates with out-of-placeness. In sum, the films indicate a form of displacement not readily accounted for via a Gothic interpretation, as the stress is on a gap in knowledge and understanding of the wilderness.

Questioning the place of humans in nature comes in another form too. The land is awe-inspiring for those traveling through it, with it variously witnessed across the three films as "God, it's beautiful" (*Dying Breed*) and "So beautiful. How can it be so beautiful?" (*Van Diemen's Land*), as well as leaving characters dumbstruck by a vista (*The Hunter*). Here, the magnificence of nature (not the associated horror of the sublime) displaces an ecocentric interpretation. Rather than evoke an operating ecosystem, these moments merely illustrate superficial splendor that connotes a quintessentially touristic panorama (Figures 4.1 and 4.2). Moreover, they fall into the trap outlined by William Cronon, whereby "Any way of looking at nature that encourages us to believe we are separate from nature – as wilderness tends to do – is likely to reinforce environmentally irresponsible behavior" (1996, 87). Cronon therefore points to a stance that "suggests that nature is only authentic if we are entirely absent from it" (Garrard 2012, 77). This is precisely what these shots visualize as they lingeringly contrast the human with the nonhuman.

The predominance of location shooting provides an additional layer of meaning, for it affirms the wilderness has been preserved in real life. The legitimacy of the landscape requires a caveat: in respect of *The Hunter*, "Filming took place entirely in Tasmania," even for the Paris Airport location (*Production Notes – The Hunter* 2018, 7), but Jonathan auf der Heide, director of *Van Diemen's Land*, states, "the majority of the film

Figure 4.1 Wilderness as touristic panorama in *The Hunter* (Dir. Daniel Nettheim; Prod. Magnolia Pictures, Screen Australia in association with Screen NSW, Screen Tasmania, Fulcrum Media Finance, Madman Entertainment & Entertainment One; 2012).

Figure 4.2 Wilderness as touristic panorama in *Van Diemen's Land* (Dir. Jody Dwyer; Prod. Noise & Light, Inspiration Studios, Screen Australia; 2008).

was shot in Victoria [mainland Australia]" (auf der Heide 2012), which also doubled for parts of *Dying Breed*. However, auf der Heide continues by claiming "We spent ten days shooting in Tasmania where we captured all of the scenes that had any sense of landscape … or water." In addition, in respect of *Dying Breed*, Stadler (2012b) records "much of the footage … [was] shot in locations that Pearce might have travelled through, had his northward escape route been successful," while it also utilizes recognizable human-made locations such as the Zeehan Spray Tunnel. The latter is a site of horror, pointing to the dangers of humans interfering with the landscape, but collectively the films (and their promotion) clearly exult the authenticity of the location, especially a pristine wilderness. In effect, it seems to say look at how wonderful Tasmania's wilderness is, even when depicting fallacious spatial configurations. By showcasing what has been conserved, it simultaneously advocates immutability. Denying an ecocentric understanding of the landscape, it privileges a dominant anthropocentric view that supports ecotourism, namely a stewardship of nature that preserves its isolation. Rather than the economically material approach associated with logging, the films appear to endorse a use value for the wilderness in respect of pleasure, while nonetheless suggesting that nature is distinct from culture.

Establishing the separation is pivotal, for it enables the depiction of culture intruding on nature. The soundscape plays an important role in the process. Allowing for the generic requirements of horror cinema in the case of *Dying Breed*, the films feature a noticeable predominance of natural noises such as wind, rain, and cascades. Daniel Nettheim, director of *The Hunter*, states "the sound design is sometimes heightened in a highly subjective manner" (in *Production Notes – The Hunter* 2018, 9).

Ironically, by noticing its naturalness, the sound becomes unnatural. As V.F. Perkins argues in respect of lighting effects in *The Red Desert* (Michelangelo Antonioni, 1964), "We are so busy *noticing* that we respond rather to our awareness of the device than to the state of mind it sets out to evoke" (1990, 85, emphasis in the original). The effect is especially pronounced in respect of silence, the most disquieting element of the three films' soundtracks, which serves as an absence alongside the natural noises. In *Van Diemen's Land,* silence is often accompanied by stillness, with static shots contemplating the wilderness, and awaiting the escapees to emerge into the landscape. We might interpret such scenes as suggesting a nonanthropocentric model of nature, acknowledging that it is not merely brought into being through its relationship to humankind, and recognizing nonhuman agency. But the emphasis does not lie here. Guinevere Narraway (2012) argues that the convicts are linked to nature in three ways: they have been expelled from civilization, their cannibalism is linked to animal savagery, and they are defined via their bodies (not minds). Moreover, Narraway (2012) sees these contemplative scenes "absorb[ing] the men into the natural environment." For me, the scenes evoke the cultural more than the natural. Conservationist and wildlife watcher Geoff King explains how in 1842, on what later became his property, "the last surviving Tasmanian Aborigines in the bush surrendered" (in Shakespeare 2005, 320). Describing his feelings, King states "There's been a quiet noise in the landscape since 1842" (320). The troubling disturbance of the absence is what is embodied in the hush, and so it goes beyond experiencing the wilderness as "lifeless" as Narraway (2012) reads the silence. What is stressed is a pervasive absence that has presence, and it encapsulates an intrusion of the cultural.

Despite the visual and aural strategies to aggrandize the natural world, it is apparent that some imagery is not realist. In respect of *The Hunter,* Nettheim (in *Production Notes – The Hunter* 2018, 9) indicates a defined esthetic that "avoid[ed] filming exteriors in the middle of the day, as we were after an atmospheric look of low light and long shadows." The style is more pronounced than limited lighting, as it often features desaturated colors, which emphasize a gloominess of setting at odds with the espoused magnificence. Similarly, *Van Diemen's Land* is described as "a landscape leached of colour" (Stadler 2012a). It is as if there is a failure in the coding, with it moving from depicting the tangible profilmic to representing a feeling about place. We might interpret this via the Gothic, but alternatively we could see it as the cultural revising the natural. Discussing the management of TWWHA, Russell and Jambrecina (2002, 131) argue, "wilderness is poorly equipped to be the central defining value … as it selectively ignores community attachments." These filmic moments, when a realist view of nature appears to break down, capture the essence of there being something more than the tangible. It therefore becomes a suggestion of both the preserved natural, and the intrusion of the history of the place. In *The Hunter*, it becomes most pronounced in the mythological moment when the extinct thylacine appears, and the scene takes on an artificial, desaturated blue-tonal quality. In a world where anthropogenic changes to the environment, such as global warming, seem to be endlessly contested, the demise of the thylacine appears to offer the indisputable impact of humankind; however, these films provocatively insert uncertainty. The filmic mode responds as if troubled by the claim: it is as if the doubt in respect of the folkloric return has overwhelmed the conviction of the natural world.

Loss and the Folkloresque

A focus on the wilderness (both by the films and by Tasmania's management of its landscapes) can be seen as overcompensatory in respect of the losses experienced by the state. Primary among these are the Tasmanian Aboriginal people, apparently wiped out with the death of the supposedly last "full-blood" Palawa, Truganini, in 1876. What George Murray called an "indelible stain upon the character of the British Government" (in Reynolds 2004, 140) has taken on a hypercharged significance, with it described as "ethnic cleansing" (145–46) and Robert Hughes claiming that it was "the only true genocide in English colonial history" (1996, 120). And yet, genocide is hotly contested. As Nicholas Smith (2012, 283) notes, the "myth of Palawa extinction denied the existence of the Furneaux 'Islander' communities and other surviving indigenous Tasmanians." In effect, there is a double extinction – first the decimation of Palawa through violence, disease, and poor living conditions, and second, through a denial of the survivors. Furthermore, Smith (2012, 283) proposes that "Thylacine narratives posit existence in the face of extinction, whereas the myth of Truganini posits extinction in the face of existence." That the historical record was incorrect in proclaiming the demise of the Palawa resonates with the repeated imagings/imaginings of the Tasmanian tiger – extinction may not be the end. Notions of loss within Tasmania are therefore located in relation to a battle between authorized accounts of events and contested disavowals that come in various retellings of traditional narratives, including myths, folktales, and the narratives of popular culture. Collectively, these can be termed the folkloresque,[2] by which I mean they utilize motifs and narratives associated with folkloric storytelling. Although featuring tales of past losses, all three films exclude Palawa from their narratives. The Palawa are, however, present by their absence, which in turn links to both the thylacine and convict history via a palimpsestic approach to the past, whereby "Like the convicts, the natives survived only in misrepresentations" (Conrad 1988, 98). Consequently, the films examine the land's meanings in respect of loss, and do so by reenacting or reimagining the loss, which sits in contradiction to the natural landscape apparently being unchanged.

The folkloresque occurs thematically through tales of thylacine sightings and convict narratives, but also via the stress on nonwritten cultural histories. The lack of dialogue, especially in *The Hunter* and *Van Diemen's Land*, places greater emphasis on when characters do speak, with voices intruding after sustained periods of quietude and natural sounds. Crucially, nonwritten communication is framed in terms of the folkloresque, including testimony, storytelling, and dissemination across generations. In *Van Diemen's Land*, the voice-over foregrounds orality, not least because of the use of Gaelic for these moments and through its integration of moments of song with the prose (reflecting an Australian ballad tradition). The story's origins in Alexander Pearce's admissions of guilt locates it within the act of narration, while the film is only one of the various iterations of his escape, thereby providing another layer to "an accumulation of the meanings and morals ascribed to this confession" (Whelehan 2015, 158). *Dying Breed*'s contribution to this accretion is through imagining a narrow gene pool threatening Pearce's descendants. The narrative harnesses a prevalent regional, settler mythology: "inbreeding is another aspect of Tasmania's insular mystique. Tasmanians love to tell stories about the endogamic clans of the midlands ... Tasmanians keep the legends alive by repeating them, and personally vouching for their truth" (Conrad 1988, 114). The rumored existence of the cannibals is suggested in the film by the repeated rhyme of "Simple Simon," which combines reference to the natural (the Pieman River where the real Alexander Pearce absconded) and the cultural (the community's (human) meat-filled pastries), via a traditional nursery rhyme. *The Hunter* also accentuates silences and relies on testimonies. Rather than speech, a drawing of a thylacine by Jarrah's young son, who pointedly refuses to speak, and whose father had witnessed the creature, first confirms its existence, and then its location. All three films evidently privilege oral or visual communication over the usually authoritative written language.

These folkloresque narratives highlight telling and retelling the wilderness, defining it as both a natural and cultural landscape. Although ostensibly devested of agency, nature is revealed to have the potency to prompt meaningful cultural responses via the folkloresque, and in turn, culture is seen to impose narratives on complicated ecosystems. The thylacine provides a heightened intersection of the two, and serves as a repository to negotiate loss.

The Thylacine

Australia's Threatened Species Day, 7 September, commemorates the anniversary of the death of the last Tasmanian tiger. But with "1 out of 3 mammal extinctions in the last 400 years hav[ing] occurred in Australia" (Australian Wildlife Conservancy 2017), the animal is emblematic of more than its own end. Its symbolic potency extends further to embody a conglomeration of loss that includes the natural and the cultural. As Nicholas Smith notes, "Extinction is the ligature that binds Palawa and thylacine in the Australian imaginary" (2012, 283). If we take Conrad's perspective, that the Palawa "weren't extinct, as we had been told; we were simply unable to see them" (1988, 103), perhaps this is what is hoped for with the thylacine. Significantly, *Dying Breed* and *The Hunter* depict the tragic image of a captive Tasmanian tiger. Scratchy film images reveal the repetitive movements of the animal pacing its cage and convey the circularity of the narratives about to unfold. Most extinct animals have not been photographed, but here the imagery at once confirms the animal and asserts its absence. Like the folkloric tradition of the revenant, it returns from the grave, yet lacks presence. An ethereal computer-generated image version later appears in both films which, because of its relationship to its referent, both attests to and denies the creature's presence (Figure 4.3). These arresting visions draw attention to culture's role in nature, including humankind's complicity in extinction and its narrating of the wilderness. The façade of a conserved landscape crumbles, but not to afford an analysis of nature based on deep ecology, which would need to address the ecological impact of the loss of the largest nonhuman predator in the ecosystem; instead, the films highlight a cultural experience of loss informed by doubt.

Smith (2012) points to there being an "unforgetfulness" in terms of the thylacine, which will see it always returning, until the trauma of colonial history is faced and reconciled. Indebted to a Lacanian reading, Smith (2012, 269) regards it as a "return of the real." I agree that the re-animated thylacine disturbs the symbolic world, visually evidenced in these films by appearing out of place, yet through the films foregrounding acts of narration, the creature is defined as coming to life through the symbolic. Moreover, the films are characterized by forgetting as much as by unforgetting, thereby suggesting that "The problem indeed is our

Figure 4.3 The ethereal thylacine in *The Hunter* (Dir. Daniel Nettheim; Prod. Magnolia Pictures, Screen Australia in association with Screen NSW, Screen Tasmania, Fulcrum Media Finance, Madman Entertainment & Entertainment One; 2012).

forgetfulness. Tasmania has unwritten its own history" (Conrad 1988, 96). Rather than a "return of the real," I would argue the emphasis is on the repression of any return – a repeated process of reencountering what has been lost, only for it to be lost again. Structurally, repetition is echoed in the films through the depiction of numerous false returns and a cyclical pattern that sees the returned thylacine being forgotten again. In *The Hunter,* circularity takes several forms, including the repeated trips by Martin up the Central Plateau in search of the thylacine, only for its presence to be denied each time, and Martin to return to his temporary abode. And then when the thylacine is discovered, he chooses to kill it, to save it from exploitation. Stadler (2012a) regards the act, with the related disposal of the animal's ashes over an imposing escarpment, as "harness[ing] a sense of the sublime to reinstate Martin's place in the web of life." But we might read it differently, as a repeated cycle of hope, followed by acknowledgement of extinction. Repetition occurs in other ways too, for instance, Lucy (Frances O'Connor), the wife of the murdered ecologist, Jarrah, cries out "You're back" when she hugs a man wearing his boiler suit, only to find it is Martin. Like the thylacine, Jarrah is there but not there. Lucy too has her own false return. She acts as a form of ecofeminist who, regardless of gender being culturally defined, seems to be linked to nature by a feminine essence. Thus, she has stopped studying for her PhD to be a wife and mother, and is delineated by her emotionality as opposed to rationality. Moreover, having become addicted to antidepressants to cope with the loss of Jarrah, Lucy is resurrected from her comatose state by Martin; in a clear echoing of the thylacine, she must die again, in a fire (as does her daughter but not her son). Such a pairing accentuates repetition and sets up an androcentric relationship that privileges the rationality of men (i.e., culture) over nature, including the thylacine/Lucy.

Dying Breed also resounds with repetitions. The narrative features zoologist Nina suffering the same destiny as her sibling, being unable to prove the thylacine's existence and becoming a sexual slave to further the bloodline of the cannibal community so that it "stay[s] pure like your tiger." But the thylacine is again denied a confirmed return, at least symbolically. Police inspecting the disappearance of the tourists align themselves with the locals ("I was born here"), and rather than fully investigating events, they nonchalantly discard a cell phone, which only the audience can see displays the fading photographic record of a living thylacine. It is therefore lost again.

Both films restrict any optimism that the historical record may be wrong, for they reject the return of the creature, privileging doubt over affirmation. Smith, writing before the release of *The Hunter,* and addressing sightings and media representations of thylacines, sees them as a focus on "ecological blunders of the past" as a possible means by which "settler's forgetfulness" is agitated (2012, 285). However, I regard this group of films as not only addressing the past, but also the retelling process, so that they depict the reencountering of the trauma, not the resolving of it. Through the application of the folkloresque, heritage and wilderness appear to achieve a mutual valency, but cultural doubt is favored over ecological enquiry. The worth of the landscape is embodied in its anthropocentric value: it facilitates a comforting ecotourist vision of an unchanging, conserved wilderness that offers glimpses of hope, plus it is a heritage space to replay cultural insecurities. Undeniably these doubts include past actions, but they also indicate uncertainty as to how heritage and wilderness might coexist as landscapes today.

Conclusion

Both *Dying Breed* and *The Hunter* form a kind of reimagining, which envisages events through folkloresque claims regarding the past returned. While the natural world is depicted as agelessly intact and lacking agency, the cultural landscape is wracked with false hopes and doubts through constant renarration. It seems to me not insignificant that conservationists die in both films. As surrogates for nature, the conservationists are reduced to the testimonies of others and flashbacks (so like nature, have no agency of their own), and are destroyed to further cultural aims (preserving the cannibal community and protecting the biotech company). We might interpret this as reflecting wider debates in Tasmania in respect of the wilderness agenda.

The focus on absent presences throughout the chapter fits easily within the Gothic, but it also maps onto the continuing battle for supremacy between wilderness and heritage status for Tasmania's landscapes. Without doubt, the films favor cultural concerns, even when focused on nature. The stories, however, could be told very differently, so that they recognize the interdependence of nature and culture to stress equally strong ecological reverberations. Geoff King describes how species that would have been the thylacine's prey, such as the Tasmanian devil, must still be hardwired to anticipate its attack: "It's like they're listening for a ghost" (in Mittelbach and Crewdson 2006, 90). The comment rethinks what some would regard as a Gothic trope, via a different understanding, that of the ecosystem; the shift is made more pronounced when placed alongside another observation by King: "If the Tasmanian tiger exists, it's in the mind of the Tasmanian devil who doesn't know that the thylacine is extinct" (in Shakespeare 2005, 322). Read in such a way, it is the connectedness, that includes those between nonhumans and other nonhumans, as well as humans and nonhumans, that sustains the thylacine's presence in the landscape.

The films withhold a full eco-gaze, such as that suggested by King. Instead, folklore, like ecosystems, creates connections with place. The thylacine serves as an intangible presence to work through prevalent concerns regarding the direction of conservation in Tasmania, as well as how post-settler society comes to terms with, or is in fact unable to come to terms with, the historical record. Interestingly, whereas the vehicle license plates from 1998 to 2008 had the tagline "Tasmania – Your Natural State," they subsequently changed to the current version which reads "Tasmania – Explore the Possibilities." The new slogan suggests hope, but equally it is about doubt, and of course, both plates contain the image of the illusive thylacine. It seems evident that alongside a preservation of the wilderness, there is a cultural desire to preserve doubt.

Coda

Being set in the past, the natural landscape in *Van Diemen's Land* is simultaneously a cultural landscape of convictism. There is no thylacine to create doubt; rather the film intervenes to renarrativize past doubts. Historically, the authorities rejected Pearce's first confession; it was too troubling to be believed. *Van Diemen's Land* offers no direct representation of the story being based on Pearce's testimony. Moreover, the denunciation of Pearce's confession is relegated to a single title slide at the end of the film, with only an oblique reference to his subsequent cannibalizing of Thomas Cox. In effect, it reconfigures doubt into visualized certainty. The stark black lettering on white proclaims indubitableness, but the background is ethereal, being the bleak sky that the camera has panned up to from the certainty of the verdant landscape. Alexander Pearce's fellow abscondees, like him, are the absent presences in the landscape, with nature once more divorced from the cultural.

Notes

1 In 2015, it was revealed that the state planned to remove Wilderness from TWWHA's title; in 2016, UNESCO recommended against it.
2 Michael Foster and Jeffrey Tolbert (2015) have utilized folkloresque to highlight connections between folklore and popular culture, with the latter discussed in terms of how it integrates folkloric material, portrays folklore, and parodies it.

Works Cited

auf der Heide, Jonathan. 2012. "*Van Diemen's Land*." *Senses of Cinema*. 65. Accessed April 28, 2017. http://sensesofcinema.com/2012/tasmania-and-the-cinema/van-diemens-land/.

Australian Wildlife Conservancy. 2017. "Wildlife." Accessed May 14, 2017. www.australianwildlife.org/wildlife.aspx.

Bullock, Emily. 2011. "Rumblings from Australia's Deep South: Tasmanian Gothic On-screen." *Studies in Australasian Cinema* 5 (1): 71–80.

Conrad, Peter. 1988. *Down Home: Revisiting Tasmania*. London: Chatto & Windus.

Cronon, William. 1996. "The Trouble with Wilderness; or, Getting Back to the Wrong Nature." In *Uncommon Ground: Rethinking the Human Place in Nature*, edited by William Cronon, 69–90. New York: Norton.

Ecotourism Australia. 2017. "A Brief History of Ecotourism Australia." Accessed May 05, 2017. www.ecotourism.org.au/about/history/.

Foster, Michael Dylan and Jeffrey A. Tolbert, eds. 2015. *The Folkloresque: Reframing Folklore in a Popular Culture World*. Logan: Utah State University Press.

Garrard, Greg. 2012. *Ecocriticism*. 2nd ed. London: Routledge.

Hughes, Robert. 1996. *The Fatal Shore: A History of the Transportation of Convicts to Australia 1787–1868*. London: Harvill.

Mathiesen, Karl. 2014. "UN Body Calls Tasmania Forest U-turn 'exceptional.'" *The Guardian*. 4 February. Accessed May 13, 2017. www.theguardian.com/environment/2014/feb/04/unesco-tasmania-forest-world-heritage-exceptional.

Milman, Oliver. 2014. "Tony Abbott Tells Tasmania Too Much Forest is "Locked Up" in-National Parks." *The Guardian*. 5 March. Accessed May 05, 2017. www.theguardian.com/world/2014/mar/05/tony-abbott-tells-tasmania-too-much-forest-is-locked-up-in-national-parks.

Mittelbach, Margaret and Michael Crewdson. 2006. *Carnivorous Nights: On the Trail of the Tasmanian Tiger*. Edinburgh: Canongate.

Morris, Simon. 2009. "Trekking Tasmania: When Driven by Hunger." *Australian Geographic* 29 June. Accessed May 03, 2017. www.australiangeographic.com.au/travel/destinations/2009/06/trekking-tasmania-when-driven-by-hunger/.

Narraway, Guinevere. 2012. "Eating and Othering in Jonathan auf der Heide's *Van Diemen's Land*." *Senses of Cinema* 65. Accessed April 28, 2017. http://sensesofcinema.com/2012/tasmania-and-the-cinema/eating-and-othering-in-jonathan-auf-der-heides-van-diemens-land/.

Norwood, Vera L. 1996. "Heroines of Nature: Four Women Respond to the American Landscape." *The Ecocriticism Reader: Landmarks in Literary Ecology,* edited by Cheryll Glotfelty and Harold Fromm, 323–50. Athens, GA: University of Georgia Press.

Paddle, Robert. 2000. *The Last Tasmanian Tiger: The History and Extinction of the Thylacine*. Cambridge: Cambridge University Press.

Parks and Wildlife Services Tasmania. 2017. "Tasmanian Wilderness World Heritage Area." Accessed May 16, 2017. www.parks.tas.gov.au/index.aspx?base=391.

Perkins, Victor F. 1990. *Film as Film: Understanding and Judging Films*. London: Penguin Books.

Production Notes – The Hunter. 2018. New York: Magnolia Pictures. Accessed March 15, 2018. www.magpictures.com/presskit.aspx?id=c352a404-2c40-4fd0-bfc2-bc581017f8bc.

Rainbow, Stephen L. 1992. "Why Did New Zealand and Tasmania Spawn the World's First Green Parties?" *Environmental Politics* 1 (3): 321–46.

Reynolds, Henry. 2004 "Genocide in Tasmania?" In *Genocide and Settler Society: Frontier Violence and Stolen Indigenous Children in Australian History,* edited by A. Dirk Moses, 127–49. New York: Berghahn Books.

Rose, Deborah Bird. 1996. *Nourishing Terrains: Australian Aboriginal Views of Landscape and Wilderness*. Canberra: Australian Heritage Commission.

Russell, Jim and Mirjana Jambrecina. 2002. "Wilderness and Cultural Landscapes: Shifting Management Emphases in the Tasmanian Wilderness World Heritage Area." *Australian Geographer* 33 (2): 125–39.

Ryan, Lyndall. 2013. "The Black Line in Van Diemen's Land: Success or Failure?" *Journal of Australian Studies* 37 (1): 3–18.

Simpson, Catherine. 2010. "Australian Eco-horror and Gaia's Revenge: Animals, Eco-nationalism and the 'New Nature'." *Studies in Australasian Cinema* 4 (1): 43–54.

Shakespeare, Nicholas. 2005. *In Tasmania: Adventures at the End of the World.* London: Vintage.

Smith, Nicholas. 2012. "The Return of the Living Dead: Unsettlement and the Tasmanian Tiger." *Journal of Australian Studies* 36 (3): 269–89.

Stadler, Jane. 2012a. "Seeing with Green Eyes: Tasmanian Landscape Cinema and the Ecological Gaze." *Senses of Cinema* 65. Accessed April 28, 2017. http://sensesofcinema.com/2012/tasmania-and-the-cinema/seeing-with-green-eyes-tasmanian-landscape-cinema-and-the-ecological-gaze/.

———. 2012b. "Mapping the Cinematic Journey of Alexander Pearce, Cannibal Convict." *Screening the Past* 34. Accessed May 03, 2017. www.screeningthepast.com/2012/07/mapping-the-cinematic-journey-of-alexander-pearce-cannibal-convict/.

Stadler, Jane, Peta Mitchell, and Stephen Carleton. 2016. *Imagined Landscapes: Geovisualizing Australian Spatial Narrative.* Bloomington: Indiana University Press.

Tourism Tasmania. 2016. "Tasmanian Tourism Snapshot: Year ending December 2016." Accessed November 28, 2017. https://tourismtasmania.com.au/__data/assets/pdf_file/0007/48148/TVS-Snapshot-Dec-16_2.pdf.

Whelehan, Imelda. 2015. "Adapting Tasmania: Terrorizing the Past." In *The Politics of Adaptation – Media Convergence and Ideology*, edited by Dan Hassler-Forest and Pascal Nicklas, 158–71. Basingstoke: Palgrave Macmillan.

Filmography

Dying Breed. Dir. Jody Dwyer, Australia, 2008.

The Hunter. Dir. Daniel Nettheim, Australia, 2012.

The Red Desert/Il deserto rosso. Dir. Michelangelo Antonioni, Italy/France, 1964.

Van Diemen's Land. Dir. Jonathan auf der Heide, Australia, 2009.

5 Perceptions of Place in an Irish Energy Landscape on Film

Pat Brereton

Introduction: Ownership versus Environmental Stewardship of Land

The trauma of the famine in Ireland and the failed revolutionary struggles to take back ownership and control of land continue to have a hold on the Irish psyche. Such concerns emerge in the nation's films and are encapsulated by the character of the farmer in *The Field* (Jim Sheridan, 1990). Alternatively *Eat the Peach* (Peter Ormrod, 1986) emphasizes the use of bogland and its excavation by the state, while also dramatizing the effects of multinationals on the countryside. Both films in different ways call attention to the economic importance of land and ownership, while testing differing models of environmental stewardship and people being rooted on the land while earning a living.

This chapter seeks to coalesce such debates through a number of environmental concepts including the land ethic, the tragedy of the commons, biophilia, and topophilia, while foregrounding how these concepts and local Irish tensions are played out through such films. In *The Field*, we witness polarized representations of farmers: either benevolent stewards of their land, or individuals pathologically fixated with owning, even polluting, their habitat. Adapted from a play and based on a true story by John B. Keane, *The Field* focuses on ownership and the power of land to corrupt its farming steward, The Bull McCabe (Richard Harris). He will do anything to nurture and protect his beloved field that he has worked on for so long, while his son Tadgh (Sean Bean) is less committed to this vocation. The story unfolds when the field is sold over The Bull's head at a public auction to a returning "Yank" who has no respect for the land and its heritage and instead wants to use it for industrial purposes. The Bull cannot allow this precious field to pass from his nurturing hands and tragic consequences follow. Meanwhile, *Eat the Peach* is a tragicomedy also based on a true story, which follows two men – Vinnie (Stephen Brennan) and Arthur (Eamon Morrissey) – who respond to the oppressiveness of their midlands existence by building a motorcycle "wall of death" [inspired by the Elvis Presley movie *Roustabout* (John Rich, 1964)] in the middle of a bog. The film captures a mood that was prevalent in the 1980s when the country was considered all but broke and emigration was very high, especially across rural areas of the country. The two protagonists believe that by building a "wall of death," they will gain a source of income and people will come to watch their daring adventure. While this feat of engineering does not finally work in the end, nonetheless they have demonstrated their ability to rise above their circumstances and discover a renewed sense of place and identity.

The complex evocations of place and landscape suggested by both these narratives are evident by the blurb for a major international conference, coordinated by Tim Collins (2016) at the National University of Ireland, Galway.

> Place is central to any critical discourse on landscape. Indeed, the landscape project, and the future of European communities and their particular landscapes that is envisaged in the European Landscape Convention, rests on the negotiation of the myriad values attaching to place. Of critical importance is how such values find expression and are considered in decision-making.

The Irish audiovisual media can be regarded as a bellwether for assessing attitudes and general perceptions across all forms of land production – from bog and turf to land usage. Historically, the conservation movement in Ireland and elsewhere has mobilized a blame narrative in which the environmentally enlightened agents act to protect nature from the environmentally deviant (Jacoby 2001, 1). In particular, representations of farmers play out these tensions and in turn help to foreground an environmental agenda, from a localized sense of place. While frequently being co-opted by environmentalists as stewards of the land, to remain economically viable, farmers on the ground have to privilege economic growth and maximizing their productive output, which can lead to tensions from an environmental perspective.

Romantic Myths of Land and Place

The Irish preoccupation and even fixation with land has been augmented by a long and troubled history as a British colony and as a contested space where her people fought for hundreds of years to regain sovereignty and ownership of the land (Slater 2009). Of late, with the economy transformed through the so-called "Celtic Tiger" renaissance, augmented by a hemorrhaging of population from the rural areas, there has been an apparent rejection of rural values, alongside a form of amnesia that draws on the traumas of the past. It is suggested that in spite of the radical transformation of the country from a predominantly rural to an urban society, such deeply felt Irish trauma, sparked by famine and forced eviction off the land, has remained a narrative specter ever since (Kiberd 1995; Crosson and Stoneman 2009). This specter is registered across Irish literature and also within the cinematic visualizations of the landscape and is most especially embodied by representations of farmers working on the land. As a primal rural profession, farming oscillates between nurturing and exploitation of the land, as articulated by poet-activists like Wendell Berry (see Slovic 1992, 128) and this tension can be used as a barometer of core ecological land values and pressures that most explicitly underpin the country's preoccupation with ownership and place.

At one level, the main protagonists in these fictional narratives are good exemplars of sustainable agriculture and model rural inhabitants, trying to deepen their sense of connection with their environment, eking out a frugal living and simply using land to survive, rather than exploit over the long term.[1] It must be noted however, much of the island of Ireland is mountainous and boggy and consequently of limited use for intensive farming. While not worth cultivating in conventional ways, such land nevertheless provides rough grazing and closely corresponds with the tourist industry's perception of "wild nature," ensuring the land's (in)tangible worth for the broader economy, rather than simply focusing on its utilitarian value, as evident in *The Field*. This type of wild topography encapsulated by *Man of Aran* (Robert Flaherty, 1934) is contrasted with manicured colonial gardens, designed primarily for easy engagement with nature, as exemplified by *The Quiet Man* (John Ford, 1952).

The dominant myth visualized within Irish rural culture has remained a pastoral one, which foregrounds an almost Arcadian evocation of the happy swain close to nature, alongside displaying the cyclical rhythms of the earth. This myth was certainly fostered and encouraged by the cultural nationalists of the newly formed independent state from the 1920s onwards. Most notably, one recalls Ireland's long-time political leader and visionary Eamon de Valera and his wholehearted endorsement of a form of primitive frugality, encapsulated by the docudrama *Man of Aran*. The unique beauty of the land(scape) as a fixed and unchanging topography was also affirmed by romantic nationalists, like the globally celebrated poet William Butler Yeats.[2] Such a preoccupation served as a bulwark in the cultural and political struggle for national independence during the first decades of the twentieth century and feeds into readings of *The Field*.

The topography of small land holdings and wild landscape sites, especially along the western coast, have been appropriated from such Arcadian myths and remain etched on the tourist's imagination, continuing to draw the attention of artists and filmmakers (see Lefebvre 2006, 19–60; Wylie 2007, 187–206). Scholarly works tend to focus on landscape and place across a wide range of cinematic output, as background within rural narratives, while the preoccupation of much environmental media investigation involves pulling such representations firmly into the foreground. The rugged coastline and encroaching sea, with its supremacy over the island's inhabitants, were often re-worked into a fatalistic trope within Revivalist Irish literature. This is most notably evident in J.M. Synge's *Riders to the Sea* and its cinematic namesake from 1987, or Robert Flaherty's *Man of Aran*. *The Field* continues in this vein and serves as an indicator of the power of wild landscape and its appeal for both a diasporic and an indigenous Irish audience.

Recently, much scholarly analysis of Irish landscape has foregrounded its touristic and heritage residue (Barton 2004), or alternatively such investigations serve as a signifier of the irrationality of terrorist agitators, as suggested by John Hill (2014), or more cogently for the purposes of this chapter, as signifiers of a postcolonial landscape. This is evident in Eamonn Slater's (2009) close reading of representations of Ashford Castle in *The Quiet Man*. Meanwhile, literary studies tend to focus on landscape as betraying an explicit or at least an implicit environmental sense of place and identity (see Smyth 2001; Frawley 2005; Leonard 2008; Wenzell 2009; Cusick 2010), while Irish film scholarship remains somewhat locked within a historical, nationalist, and romantic paradigm.

Readers recall the celebrated image of a stoical farmer-fisherman, heroically breaking stones in a barren landscape on the Aran Islands in *Man of Aran* to literally create fertile soil, or the use of seaweed to help fertilize a green field, as it sparkles in the mountainous landscape during the opening sequence of *The Field*. The Irish creative imaginary has remained fixated with a romantic vision of (agricultural) land carved out of a barren landscape, which can help economically sustain households within such otherwise inhospitable regions.[3] Alternatively, the more commercially acceptable and audience-pleasing images of group solidarity often demonstrate a lack of fruitful agricultural labor. This is evident in *The Quiet Man*, where the only evidence of farm work is the communal threshing imagery that is used as a backdrop for a final fight sequence.

Meanwhile, *Eat the Peach's* representations of a flat midlands bogland recalls Seamus Heaney's celebrated nature poetry, which successfully used landscape not in a fatalistic manner like in *The Field*, but to speak more positively and eloquently through a troubled political past and present. *Eat the Peach* presents one of the few examples in Irish film that actively bring the landscape and place of a large bogland habitat into the narrative's diegesis while addressing a number of contemporary issues. In particular, the film seems to question Heaney's claim that "Irish bogland cannot hope to emulate the vast American prairies which slice a big sunset evening" (cited in Rockett et al. 2014, 241–42). For Heaney, unlike the romanticizing of farmland, Irish bogs are compressed layers of history, forcing the eye inwards rather than drawing it toward the horizon. In a country where "The Troubles" loomed large in the Irish consciousness, as violence continued to flare in the North of Ireland during this (1980s) period, revisionist cultural artifacts like this tale attempt to find new ways of appropriating and therapeutically using the landscape to address the needs of its inhabitants.

First-Wave Environmental Preoccupations and Debates

To help textually examine *The Field* and *Eat the Peach* as exemplary environmental narratives, we will use a number of well-honed environmental theories, including the land ethic, biophilia, and topophilia, which underpin much "first wave" environmental scholarship (see Brazeau et al. 2014), before applying them onto an Irish context using more recent critical evaluation of environmental agency and representation, highlighted by scholars like Donna Haraway (1992) and John Barry (1998). Organic modes of sustainable farming are further highlighted as a pragmatic way forward toward promoting new forms of environmental engagement with farming.

Aldo Leopold's "land ethic" rests upon a single unifying premise: "that the individual is a member of a community of interdependent parts" (1947, 204). His vision served to enlarge the boundaries of community to include soils, water, plants, animals, and so forth. Especially since his "rediscovery" in the 1960s, Leopold's thesis has become a central tenet of environmental thinking, and the symbiotic relationship he proposes between humans and nature has remained the dominant orthodoxy of much ecological thinking. Such a simple notion helps create a more sustained and long-term beneficial environmental sense of place, which can apply to farming as well as bogland. The work and agency of the farmer most effectively play out many of these tensions, as they cope with issues around maximizing productivity of the soil, while at the same time ensuring long-term holistic balance. In particular, The Bull's labor in transporting seaweed as a form of organic fertilizer across the mountain to his precious field seems to embody this measured response in nurturing the soil.

This recuperative notion of a land ethic is most clearly manifested in the "Tragedy of the Commons," which, in turn, serves to frame cautionary representations of farmers as stewards of the land that are sharing a resource held in common. Yet especially within our contemporary agricultural industry, they sometimes appear to only act in their own short-term self-interest, and progressively degrade the collective resource of their land holdings (see Brereton 2016).

Alongside the land ethic, the utopian celebration of sustainable land management is echoed by E.O. Wilson and his controversial theory of "biophilia" (1984), which insinuates that because humans evolved from nature, we still carry a part of nature in our hearts and this is where humans feel their relationship with and responsibilities to the land, through the complexity of human-land relations. While some Irish farmers might be familiar with such idealistic rhetoric, most remain sanguine following their lived experience, only a small few I believe embrace such a love of the land that edges toward the psychotic extremes evident in *The Field*. There are relatively few examples where farmers actively fight to secure ownership of land at all cost, as evident by this story of land dispute. Nonetheless, one could argue, this specter continues to have a magnetic pull for farmers, who are seen to be environmentally compromised by their commercial stake in the land and their unique conceptualizations of space and place. Furthermore, this lays an idealistic burden of responsibility on the shoulders of farmers to express their "love of the land" and at the same time maintain a more environmentally driven, long-term and holistic strategy of mixed and sustainable farming, rather than accepting the dominant model set out by Government and farming organizations promoting increased herds and throughput, while maximizing soil productivity, using (excessive) artificial fertilizers.[4] All of these measures are ostensibly environmentally bad for the habitat and seem at odds with sustainable farming methods that are embraced by the environmental movement.

Together with biophilia, another related concept which underpins an environmental philosophy is Yi-Fu Tuan's notion of "topophilia" and the idea that humans have culturally mediated affinities for certain types of landscape (cited in Buell 2001, 26). Such a notion helps to capture local variables evident in Ireland and elsewhere and highlights how land and place as a concept have very different meanings for The Bull, or his son for that matter, in *The Field*. In turn this love of nature is very differently cast for the two pleasure-seeking protagonists in *Eat the Peach*. Attempting to tease out tensions around environmental conflicts and how they are depicted across a range of audiovisual texts remains challenging. As a core environmental concept, topophilia can also be used to illuminate a historical comparison between the rugged primitivism of *Man of Aran* as against the pastoral farming beauty of *The Field* (Gibbons 2002). While Luke Gibbons in his astute analysis does not see beyond a nationalist mode of romantic engagement with land and ownership, I suggest that adding an environmental register embedded within notions like topophilia or biophilia affords a further layer of place identity attributes to engage with. By not foregrounding the deep environmental sense of nurturing land through fertilizing it and only remaining preoccupied with representations of ownership and control, such scholarship is missing the inherent (and transnational) attribute of stewardship of the land and an appreciation of the protagonists' unique connection with their land. Furthermore, such representations can be contrasted with the rare construction of the flat bogland in *Eat the Peach*, which has been also farmed and excavated for energy since the founding of the state. Yet at the outset the protagonists portrayed in this peat landscape appear to have little biophilic or topophilic tendencies, nonetheless this eco-reading will serve to question such assumptions.

Eat the Peach captures a unique topography, which plays a key role in the global carbon cycle and "provide[s] important ecosystem services including carbon sequestration and storage" (Connolly and Holden 2017, 1). Representations of place, be they mountains, sea, or other conventional pictorial farming images, by all accounts suggest that

> place meanings are malleable, interlinked within integrated discourses of social and cultural meanings that persist in personal and collective memory. Environmental interpretation as a mode of interrogation of place can further be considered as another discursive arena in which such place meanings are constructed.
>
> (Derrien and Stokowski 2017, 277)

Consequently, inhabitants who live in bogland regions, together with those who maintain their livelihoods on the land as farmers, often might have more in common than one thinks, while having very different attitudes to environmental conservation, or sense of place than, for instance, tourists. The Japanese manager from the multinational company comments effusively on the inherent beauty of the Irish landscape as he is about to leave, an irony which is not lost on the local protagonists. Such visitors, including I would add some outside environmental activists, frequently wish to preserve these rural landscapes for posterity while not having to live there, much less eke out a living.

Furthermore, the Irish farming communities, which by definition remain fixed in a place, often appear wary of outsiders telling them what to do with their land and sometimes appear a long way from endorsing ethical forms of organic farming, together with the strict application of deep environmental principles involving co-existing with, rather than dominating, natural systems. Organic farming also includes sustaining or building soil fertilizer; minimizing the danger of chemical pollution to the environment; minimizing the use of nonrenewable resources; and ensuring the ethical treatment of animals in their work. All of these principles incorporate the ultimate manifestation of environmental husbandry, alongside recalling a more holistic and close identification and engagement with place. Contemporary farmers in general, together with these pragmatic employees in *Eat the Peach*, resigned to an uncertain future on bogland are less certain regarding the way forward. Surprisingly in ways, such radical environmental connection with land and green husbandry is encapsulated and visualized by an otherwise romantically driven and backward-looking tale like *The Field*. The Bull's careful nurturing of the land with seaweed remains a memorable example of proactive organic husbandry, in spite of the series of events that is about to engulf this tragic farmer as the story develops.

At the same time, as environmental scholar John Barry asserts, the majority of people in modern society "have no direct transformative experience of nature" (1998, 257), and have little direct connection with the land, except as some dramatic natural disaster. Coincidentally, the wage-earning protagonists in *Eat the Peach* are probably closer to the average contemporary Irish citizen with regard to their engagement with place. Such filmic evocation of ecological debates and the privileging of organic modes of production can furthermore help sow the seeds of good stewardship and at least kick-start and promote awareness of our interdependence with our environment.

I would nonetheless agree with Donna Haraway who argues that "we must find another relationship to nature besides reification, possession, appropriation and nostalgia" (1992, 65). Unfortunately, in many ways, Irish representations of farming and the visualization of landscape are often dramatized, codified, and reduced to such precepts, including a legal commodification of land while upholding its monetary value above all else. Consequently, as we further examine the films, a productive nature esthetic and a growing ecological preoccupation and reevaluating of place and landscape need to be constantly recalibrated and reimagined to help keep environmental concerns high on the representational agenda.

Contextual Analysis of Eat the Peach and the Field

Recalling the use of leisure and touristic space evoked in *The Quiet Man*, *Eat the Peach* foregrounds how two male protagonists become preoccupied with appropriating landscape – whether racing each other on their bikes across the vast flat bogland, or trying to control vertical space as they race each other up the sides of the "wall of death." Both of these modes of traversing space are simply driven by the vicarious pleasure of fast movement and the excitement of danger, as evident in much male-addressed generic media such as road movies (Brereton 2005). This excitement is augmented by a lively musical score and fast-paced editing, designed to capture and replicate such palpable pleasure. This is a long way from the stoical reverence for land and labor evoked in *Man of Aran* and *The Field*, where the farmer puts all his solitary energies into fortifying the nurturing potential of his beloved ultra-green field.[5] Meanwhile, locked into a precarious rural economy with farming in decline, as depicted in *Eat the Peach* the wage-employees have apparently little to anchor them to the land (or for that matter to the commons as bogland), since they have no direct connection with or ownership of the land. At least this appears to avoid the inherent dangers of such desire for ownership at all cost and its potentially dire consequences, as witnessed in *The Field*.

As illustrated in "Farming on Irish Film: An Ecological Reading" (Brereton 2009, 193), *The Field* opens with "two men in picturesque silhouette, pushing a cart over mountainous fields and unceremoniously ridding the carcass of a donkey into deep water below, thereby polluting the environment." The farmer and his son are shown to be both complicit in abusing nature by disposing of the carcass, while at the same time working hard to collect seaweed to fertilize their own precious land.[6]

The Field ostensibly remains a primal text for exploring Irish national identity, as it applies to the political and historical "land question" around ownership, which as cited above has plagued the island for centuries. Nevertheless, in spite of a number of caveats mentioned earlier, this reading remains more positive toward developing a model of fruitful ecological representation to help recuperate and foreground a more universal environmental discourse around a farmer's relationship with his land. At the same time, this primal conflict-ridden drama also works at a mythical level, by ensuring the personification of The Bull and his (albeit psychotic) love of the land lives on in popular consciousness, as the story resonates across geographical space and time.

Alternatively, observing the strong buddy relationship established between the two brothers-in-law in *Eat the Peach*, as they ride through the bog on their contrasting motorcycles and witness the harvesting of the bog by massive industrial machines, such activity is also calling attention to a number of environmental difficulties. While at a distance there appears to be little direct environmental critique within the *mise-en-scène*, nevertheless an eco-reading can help reexamine and reconstitute such powerful representational motifs. For example, memorable images of technology and machinery are used to expose fractures around the shock of a multinational Japanese company pulling out of the region: the helicopter that flies overhead suggests desertion, while also providing a celebratory bird's-eye view of the landscape below. Concurrently, we witness the slow-grinding erosion of moss peat by heavy industrial machinery, literally cutting away the surface down to the solid rock base underneath; all of which is carried out by a semi-State-owned company Bord na Mona that was set up to exploit this precious habitat for national economic benefit (Malone et al. 2009). As alluded to earlier, while the Japanese visitor might recognize the inherent beauty of the landscape, the long-term survival and environmental stability of the region is being put in peril by such industrial abuse on a massive scale.

The open flat but constantly eroding landscape is filmed in wide-shot with dramatic skies, calling attention to its material organic surface, which stands out even within a European perspective as an environmental black spot. A Western generic strategy is used as shorthand to capture the romantic appeal of the landscape, recalling the tenets of biophilia and topophilia discussed earlier, which in turn echo the findings of a number of recent environmental studies of Hollywood films (Carmichael 2006; Moore 2017). Noting the European Union's strict preservation rules for bogland, such a visual esthetic needs to be reimagined beyond the merely instrumental and economic bottom line use value assessment.

While these wage laborers appear to have a relatively tentative hold on their habitat and landscape in not legally owning or actively working the land, farmers, on the other hand, remain the quintessential embodiment of long-term stakeholders and custodians of land and are thereby expected to have deep connections with and a close appreciation of place. Yet from the "hard primitivism" of *Man of Aran* to the more fractured connection with land and ownership in *The Field*, this romantic trajectory might appear to further increase urban-rural tensions within the bog landscape, where a corresponding appreciation of the struggle to discover a sense of place and environmental connectivity is less frequently recorded.

When becoming redundant from their well-paid multinational jobs, the two men respond in a manner that both stave off boredom and allow them to maintain a more self-controlled sense of place and identity: they decide to build a fantasy escape in the form of the "wall of death" carnival attraction. Although promoting a fresh sense of place and identity, it is still framed and embedded within a bogland habitat that is being literally destroyed to service local and national electricity power stations.[7] The representation of Bord na Mona and the overharvesting of bogland can be allegorically read – at least in hindsight – as signaling an environmental cautionary tale of mismanagement.

The specter of Ireland's national energy policy and its effect on the landscape is evident by the recurring images showing the harvesting of the environmentally sensitive boglands. This large open habitat, which encapsulates a self-contained ecosystem, has slowly been destroyed. Concurrently, on dry land, the equally precarious lure of high-risk multinational investment to create jobs for the region is also shown as being unsustainable. Both specters have direct negative environmental consequences for the land and explicitly affect the workers' hold on their sense of place and identity through long-term unemployment and the perennial prospect of migration.

The multinational company is most clearly codified and visualized by the appearance of an "alien" helicopter (registered as an uber-modernist mode of transportation during the 1980s and symbolically the two protagonists end up appropriating the iconic helicopter by attempting to build their own), which is used at the start and end to quickly and efficiently transport the Japanese officials to the site and deliver the bad news. On landing and taking off, the observing natives have to literally cower in its presence, as it violently disturbs the natural equilibrium, forcing the long grass to wave violently. Similarly, the towering machines used to harvest the peat appear in the landscape like futuristic science fictional beasts, as they totally destroy the bogland.[8]

Even after 30 years, this film remains one of the few that dramatizes the work of Bord na Mona within a fictional narrative, which in itself is significant. Traces of such an environmental engagement or critique within a publically owned commons can be actively excavated through the pictorial forms of framing, using a broad range of wide and long shots from various angles, coupled with uplifting and celebratory-themed Irish music, across such landscape sequences. In turn, these appear to be punctured by the ensuing narratives of closure and hopes dashed for the two main protagonists.[9]

Somewhat pointedly, the "wall of death" imaginary, as a saving intervention in the landscape while striving to help create a sense of investment if not ownership in place, is being currently replaced in Ireland's contemporary landscape by the physical installation of more sustainable wind and solar farms. Such alternative energy iconography also includes a new brand of ecotouristic walking and leisure parks dotted across the otherwise scarred site of these massive cutaway boglands. Bord na Mona has radically reimagined its business model, which some might dismiss as a form of greenwashing. Nonetheless, the powerful semi-State organization, which owns the land in common for the people of the country is actively repurposing such "waste land" to construct alternative energy sites and in developing new types of ecotourism. Consequently, new forms of biophilia and topophilia are being imagined and engineered, which can be reinforced by creating a number of environmental learning projects situated within this otherwise exploited landscape. Beyond signaling memorial sites of environmental pollution, such spaces can be reimagined to help develop a low carbon energy future and provide renewed purpose to such heritage sites. Unfortunately, however, providing new modes of economic development and an effective use of land for all citizens living in such rural areas remain more of a challenge, as the flight from the land continues unabated across the island.

Promoting Effective Environmental Stewardship and Literacy

Such overly dramatic and iconic films certainly emphasize the economic value of land and landscape, while almost remaining complicit with the often intangible economic value of a farming or touristic landscape. Moving from land and soil as a raw material for farming to bogland and peat as a natural resource used for energy production also dovetails with the pervasive economic bottom line that is set up to critique a lack of sustainable environmental engagement in such areas, while raising the prospect of preserving such habitats and topographies for the future. *Eat the Peach* and even *The Field* provide some useful pointers to the complexities of engaging with environmentalism and place while, as suggested by Haraway, problematizing the dangers around such representations of land and bog remaining preoccupied with contentious issues of reification, possession, and appropriation, as well as wallowing in romantic forms of nostalgia for a rural idyll.

Through their portrayal of creative imaginaries around landscape together with specific usage of extractive technology in *Eat the Peach*, these fictional narratives insinuate a range of cautionary allegories around land management and energy production and employment. These stories help to initiate a debate concerning the central importance of place, environmental awareness, and sustainability for the country and by extension the planet.[10] Some engaging ways of communicating with audiences are presented, which draw on generic romantic strategies, yet such singular narratives cannot do much more than sow some seeds of engagement. While only a small start has been made with such examples, effective engagement with place and promoting critical representations of Irish (and world) energy landscapes are needed more than ever.

I instinctively believe that Irish audiences, at least, remain connected with and are "emotionally moved" by so-called first-wave environmental preoccupations because of their ongoing deep connection with their habitat, including the land ethic, biophilia, and topophilia in particular, much of which appears to be embodied by American and Irish romantic poets and their evocative espousal of a rural idyll. This trajectory has fed directly into the visualization of Irish filmic narratives, including a tentative environmental reading of *The Field* and *Eat the Peach*. Such national celebration of a rural idealist sense of place and landscape can, of course, be accused of being naïve, while even reifying a rural-urban divide; nonetheless, the dominant tenor of many Irish rural landscape films – recalling early American nature writing – remain preoccupied with an epiphanic sense of place connection. In the end, powerful images of place stay in the memory across such landscape films and continue to affect their audiences.

Notes

1 All of which is a long way from the industrial model of land management encouraged by modern farming methods and seldom if ever witnessed within fictional narratives.
2 For an eco-reading of Irish literature, see Brazeau et al. 2014.
3 Most recently, there is evidence of new modes of farming on film, evident through what could be characterized as "misery porn" in, for example, *Pilgrim Hill* (Barrett 2013).
4 See Harvest 20/20 for Ireland's official policy to develop Agriculture. www.agriculture.gov.ie/publications/2011/annualreviewandoutlookfor-agriculturefisheriesandfood20102011/nationaldevelopments/foodharvest2020/
5 Incidentally in *Man of Aran*, it is the woman who carries the seaweed to help nourish the land.

6 Yet surprisingly little cultural or literary analysis is afforded to this often-contradictory agency of farming – be it organic or factory-type mass production – remaining frequently locked into a one-dimensional romantic abstraction.
7 Their attempts to construct a timber edifice – believed by some to be a form of male-hubris – incidentally also appears to disrupt the organic vegetable garden that is beloved by the main character's wife and leads to a temporary break in their relationship.
8 But, of course, from a business and land management perspective, like with large modern tillage harvesters, such machines remain both efficient and effective. For a comprehensive overview of Bogland in Ireland, see www.npws.ie/sites/default/files/publications/pdf/NationalPeatlandsStrategy2015EnglishVers.pdf
9 At a structural level, the subsequent dramatic form of destruction of their timber edifice using the primary elements of fire can be contrasted with the theatrical use of wild seas and drowning at the end of *The Field*.
10 This preoccupation with environmental analysis of audiovisual narratives has been addressed across a range of studies (see Brereton 2005, 2016).

Works Cited

Barry, John. 1998. *Rethinking Green Politics: Nature, Virtue and Progress*. London: Sage.
Barton, Ruth. 2004. *Irish National Cinema*. London: Routledge.
Brazeau, Robert and Derek Gladwin, eds. 2014. *Eco-Joyce: The Environmental Imagination of James Joyce*. Cork: Cork University Press.
Brereton, Pat. 2016. *Environmental Ethics and Film*. Oxon: Routledge Earthscan.
——— 2009. "Farming on Irish Film: An Ecological Reading." In *Ecosee: Images Rhetoric, Nature*, edited by Sidney Dobrin and Sean Morey, 185–202. Albany: State University of New York Press.
——— 2005. *Hollywood Utopia: Ecology in Contemporary Cinema*. Bristol: Intellect Press.
Buell, Lawrence. 2001. *Writing from and Endangered World: Literature, Culture and Environment in the US and Beyond*. Cambridge: Belknap Press of Harvard University Press.
Carmichael, Deborah A., ed. 2006. *The Landscape of Hollywood Westerns: Ecocriticism in an American Genre*. Salt Lake City: University of Utah Press.
Collins, Tim, ed. 2016. *Landscape Values: Place and Praxis. Proceedings*. Galway: Center for Landscape Studies. NUI. Galway, Ireland.
Connolly, John and Nicholas H. Holden. 2017. "Detecting Peatland Drains with Object Base Image Analysis and Geoeye-1 Imagery." *Carbon Balance and Management* 12 (7): 1–13.
Crosson, Sean and Rod Stoneman. 2009. *The Quiet Man … and Beyond: Reflections on a Classic Film, John Ford and Ireland*. Dublin: The Liffey Press.
Cusick, Christine, ed. 2010. *Out of the Earth: Ecocritical Readings of Irish Texts*. Cork: Cork University Press.
Derrien, Monica and Patricia A. Stokowski. 2017. "Discourses of Place: Environmental Interpretation about Vermont Forests." *Environmental Communication* 11 (2): 276–87.

Frawley, Oona. 2005. *Irish Pastoral: Nostalgia and Twentieth-Century Irish Literature.* Dublin: Irish Academic Press.

Gibbons, Luke. 2002. *The Quiet Man.* Cork: Cork University Press.

Haraway, Donna. 1992. "Otherworldly Conversations: Terran Topics: Local Terms." *Science as Culture* 3 (1): 64–98.

Hill, John. 2014. "Images of Violence." In *Cinema and Ireland,* edited by Kevin Rockett, Luke Gibbons and John Hill, 147–93. London: Routledge.

Jacoby, Karl. 2001. *Crimes against Nature: Squatters, Poachers, Thieves, and the Hidden History of American Conservation.* Berkley: University of California Press.

Kiberd, Declan. 1995. *Inventing Ireland: The Literature of the Modern Nation.* London: Jonathan Cape.

Lefebvre, Martin, ed. 2006. *Landscape and Film.* London & New York: Routledge.

Leonard, Liam. 2008. *The Environmental Movement in Ireland.* New York: Springer.

Leopold, Aldo. 1947. *A Sand County Almanac and Sketches Here and There.* New York: Oxford University Press.

Malone, Sarah and Catherine O'Connell, 2009. *Ireland's Peatland Conservation Action Plan 2020- Halting the Loss of Peatland Biodiversity.* Kildare: Irish Peatland Conservation Council.

Moore, Ellen E. 2017. *Landscape and the Environment in Hollywood Film: The Green Machine.* London: Palgrave.

Rockett, Kevin, Luke Gibbons, and John Hill. 2014. *Cinema and Ireland.* London: Routledge.

Slater, Eamonn. 2009. "The Hidden Landscape Aesthetic of *The Quiet Man.*" In *The Quiet Man ... and Beyond: Reflections on a Classic Film, John Ford and Ireland*, edited by Sean Crosson and Rod Stoneman, 139–58. Dublin: Liffey Press.

Slovic, Scott. 1992. *Seeking Awareness in American Nature Writing: Henry Thoreau, Annie Dillard, Edward Abbey, Wendell Berry, Barry Lopez.* Utah: University of Utah Press.

Smyth, Gerry. 2001. *Space and the Irish Cultural Imagination.* London: Palgrave.

Wenzell, Tim. 2009. *Emerald Green: An Ecocritical Study of Irish Litera*ture. Newcastle: Cambridge Scholars.

Wilson, Edward O. 1984. *Biophilia.* Cambridge: Harvard University Press.

Wylie, John. 2007. *Landscape.* London and New York: Routledge.

Filmography

Eat the Peach. Dir. Peter Ormrod, UK/Ireland, 1986.

The Field. Dir. Jim Sheridan, Ireland, 1990.

Man of Aran. Dir. Robert Flaherty, UK, 1944.

Pilgrim Hill. Dir. Gerard Barrett, Ireland, 2013.

The Quiet Man. Dir. John Ford, USA, 1952.

Riders to the Sea. Dir. Ronan O'Leary, Ireland, 1987.

Roustabout. Dir. John Rich, USA, 1964.

6   Walking the Mythical Path
Thoreau's Old Marlboro Road

David M. Robinson

"Walking" and Sauntering

Henry David Thoreau's elevation of Walden Pond into a place of reverence, pilgrimage, and cultural myth in *Walden* (1854) is widely acknowledged as a foundational document in the history of American environmental thought. In pursuing his own self-reformation, Thoreau (1971, 192) took note of the stability of the pond, which always remained essentially unchanged. He called the pond a friend, the character who "best preserves its purity," seeing in it his aspiration for a life with principle (192). Lesser known is Thoreau's homage to the Old Marlboro Road in "Walking" (1862), an essay drawn from versions of a lecture Thoreau had delivered in the earlier 1850s, entitled first "Walking or the Wild," and then simply "The Wild" (Thoreau 2007, 561). Rather than praise the act of settling in a particular place, "Walking" explored unending transformation, depicting Thoreau's daily walks as mythical quests, efforts to know the ever-renewing unknown in nature. Central to these walks was the largely abandoned "old" road from Concord to Marlboro, whose neglect and seclusion constituted its appeal. To walk the road was to be in the immediate present, but also in the era of myth, performing the acts that ground human experience.

The Old Marlboro Road was the path of the "saunterer," the heroic knight forever in search of new and liberating experiences (Thoreau 2007, 185). It was, for Thoreau, not a road from one *place* to another, but a Taoist's perpetual *way* forward. Like the boundaried, but infinitely rich Walden Pond, the Old Marlboro Road opened itself to life, thereby re-enchanting the ordinary world. The road provided the saunterer access to "a subtle magnetism in Nature" (195), and thus to the ever-present wild that defines and animates us. Thoreau walked this road assured that "life consists with Wildness," and assured that "the most alive is the wildest" (203). To bring the idea of sauntering to life, Thoreau inserted a poem, "The Old Marlboro Road," into the text of "Walking," thereby investing the Old Marlboro Road with multiple imaginative dimensions. He made it a place infused with myth, lore, sanctity, and most importantly, the vitality of the wild. The road embodied the trek into wild nature as the new form of the religious pilgrimage in the modern age. This essay will focus on the correlations and disjunctions between the essay's defense of the wild and the description of the complex and somewhat secretive world of the saunterer's path encapsulated in the poem.

The Poem and the Essay

As a lengthy poem interpolated within the larger essay "Walking," "The Old Marlboro Road" poses interesting generic questions. How does the poem illuminate, or complicate, the essay? Thoreau placed the poem within the text of "Walking" to emphasize sauntering as a demonstrable, place-oriented physical activity, as well as a transcendent process of thought. I saunter *here* Thoreau seems to be saying. The road itself thus becomes a major feature of the essay, and its qualities help to define the art of sauntering. In explaining his connection with the road Thoreau suggests that he is drawn, will-less, to the road rather than selecting it deliberately. "I believe there is a subtle magnetism in Nature, which, if we unconsciously yield to it, will direct us aright" (2007, 195). The modern reader may overlook the significance of Thoreau's linking "magnetism" to nature. He wrote the essay at a period in which the phenomena of magnetism was being intensely studied by both scientists and spiritualists. Michael Faraday's early nineteenth-century experiments in electromagnetism had a shaping impact on the field of physics, and Franz Mesmer's theories of animal magnetism had generated an entirely new sensibility of a living world of physical objects and organic beings, interconnected by currents of unseen but dynamic force. Thoreau, aware of these theories and intensely responsive to the processes of constant natural transmutation, entered the realm of nature as if it were a field of attractive force. Thoreau connects this magnetic pull of the green world with the west, and ultimately with "the Wild." "In Wildness," he wrote, "is the preservation of the World" (2007, 202).

In reading the essay "Walking," the presence of "The Old Marlboro Road" can be disconcerting. It interrupts "Walking" with writing that in no way resembles the lucid flow of Thoreau's prose. The long, deftly shaped sentences are replaced by blunt stubs of verse, heavily rhyming couplets, with some poetic lines no longer than two or three words. There are sixty-five poetic lines in all, visually snaking down the pages and forcing the reader to retune her auditory settings, and most importantly, slow her pace. On the page, the poem visually suggests a path or road, narrow in places and wider in others, leading the eye down the page to a yet unknown objective. "The Old Marlboro Road" vies with its prose surroundings in particularly notable ways. Its principal impact is rhythmic, and in temporarily derailing the flow of Thoreau's forcefully developing theory of sauntering, the poem grounds the concept in material ways. While the destination of a walk may not be predetermined at the outset, the excursion ultimately achieves a purpose through a spontaneously unfolding process. "The Old Marlboro Road" embodies the evolving organic structure of a saunter. Thoreau compares such a venture with the pilgrimage and the crusade, intensely purposeful religious journeys in which routine patterns of life are discarded for deeper purposes. These ancient pilgrimages are solitary quests in one sense, but solitary only in the sense that the walk ultimately leads the lone walker to be a part of something larger than a solitary self.

The Old Marlboro Road was not the only isolated and little traveled road that Thoreau praised poetically. Randall Conrad (2013) called attention to a series of passages in Thoreau's 1859 Journal that sing the praises of the old Carlisle road, which cuts through the wild area of Estabrook Country. Conrad explicates the Journal passages as closely as one would explicate a poem by Emily Dickinson or Robert Frost. The key paragraph comprises a succession of fragmentary and complex sentences, a dream-like meditation on the inspirational power of this utterly remote road. The passage seems in some places like the notes Thoreau might have made for a poem in the works. In other sections, it resembles a stream of consciousness series of observations that appear to be a web of associations that he wants to preserve after a particularly stimulating ramble. Estabrook Country, now known as the Estabrook Woods several miles north of Concord, still remains "a wild tract of more than 1,200 acres (4.9 square kilometers) of woodland, hills, ledge, and swamp." It constitutes "the largest contiguous and undeveloped woodland within thirty miles of Boston" ("Estabrook Woods" 2017). As Conrad (2013, 98) writes, the old Carlisle road "is the road of imagination," but one "where we never reach our ethereal destination (heaven's gate) because our heaven is our presence in the moment." Conrad's perceptive comment also offers insight into "The Old Marlboro Road," a poem that shares this imaginative dimension.

Both roads are akin to Thoreau's best-known holy place, Walden Pond. He saw these roads as sacred places not only because of their rural natures, but because they also served as a passage to many other wild places. These roads were gateways to the wild, whose locations and destinations restored men and women to their vital natural roots.

Thoreau's reverence for life on the road grounds the signal term of his essay: to *saunter*. He presents it as an amplified and glorified form of walk that has deep historical, mythical, and philosophical roots. Calling the true walker a saunterer, Thoreau writes a declaration of independence that celebrates the abandonment of all the constraints that detract from a spiritual life. "Walking" captures some of the celebratory mood of Walt Whitman's 1856 poem "Song of the Open Road," which offers its reader an unlimited sense of liberty and discovery. The great escape of the limitless road was thereby transformed into the route to new possibilities. Whitman writes of freeing oneself from a particular place in order to discover the unlimited possibilities of the earth, while Thoreau, as we usually consider him, writes of the liberating experience of the intensive study of a single place, Walden Pond, whose qualities are limitless. Both these perspectives share the imperative of the cultivation of the inner self as the process of spiritual growth. Thoreau asserts that he has known only one or two persons who have "understood the art of Walking," or "had a genius, so to speak, for *sauntering*" (2007, 185). He does not mean the casually bold and relaxed walk that the thesaurus groups with "stroll," "amble," "ramble," and "meander." For Thoreau, sauntering is an ancient artistry connected with the Medieval pilgrimage "*à la 'sainte terre*,' to the Holy Land" (185). Even though Thoreau began the essay by proclaiming that he hoped "to speak a word for Nature, for absolute freedom and wildness" (185), he connects sauntering with a religious practice of the most traditional and rigorous kind. The true walker is the steadfast seeker or "'*sainte-terrer*', a saunterer a holy-lander" (185). We should recognize that the etymology for the word saunter that Thoreau offers here, as well as a further suggestion that saunter can be derived from the French term "*sans terre* without land or a home," is a fanciful or poetic invention, with no linguistic or historical backing (185). These imaginative inventions make their point, however, and link walking with spiritual questing, an activity far deeper than the daily walk, or even the most ambitious hike or climb.

Thoreau's most radical assertion is that no walk is a true saunter unless the walker is willing never to return. "We should go forth on the shortest walk, perchance, in the spirit of undying adventure, never to return" (207, 186). To saunter is to separate yourself from the possessions, and even the relationships and commitments that you cherish, in order to experience the world in a wholly fresh and receptive way. "If you are ready to leave father and mother, and brother and sister, and wife and child and friends," he writes, adding for emphasis the clause "and never see them again," then and then only "you are ready for a walk" (186). This severe demand is an effective rhetorical device, calling readers to think of what they most cherish. The experience of the saunter must be grounded in the familiar and the domestic as well, since the walk has the power to remake the saunterer into a person worthy of those vital connections. While it is true that one must usually leave home to see the wild, such experiences, if thoughtfully undertaken, can transform individuals into richer spiritual contributors to the family's soundness and equity.

Society and Solitude

Thoreau begins the poem with several references to those few who have lived along the secluded Old Marlboro Road. Through them, Thoreau poetically evokes the crucial importance of solitude and self-reliance,

but also establishes the road as a place of struggle and failure. The saunterer must recognize it as a road of suffering as well as independence,
defined by history and lore, and wilderness, and freedom. The road is
the place "Where sometimes Martial Miles/ Singly files," and where he
finds "Elijah Wood," a man for whom "I fear no good" (2007, 193). In
his informative recent research on the history of the road and its current
location and condition, David Mark (2017) identified Martial Miles as
a landowner of areas "near the road," including a swamp that Thoreau mentions in his Journal. Of Elijah Wood, "a life-long resident of
Concord, descendant of one of the founding families," Mark considers
Thoreau's "fear no good" comment something of a "mystery," but spec-
ulates that Thoreau, a contemporary of Wood's son, may have known
"of Wood's pending death" (2017, n.p.). Perhaps the most interesting of
the figures connected with the road is Elisha Dugan, the son of a run-
away slave who had settled in Concord. Thoreau's description of Dugan
is one of the most vivid passages in the poem: "Elisha Dugan – /O man
of wild habits, / Partridges and rabbits, / Who hast no cares/ Only to
set snares, / Who liv'st all alone, / Close to the bone; / And where life
is sweetest/ Constantly eatest" (2007, 193). Thoreau describes a man
existing in a life of subsistence, living meal to meal by hunting and trap-
ping the small animals in the woods near Concord. He resembles in
some ways the persona of the "Economy" chapter of Thoreau's *Walden*,
who advocates an unencumbered life free of unnecessary luxuries and
responsibilities. It is perhaps for these reasons that Thoreau calls Dugan
a man with "no cares," who lives "where life is sweetest" (193). He is,
however, a man at the margins of human society, alone and drastically
poor, whose condition would seem pitiable to most. Even so, Thoreau
values his closeness to the wild, connecting him with the Old Marlboro
Road's emblem of freedom in the green life.

Elise C. Elmire (2016, 59) has shed some new light on Elisha Dugan
in an essay on Thoreau's efforts at "repeopling the woods" around Concord in his writings. Elmire is particularly interested in Thoreau's contributions to the work of "reconstructing the long overlooked lives of the
enslaved and formerly enslaved in the town claiming to be the birthplace
of American liberty" (59). Elmire explains that Elisha's father Thomas
Dugan had escaped from Virginia and settled near Concord, where he
was able to own a relatively small farm. Elisha was the sixth of Thomas
Dugan's ten children and was ten years old when his father died in 1827,
leaving his family "teetering on the brink of poverty" (67). He was eventually able to own a house and a farm, but only for a period, after which
he turned to work as a laborer in the woods. Elmire's work in the archives
raises serious questions about Elisha Dugan's range of choices in living
his subsistence life, and requires us to reconsider the implications of
Thoreau's sense that he was a man with "no cares" (Thoreau 2007, 193).
We can see Thoreau's limitations as an observer of social life in this

description of Elisha Dugan. Thoreau advocated a life of Spartan economy that denied the use of all material goods except those that could be deemed necessary. He condemned the pursuit of unnecessary luxuries that he saw as a barrier to a pure focus on the spiritual life. He seems to praise Elisha Dugan for his poverty here, a condition that Dugan apparently did not choose. This blindness to Dugan's suffering strikes modern readers as a troubling insensitivity.

Thoreau used Elisha Dugan as a representative of the human capability to survive, and in some ways thrive, outside the organized social economy. His strength is drawn from nature itself, and in that sense, he lives "close to the bone" (2007, 193), at the core of the natural force that drives life itself. With this in mind, we can understand the sense of energy and empowerment that Thoreau connects with both sauntering and the Old Marlboro Road. The act of sauntering and the presence of the road that enables it combine to reflect the seasonal upsurge of strength and happiness brought by spring, with its urgings for new places and experience. In the "The Old Marlboro Road," Thoreau also calls up the time "When the spring stirs my blood/ With the instinct to travel," an impulse that leads him to the ever-unchanged Old Marlboro Road: "Nobody repairs it, For nobody wears it" (193). He calls the road "a living way," relating it to the New Testament's narrow way of faith. "As the Christians say, / Not many there be/ Who enter therein" (193). In fact, the road is ultimately less a built structure than a moral attitude or a spiritual bearing. "What is it, what is it /But a direction out there, and the bare possibility/ Of going somewhere?" (194). Thoreau also emphasizes that this itch to travel is not of the tourist variety. The nearest road will suffice. "I can get enough gravel/On the Old Marlboro Road," he writes (193). This wry insistence on the sufficiency of what is at hand – the principle that guided his experiment at Walden Pond – defines the usage of the Old Marlboro Road as well. Distance does not define sauntering. "You may go round the world/By the Old Marlboro Road" (194).

Thoreau's declaration of the limitless possibility of the road clashes directly with his portrayals of the people living along it, especially the brave but impoverished Elisha Dugan. His peopling of the Old Marlboro Road establishes it as a lived-in social place, despite its abandonment and obscurity. Yet the peopling of the road with those who have been socially and economically marginalized also serves to remind his readers that society has margins and boundaries, and that these boundaries are critical in defining both the shape and the nature of a place. At the heart of the poem, and we might say at the heart of the entire essay "Walking," is Thoreau's redefinition of the Old Marlboro Road as a place of freedom from the barriers of society. Thoreau declares the road a place of "bare possibility" (2007, 194), suggesting that the saunterer must not merely *observe* the open road and the wildness around it, but *imagine* its possibilities and, in effect, bring to the road an identity. In this sense, Thoreau is naming the Old Marlboro Road a place of meditative inspiration and poetic experimentation.

Thoreau's own walks or saunters became the chief sources of his literary production. Laura Dassow Walls (2017, 305) writes that, in the early 1850s, when he had returned to Concord life after the Walden Pond experiment, his "walks became a form of meditation, a spiritual as well as physical discipline. He worried about walking bodily into the woods without getting there in spirit, some piece of business in his mind literally blinding his eyes." In this context, we could call the Old Marlboro Road a place of mental refreshment and renewal, a place in which the chains of routine and superficial distractions can be cut away, while the imagination is released. For Thoreau, this did not mean an escape into the clouds of abstraction, but a sharpened awareness of what is near, and how the near is connected with the far. For Thoreau, these saunters became increasingly akin to botanical fieldwork, in which he observed the cycles of the budding and flowering of the forests and fields around Concord, taking extensive notes and compiling valuable seasonal data (Walls 2017, 303–11). He, of course, continued to write poems, lectures, and essays, fueled in part by his growing mastery of the earth's processes. The Old Marlboro Road, where many of his observational rambles took place, in this sense became a combined laboratory and library, a place where "bare possibility" yielded new knowledge and deeper inspiration.

A Living Way

Clearly, the road that Thoreau celebrates poetically is in part a creation of his transcendental imagination, the product of the more elevated and elaborated methods of seeing the world that he describes in *Walden*. Perhaps the most significant illustration of the enlarged vision for which Thoreau strived during his two-year stay at Walden Pond appears in the chapter "Spring," the season of new awakening for both the earth and the author who witnesses it. Thoreau offers a detailed description of the uncanny event of "thawing sand and clay" warmed by the sun that pushes up to flow over the snow cover above them (Thoreau 1971, 304). The sand forms "innumerable little streams" in "various shades" in a myriad of forms – "coral"; "leopards' paws or birds' feet"; "brains or lungs or bowels"; and "acanthus, chicory, ivy, vine, or any vegetable leaves" (305). This seems a bit like cloud gazing, but Thoreau elaborates how these streams of sand follow the same laws of shaping and development of all organic and inorganic processes that formulate the earth. He sees, in this obscure and overlooked phenomenon, a fact that multiplies itself into a law. "Thus it seemed that this one hillside illustrated the principle of all the operations of Nature. The Maker of this earth but patented a leaf" (308). The Old Marlboro Road is a conduit not only from place to place, but also from idea to idea, an infinitely expansive intellectual construction that transcends the given boundaries of what a "road" ordinarily means. In one brief phrase of the poem, Thoreau offers a particularly insightful observation by referring to the Old Marlboro Road as "a living way" (2007, 193). This is the most evocative phrase in the poem, richly suggestive of both daily experience and spiritual aspiration. Thoreau describes the road as magically or mystically unchanging when he writes, "Nobody repairs it, / For nobody wears it" (193). The road cannot *wear* or be *worn* in a double sense – it is impervious to damage and impossible to own or possess. The road is a continuously present place, alive through the plants and creatures that surround it, and sometimes overgrow it. The road also lives because of the human travel that it enables, including those enlightenment seekers who find the road not only as a path to truth, but also as itself an embodiment of truth, regardless of their destination. These are the devoted ones, the ancient and now contemporary seekers symbolized by the early "Christians" who abandoned everything to walk this "living way" of truth (193). The paucity of traffic on the road is a sign of its vigor, since its seclusion nourishes the traveler in ways that a busy thoroughfare could not.

As the reader considers the poem two centuries after Thoreau's birth, the question inevitably arises: "What of the road today? Does the Old Marlboro Road actually live on in the twenty-first century?" Pondering this question, I did what most twenty-first-century persons do – I googled it. I found that when we search the "Old Marlboro Road," expecting to find hits of a literary and poetic nature, we instead encounter Zillow.com, the prominent real estate web page. Browsing through the homes for sale, I quickly recognized that no matter how much research I did on the Old Marlboro Road, I certainly would never be able to afford a house on it.

I also found, however, another document of real interest, David Mark's writings on the history of the Old Marlboro Road, and the way that it takes today. Mark's photo of one of the huge stone direction markers along the way – Thoreau refers to them in the poem, as we will see – confirms the continuing presence of the actual road that Thoreau walked and praised. Mark details how the road

> wends west from near Emerson Hospital, cuts across the north corner of Sudbury as Powers Road, continues as Old Marlboro Road in Maynard, where it ends at the east corner of the Assabet River National Wildlife Refuge [Thoreau would applaud at that!]. It continues as a trail called Winterberry Way [Thoreau would also like that!]; then out the west site yclept Bruen Road, White Pond Road and finally Concord Road all the way to the center of Marlborough.
> (2017, n.p.)

Things have clearly changed on the ground since Thoreau's day, but the traces of history mark the past, and the road itself continues. The Old Marlboro Road remains a "living way" indeed, and as Mark's article also shows – a road full of history, legend, and mystery.

Many readers will also detect another dimension of Thoreau's description of the Old Marlboro Road as "a living way." Thoreau uses that phrase to suggest the unfolding spiritual life, in which the seeker of the transcendent undertakes the stages of human experience as both an advance in understanding and an ever-renewing imperative to continue. Thoreau refers to the rare Christian who is able to follow this narrow path. The path or the way to righteousness or enlightenment is, of course, a concept shared by all the major religions. It is particularly consonant with Thoreau's engagement with Asian religions. The Asian tenor of Thoreau's spiritual vision has spurred an informative strand of the scholarly comment, which helps to clarify Thoreau's concept of the spiritual saunter. Thoreau and his close friend Ralph Waldo Emerson encountered translations of Indian, Chinese, Persian, and other ancient religious texts at key points in their own intellectual development, and became strong advocates of these texts as they moved toward a post-Christian religious stance. "Europe has always owed to oriental genius, its divine impulses," Emerson declared in his 1838 Divinity School Address, arguing that the idea of the moral sense "arose from the devout and contemplative East; not alone in Palestine, where it reached its purest expression, but in Egypt, in Persia, in India, in China" (1971, 80). The spiritual mood of "The Old Marlboro Road," and the entire essay "Walking," reflects this Asian influence, and corresponds remarkably with the ethos of the "way" of Taoism. The Tao, often rendered as the "way" in English, provides a vision of experience consonant with what Thoreau means when he offers his Credo: "I believe in the forest, and in the meadow, and the night in which the corn grows" (Thoreau 2007, 202). This is the Thoreauvian Holy Trinity, the reverence that the saunterer both seeks and always already possesses through the discipline of the complete acceptance of the way of existence.

A number of scholars have recognized the Taoist qualities of Thoreau's philosophy, but research on Thoreau's reading has led to the conclusion that he did not have access to the *Tao Te Ching* of Lao Tzu, or to other Taoist texts (Ch'en 1972). This conclusion was confirmed in Robert Sattelmeyer's extensive study of Thoreau's reading (Sattlemeyer 1988). As Hongbo Tan (1993) and Lyman V. Cady (1961) have explained, Thoreau had a deep immersion in M.J. Pauthier's French translations of Chinese texts in *Confucius et Mencius* (1841), a work from which he translated ninety-six paragraphs from French into English. As Tan notes, Chu Hsi's compilation "altered the entire course of the Confucian classics" (1993, 227), and restored an emphasis on "the problems of human nature and the cultivation of the self" (279). These were fundamental themes in Thoreau's works. Even if Thoreau drew much from the Neo-Confucianism of Chu Hsi, a sense of a harmony between Thoreau and Taoist principles has been amply documented. Ch'en (1972, 406) articulated what many have felt when he described the ideas of *Walden* as "essentially Taoist." In an essay tracing parallels between Thoreau's writings and Taoist philosophy, Gary Simon (1972, 253) observed that Thoreau's work reflected "a greater affinity for Taoism than for any other Oriental religion." Aimin Cheng (2000, 207) also noted Thoreau's "absorption of the Chinese conception of the relationship between humanity and nature," stressing its close kinship with Taoist principles. The disciplined way of the Tao, with its reverence for the structure of reality and its stress on cultivating a consenting recognition of the poised wholeness of nature, harmonizes strikingly with Thoreau's most revelatory avowals. We must perhaps accept a Taoist Thoreau who never read *Tao Te Ching*. Contradictory as that may seem, it is a reminder of how Thoreau, Emerson, and other New England transcendentalists and Free Religionists in the nineteenth century began to look to Asian religions to rearticulate a Western religious vocabulary that was no longer adequate to express spiritual experience. Thoreau's spiritual practice of sauntering is an able illustration of this process of religious syncretism, in which the holy and the divine are continuously being rediscovered and renamed.

The *way*, the *path*, the *journey*, the *quest* – these are terms that have expressed religious experience and religious instruction throughout world history. In the sense that they connote movement from one place to a new and different place, and a better place, they capture the sense of striving that is commonly connected with the spiritual life. Place and path, or place and journey, seem inseparable concepts in human experience, each defining or completing the other. When Thoreau established The Old Marlboro Road as the site for most of his intensely spiritual saunters, he was actually naming a *place* that was concurrently a *path* to many other places, both geographical and imaginative. We might consider Thoreau's Road as many places, the sum of the locations to which it could lead us.

Graves, Swamps, and the Way of the Road

The mood of "The Old Marlboro Road" shifts significantly in the second half. From a declaration of "spring stir[ring] my blood" (Thoreau 2007, 193) with the call to saunter, the poet turns a meditative eye to the gigantic stone markers along the way. These monoliths, bearing only the most essential words to guide the traveler, provide another perspective on the change of the seasons, reminding us that spring eventually brings winter, and that all human paths lead finally to the grave. "What is it, what is it/ But a direction out there, / And the bare possibility/ Of going somewhere?" (194). With this quatrain, Thoreau pivots from a celebration of the open road to a skepticism that questions the worth of all human endeavor. The possibility of "going somewhere" is now seen as "bare" or empty. The bleaker and gloomier side of Thoreau emerges here, a strand of his thinking that has drawn comment from a number of critics, notably Richard Bridgman (1982), and more recently, Branka Arsić (2016). This grimmer Thoreau is evident in the description of the stone direction markers along the Old Marlboro Road – "Great guide boards of stone/ But travelers none" (2007, 194). The granite direction markers have stood their ground, but those who once depended on them for guidance *are* no more. The stones thus become tombstones, turning the road itself into a kind of cemetery (Mark 2017, n.p.). They suggest the death of the very towns to which they point, and whose names are graven on them, becoming "Cenotaphs of the towns/Named on their crowns" (Thoreau 2007, 194). Thoreau asks who the once-living persons were who erected these markers. "I am still wondering – / Set up how or when, / By what select men, / Gourgas or Lee, Clark or Darby?" (2007, 194). Their work has not preserved them or their memory. The markers are now only "Blank tablets of stone," Thoreau writes, which stand as the emblem of futile human endeavor. These tablets, as he sees them, "in one sentence/ Grave all that is known" (194). Thoreau's word-play here is darkly resonant, and rich in irony. He suggests that these monuments bury, or "Grave," all human knowledge. These stones from the past prophesy the inevitable futility of knowing. The taciturn monuments "Grave [engrave, gave]" all wisdom in only "one sentence." Such wisdom could be the simple fact of the name of a town or direction, but it also conjures the equally simple but chilling fact of mortality, spoken through the gravestone-like appearance of the stone direction markers. The single "sentence" that the markers give – the word "sentence" carrying both a grammatical and a legal connotation – is en*graved* on them. That engraved sentence must be the very line itself in Thoreau's poem: "Grave all that is known" (194). Thoreau's *grave* symbolism adds a new dimension to the Old Marlboro Road's many destinations, if we understand the road itself as a place of death, or a pathway to death. This is indeed a *grave* meditation on human life.

In these passages on mortality, Thoreau can also be seen as adapting a Taoist outlook. Kichung Kim, one of the several scholars who has noted what he terms "the vague feeling of similarity one experiences in the works of Chang Tzu and Thoreau" (1973, 275), has emphasized "Thoreau's serene acceptance of our own life-and-death as part of nature's immutable cyclic process" (276) as part of his kinship with Taoism. He compares Thoreau's sense of death's rightness, as we might say, with Taoist philosopher Chang Tzu's doctrine that "Death is but the continuation of the process that life" in the same way that "winter is of autumn and sleep is of waking" (Kim 1973, 276). Both these connections are grounded in nature, particularly its seasonality. Kim's observation reinforces the idea that Thoreau employed the Old Marlboro Road as a deeply spiritual emblem of the journey of life, in some senses an encapsulation of the essay "Walking" as a whole, but one that softly answers Thoreau's buoyant mood in "Walking." Sauntering must have its autumn and winter as well as its spring and summer in order to be whole, and to be holy. Sauntering, however carefree and wild, is also humble and reverent in its sense of the human experience and its ultimate end. Sauntering, as Thoreau evokes it in "Walking," thus suggests modernity's version of the ancient pilgrimage.

Dark as his thoughts are in describing the road marker/gravestones, it seems clear that Thoreau thoroughly enjoyed his agile poetic play. Melancholy distinguishes the later movement of "The Old Marlboro Road," moving the poem itself away from the brighter treatise on sauntering that begins "Walking." The result is a unique tension between the poem, read in full, and the essay itself. This is a productive tension that sharpens the attitude of brazen defiance that principally reigns in the essay. To add a third mood to this mixture, I would designate Thoreau's discourse on the swamp as a subject of both analysis and celebration. It is significant to remember that a swamp is located in the vicinity of both the Old Marlboro Road and the old Carlisle road. Both abandoned roads and swamps are secluded rural places, which serve as protective and spiritually nurturing resources for the Thoreauvian saunterer. The differences between road and swamp, however, are clear. The road is the means of travel, connecting places and changing its actual identity or "placeness" as it unfolds. The swamp is fixed, an impenetrable and forbidding place that remains ever detached from human endeavors. Thoreau, however, is intent on overturning this conventional dread of the swamp by calling it a holy place, and associating it with the primal energies of life itself. He brings the swamp into focus shortly after his hymn to wildness, one of the central moments in "Walking," and an increasingly important text in our Anthropocene era. "Life consists with Wildness," Thoreau declared. "The most alive is the wildest" (2007, 203). Here, he directly challenged the idea that progress is defined by human expansion and civic development. "Hope and the future for me are not in lawns and cultivated fields, not in towns and cities, but in the impervious and quaking swamps" (204). The very fact that the swamp is impervious – inaccessible to humans (except for Thoreau) – gives it value. "If it were proposed to me to dwell in the neighborhood of the most beautiful garden that ever human art contrived, or else of a dismal swamp, I should certainly decide for the swamp," he commented (2007, 205). It is "a sacred place – a *sanctum sanctorum*" (205), whose mucky decay represents the ever-renewing fertility of nature's process. By the early 1850s, when Thoreau had begun to write the lectures that eventually constituted "Walking," he was beginning to see the swamp as a body of water as revelatory, and even as beautiful, as Walden Pond. The pond was one emblem of the vitality of nature, the swamp another. Its workings were even closer to the heart of wild nature. In "Walking," the swamp answers the dim message of mortality of the great stone markers along the Old Marlboro Road. The swamp is the place from which new life continues to emerge. The swamp is the vital and "sacred" spring of nature's process of life-nurturing death and decay. It is the "most alive" place and "the wildest" (203).

Thoreau's Old Marlboro Road thus stands as an engaging, but surprisingly deep meditation on holy places, secluded places, abandoned places, and places yet to be discovered. He brought the road to life as the ideal place for the true saunterer, the walker whose walks become imaginative quests and deeply spiritual pilgrimages. He also described it as a tangible location, a walkable road that led west from Concord to Marlboro. A place in itself and a gateway to other places, this still traversed pathway converted the ordinary activity of walking into a profound meditation on the quest for the holy. Thoreau's poetic portrait of the road makes us acutely aware of the landscape it traverses. He grounds the supposedly abandoned road in its disclosure of the lives of men and women who have taken these neglected lands as homes. Yet he made the neglected road a spiritually powerful place, whose winding path freed his imagination and elevated his sense of both the inner life of spiritual endeavor and the always present life of the natural world. We think of pilgrimage as the journey to a revered or sacred place, but Thoreau reminds us that the pathway itself is also sacred.

Works Cited

Arsić, Branka. 2016. *Bird Relics: Grief and Vitalism in Thoreau*. Cambridge, MA: Harvard University Press.

Bridgman, Richard. 1982. *Dark Thoreau*. Lincoln, NE: University of Nebraska Press.

Cady, Lyman V. 1961. "Thoreau's Quotations from the Confucian Books in *Walden*." *American Literature* 33: 20–32.

Ch'en, David T. Y. 1972. "Thoreau and Taoism." In *Asian Response to American Literature*, edited by C. D. Narasimhaiah, 406–16. New York: Barnes & Noble, 1972. Reprinted at "The Web of American Transcendentalism," edited by Ann Woodlief. Accessed March 28, 2018. http://transcendentalism.tamu.edu/thoreau-and-taoism.

Cheng, Aimen. 2000. "Humanity as 'A Part and Parcel of Nature': A Comparative Study of Thoreau's and Taoist Concepts of Nature." In *Thoreau's Sense of Place: Essays in American Environmental Writing*, edited by Richard J. Schneider, 207–20. Iowa City, IA: University of Iowa Press.

Conrad, Randall. 2013. "An Infinite Road to the Golden Age: A Close Reading of Thoreau's 'Road—That Old Carlisle One' in the Late Journal (24 September 1859)." In *Thoreauvian Modernities: Transatlantic Conversations on an American Icon*, edited by François Specq, Laura Dassow Walls, and Michel Granger, 82–101. Athens, GA: University of Georgia Press.

Elmire, Elise C. 2016. "Repeopling the Woods: Thoreau, Memory, and Concord's Black History." In *Thoreau at 200: Essays and Reassessments*, edited by Kristen Case and K. P. Van Anglen, 59–74. New York: Cambridge University Press.

Emerson, Ralph Waldo. 1971. *The Collected Works of Ralph Waldo Emerson, Volume I*, edited by Robert E. Spiller and Alfred R. Ferguson. Cambridge, MA: The Belknap Press of Harvard University Press.

"Estabrook Woods." 2017. *Wikipedia*. Accessed March 28, 2018. https://en.wikipedia.org/wiki/Estabrook_Woods.

Kim, Kichung. 1973. "On Chang Tzu and Thoreau." *Literature East and West* 17 (2, 3 and 4): 275–81.

Mark, David A. 2017. "Thoreau's 'The Old Marlborough Road." In *Maynard Life Outdoors and Hidden History of Maynard*. Accessed October 20, 2018. http://www.maynardlifeoutdoors.com/2017/03/. Posted March 12, 2017.

Sattelmeyer, Robert. 1988. *Thoreau's Reading: A Study in Intellectual History with Bibliographical Catalogue*. Princeton, NJ: Princeton University Press.

Simon, Gary. 1972. "What Henry Didn't Know About Lao Tzu: Taoist Parallels in Thoreau." *Literature East and West* 16: 253–71.

Tan, Hongbo. 1993. "Confucius at Walden Pond: Thoreau's Unpublished Confucian Translations." In *Studies in the American Renaissance*, edited by Joel Myerson, 275–303. Charlottesville, VA: University of Virginia Press. *JSTOR*. Accessed March 28, 2018. www.jstor.org/stable/30227643.

Thoreau, Henry David. 1971. *Walden*. Edited by J. Lyndon Shanley. Princeton, NJ: Princeton University Press.

——— 2007. *Excursions*. Edited by Joseph J. Moldenhauer. Princeton, NJ: Princeton University Press.

Walls, Laura Dassow. 2017. *Henry David Thoreau: A Life*. Chicago, IL: University of Chicago Press.

Part III

Cityscapes: Movements, Ideology, and Discourse

Introduction

Steven Allen and Kirsten Møllegaard

With more than 50 percent of the world's population living in urban areas, the centrality of the city to the human condition is undisputable. In comparison to the natural landscapes discussed in Part II, the city is all about spaces created for and by humans. The overwhelming, often confusing and intimidating features of the modern city, with buildings reaching dizzying heights, bright lights, busy streets, angles and corners, constant hustle, and anonymous masses of people have frequently framed narrative spaces in literature and film. The city has served to represent the grittiness of urban life or by contrast to externalize internal states; it has operated as a place of desire, power, crime, and optimism; it is seen as both utopian and dystopian, sometimes at the same time. Aldous Huxley claimed, "A large city cannot be experientially known; its life is too manifold for any individual to be able to participate in it" (1950, 271); and yet, the urge remains for writers and filmmakers to endeavor to capture the essence of the metropolis.

Matthew Kerry's chapter focuses on three feature films in which urban spaces play significant roles: *Girl with Green Eyes* (Desmond Davis, 1964), *I Was Happy Here* (Desmond Davis, 1966), and *The Country Girls* (Desmond Davis, 1984). These films, which were created by film director Desmond Davis in collaboration with Irish novelist Edna O'Brien, frame their stories of burgeoning female sexuality and eventual disillusionment in a series of contrasting environments that contextualize regional and national identity. The films (and O'Brien's novels that the films are based on) not only explore gendered spatialities, but also examine notions of belonging and displacement, memory and history, violence, and oppression. Kerry explores the films' industrial, historical, and social contexts in order to analyze what the films reveal about gendered places and changing identities for Irish women in the mid- to the late twentieth century. Kerry's chapter highlights the many social strictures and patriarchal norms Irish women faced when they left their homes in the country to work in the big city, or when they left Ireland to work in the United Kingdom. He discusses how rural and urban spaces, as well as the confined spaces of home, structure the women's perception of themselves, often under the yoke of a nationalist agenda where their struggle to achieve sexual and personal freedom is weighed against the haunting presence of Catholicism and the motherland. Davis' films and O'Brien's novels show how women's agency and determination can liberate and empower them, even in places dominated by patriarchal discourses.

Narrative cinema employs musical score to "tell" something about land- and cityscapes. *The Country Girls* famously opens with two girls skipping down a country lane, singing a children's song about finding a mate, followed by melancholy flute music that suggest a desire for something more, somewhere else. The narrative power of song lyrics and poetic language are significant, though often overlooked, elements of cinema. C. Yamini Krishna's chapter "Singing about the City: Imaginations of the City in Telugu Film Songs" investigates how India's sixth largest city, Hyderabad, has been imagined through the medium of film songs. Krishna's analysis explores how film songs accompany images of Hyderabad's physical cityscape and how they artfully supplement the moving camera with narrative as it weaves through the city's labyrinthine streets and alongside historical monuments. The Telugu song lyrics comment on the city's multiethnic population and complex history. Krishna points out that many film songs have a wide circulation long after the films in which they emerged are forgotten and that they have achieved an independent status in popular culture as poetic symbols of the city. She analyzes songs from the successful Telugu films *MLA* (K.B. Tilak, 1957), *Mattilo Manikyam* (P.V. Prasad, 1971) and *Happy* (A. Karunakaran, 2006) to articulate how they deeply engage with urban space. Krishna reads the film songs in conjunction with Hyderabad's sociopolitical context and discusses how the musical imaginary of the city in cinema overlaps and sometimes challenges official narratives, thus creating a fluid narrative of the city.

Fluid narratives and urban journeys also feature prominently in Michael Moreno's chapter "The Dao of the East-West City: Globalizing Identities and Urban Harmonies in Xiaolu Guo's Literature," which examines Chinese-British writer and filmmaker Xiaolu Guo's novels *A Concise Chinese-English Dictionary for Lovers* (2007) and *Twenty Fragments of a Ravenous Youth* (2008). Moreno analyzes how Guo's novels situate urban spaces in a yin-yang of identities through the local and global journeys of their characters. While *Dictionary for Lovers* demonstrates how a young Beijing woman's year-long English grammar education in London pits her Confucian and post-Maoist sensibilities against her older British boyfriend's Western mores of individuality, sexuality, and humanism, *Twenty Fragments* shows how Westernization collides with twenty-first-century Beijing as a young female film-extra/would-be-screenwriter struggles to capture the morphing of East-West culture now taking hold in the urban pockets surrounding her acquaintances. The East-West city is seen to be in flux, redefining itself in a globalizing world, while provoking its inhabitants to reconcile divergent worldviews. The characters' urban journeys and sojourns provide moments of harmony between traditionally contested cultural and ideological places. Moreno analyzes how Guo employs the cityscapes of London and Beijing as literary instruments of a contemporary East-West zeitgeist and a broader, global ethos. The novels show globalization as a complex process and deconstruct the East-West binary in various ways. Moreno argues that urban landscapes complicate the notion of place as monolithic in its identity and that London and Beijing's distinct cityscapes generate multiple narratives of power and consciousness, further contributing to the modern metropolis as actively participating in ever-evolving global and local identities.

This section on global cityscapes explores how big cities frame the formation and transformation of human identities globally and locally. Urban spaces are always-already imbued with social, historical, and cultural meanings and are, as these chapters demonstrate, rich sites of literary and cinematic production.

Work Cited

Huxley, Aldous. 1950. *Beyond the Mexique Bay: A Traveller's Journal*. London: Chatto & Windus.

The Country, the City, the Sea, and Girls with Green Eyes

The Films of Desmond Davis and Edna O'Brien

Matthew Kerry

Introduction

Film director Desmond Davis and Irish novelist Edna O'Brien collaborated on three feature films together: *Girl with Green Eyes* (1964), *I Was Happy Here* (1966), and *The Country Girls* (1984). These films frame their stories of burgeoning female sexuality and eventual disillusionment in a series of contrasting environments that help to construct regional and national identity. The films (and O'Brien's novels that the films are based on) not only explore gendered spatialities, but also examine notions of belonging and displacement – the pressure of the "Mother Ireland" fantasy immobilizing the female protagonists (Obert 2012, 292).

In *Girl with Green Eyes*, Kate (Rita Tushingham) is excited by Dublin. To her, the city "represents the possibility of escape from the oppressiveness of her childhood and of satisfying her romantic impulse to feel swept up into something larger than herself" (Weston 2010, 93). A sense of place is drawn more acutely in *I Was Happy Here*. In this film, Cass (Sarah Miles) has taken residence in a tiny flat in central London. As I discuss later, the city is a stifling place, and the film's narrative is punctuated by flashbacks to Cass's idyllic youth on the Irish coast. Ruth Barton's argument is pertinent here. She stresses that:

> In the Irish context, the extraordinarily picturesque and photographic quality of the landscape has combined with an immigrant culture predicated on nostalgia and a history of tourism to endow the romantic vision of the landscape and its people with an enduring potency.
>
> (Barton 2004, 7)

Cass's experience as an exile intensifies her feelings of homesickness and draws her back to Ireland. *The Country Girls* focuses on Kate's early experiences in the country, the convent, and her subsequent move to Dublin where she finds the freedom to pursue her clandestine relationship with an older man. The films are relatively faithful adaptations of O'Brien's work. *Girl with Green Eyes* and *I Was Happy Here* were produced in the context of the British new wave, which Davis was a part of, and contemporaneous with O'Brien's novels. The Channel 4 TV movie *The Country Girls*, however, was released twenty-four years after the novel was first published, and tends to present its characters and its landscapes through the prism of nostalgia. This arguably diminishes some of the political authority that the original novel had in 1960, as I discuss later.

Steven Adams and Anna Gruetzner Robins argue that the rural West of Ireland is traditionally gendered as feminine and that "the Irish peasant female, seen as passive, pure and nurturing" has been "co-opted as a personification of that authentic landscape" (Adams and Robins 2000, 9). O'Brien herself argues that "Ireland has always been a woman," but her heroines provide an antidote to the passive females mentioned by Adams and Robins (O'Brien 1978, 11). They can be aligned with the "wild Irish girl figure," played "with varying emphasis on her rebelliousness, seductiveness, tragic potential, [and] moral ambiguity," who genders the landscape as "feminine" (Meaney 1998, 238–40). The female protagonists of O'Brien's novels attempt to liberate themselves from the family and the Catholic Church and this is largely conducted through variations in narrative space as they move from one distinct place to another. Kate and Cass look for independence by moving away from the country to the city, or by moving away from Ireland to England. As Obert reveals, O'Brien's memoir diagnoses "the palpable 'psychological choke' experienced by women who find themselves trapped in Ireland's political vice, and suggest[s] 'escape' (in her own case to England) as a re-enfranchising alternative" (Obert 2012, 292). The pattern of migration in her novels and in their film adaptations, however, seldom offers a resolution from the strictures of Church and family. Ellen McWilliams argues, for instance, that it is "important to avoid plotting [Kate's] escape to Dublin in *The Country Girls* novel as a simple transcendence of the limits of rural Ireland for the freedom of the city" (McWilliams 2011, 53). Her move to Dublin provides "a space that initially seems liberating but quickly becomes cloyingly claustrophobic," and therefore presents a new set of problems for a protagonist who has such a quixotic outlook on life (Obert 2012, 286). This preliminary feeling of freedom transforming into eventual containment becomes a familiar pattern represented throughout O'Brien's novels and in the three films directed by Davis.

According to Graeme Harper and Jonathan Rayner, "all notions of landscape are produced by human interpretation which, simply due to human physiology or due to political or cultural bias, is selective" (Harper and Rayner 2010, 16). They continue by arguing that,

> A definition of landscape... needs to acknowledge different kinds of environments, from the rural to the urban, from the macro-environment of expansive ecology to the micro-environment of human habitation.
>
> (Harper and Rayner 2010, 16)

The narrative landscapes that I discuss in this chapter include rural and urban spaces, as well as the micro-environments of the home. These landscapes are repeatedly constructed in the O'Brien/Davis films through representations of gender or nationality, and, importantly, a combination of the two. I will also consider the films' industrial, historical, and social contexts in order to discover what these films reveal about place and the changing identities of Irish women from the 1960s onwards. Eileen Morgan argues, for instance, that O'Brien's novels posed a threat to "the weakening conservative establishment in the Republic of the '60s" and that "simply by representing women from rural Ireland as desiring subjects with sexual fantasies and habits," the author "challenged the nationalist image of Irish women as chaste, ethereal beings" (Morgan 2010, 450). Significantly, O'Brien's and Davis's films of the 1960s succeed in communicating narratives from the point of view of the female leads, rather than from the point of view of the "middle-class male protagonists" that Carrie Tarr argues is the case in the contemporaneous *Darling* (John Schlesinger, 1965) for example (Tarr 1985, 65). However, it is important to point out that in O'Brien's novels, migration does not offer complete emancipation for her heroines. As Obert suggests, "even in London, they cannot escape the demands of submissive Irish femininity" (Obert 2012, 284). In these texts, women endeavor to gain more control of their lives and bodies through migration from country to city, and from Ireland to London, yet these voyages of self-discovery ultimately end in disillusionment. Themes of place, movement, emancipation, and containment are common throughout O'Brien's and Davis's films, and provide the contexts for the narratives of place explored in this chapter.

Dublin and *Girl with Green Eyes*

Desmond Davis was one of the key figures to emerge from the new wave of British filmmaking in the 1960s. Davis worked as a camera operator on *A Taste of Honey* (Tony Richardson, 1961) and *The Loneliness of the Long Distance Runner* (Tony Richardson, 1962). *Girl with Green Eyes* was his first film as a director. Each of the above were made by Woodfall Films, a company originally formed by Tony Richardson, John Osborne, and Harry Saltzman to produce the film version of Osborne's play *Look Back in Anger* (Tony Richardson, 1959) (Murphy 1992, 16). *A Taste of Honey* made a refreshing change from the Woodfall Films associated with the "angry young man" movement. Its female writer, Shelagh Delaney, ensured a move away from the "male-centred and potentially misogynist expressions" of much of the new wave films (Hutchings 2009, 305). *Girl with Green Eyes* follows a similar formula, and, like *A Taste of Honey*, stars Rita Tushingham (as Kate Brady) whose "unconventional and quirky" qualities described by Christine Geraghty emphasize the heroine's "outsider" status (Geraghty 2009, 315). Woodfall Films were notorious for producing films based on controversial novels and plays, so choosing one of O'Brien's works for adaptation was fitting, because:

> O'Brien's first novels met with a divided response in the liberalizing Ireland of the '60s. Her frank portrayal of sexuality incensed conservatives, including the state censors, who banned her first five novels.
>
> (Morgan 2010, 451)

The narrative of *Girl with Green Eyes* centers on the relationship between Kate and an older man, Eugene Gaillard (Peter Finch). Kate has moved to Dublin with her best friend Baba Brennan (Lynn Redgrave) to escape from the domineering clutches of her alcoholic father. The opening scene of the film establishes the city as a vibrant and bustling place. As we see Kate walking briskly through a busy street back to her lodging house in an almost *cinema-verité* style, her voice-over divulges her love of Dublin, and her escape from the country:

> I love the city. I feel inside the life of it because there is always some face, some noise to interest me. It must be because I grew up in the country, a farm we had, and the house was in the middle of a field. Trees and wind and dogs barking was [*sic*] the noises I heard most.

Although we do not see any significant Dublin landmarks at the beginning of the film, the city is defined by the volume of its people as Kate passes shops and traffic. As O'Brien suggests the "enormous vitality of people hurrying to somewhere" is a far cry from the windswept, desolate farmhouse that Kate grew up in (O'Brien 2007c, 169).

The scene continues with an upbeat montage of Kate and Baba in their lodging house getting ready to go out for a night on the town. This parody of cosmetic commercials celebrates femininity knowingly and humorously. It does not critique consumerist culture as a negative feminine trait in the way referred to by John Hill (1986, 154). As Geraghty asserts, "feminine discourses of beauty and fashion are not the property of the establishment but a way of claiming a feminine identity which can be used as a mode of self-expression" (Geraghty 2009, 317). Baba blows soapsuds, fingernails are polished, and the girls fortify themselves with a gin and tonic before being collected for their date to the cinema. Although far from luxurious, the shared lodging room has at least been made to feel contemporary by the two young women – particularly by Baba who has pinups of men around her bed. This seems worlds apart from the "damp, dilapidated house" in which Kate was brought up, and which her aunt says has had a curse put upon it (O'Brien, 2007c: 97). If Baba is constructed in this film as self-assertive and confident, Kate is more contemplative and romantic. The young men who take Kate to the cinema and who approach her in the Dublin dance halls do not interest her. Instead, Kate prefers to read romantic fiction and "loses herself in daydreams about a man who will lift her out of her rural and tradition-bound Irish origins" (Weston 2010, 90). Morgan highlights how Kate desires "non-Irish men, precisely because she assumes that they will take care of her better than her own countrymen would" (Morgan 2010, 463). Eugene represents a life far removed from that which Kate has been used to. He is middle-class, part-Hungarian, and works in the film industry. After a couple of chance encounters, Kate takes the initiative to invite Eugene to join her in a Dublin teashop. This place, like the lodging house bedroom, appears to be a space where women may assert power. Kate feels confident enough to invite the older man without Baba as chaperone. In the early stages of their relationship, she displays confidence and takes agency by ordering the tea, toast, and cakes, reminding Eugene that it was *she* who invited *him*. O'Brien's heroines are able to break cultural norms in the spaces in which they feel comfortable. However, when Kate moves into Eugene's house, her assertiveness is diminished. A recurring theme of these films therefore is the representation of the heroines' sense of agency turning to inadequacy in places where men claim ideological control.

Eugene's House

If the city in *Girl with Green Eyes* offers Kate and Eugene a neutral space with which to acquaint themselves with each other, Eugene's imposing Georgian house in the hills beyond Dublin is a space where Kate is less self-assured. O'Brien's intertextual references to Daphne du Maurier's *Rebecca* (1938) abound here. Eugene's housekeeper, Josie – "a rural Irish Mrs. Danvers" – regales Kate with tales about the sophisticated parties that his wife Laura had there before they separated, and Kate finds a box under the bed with items belonging to Eugene's daughter whom he omitted to tell her about (Greenwood 2003, 27). Kate's aunt's comments regarding the curse on the Brady farmhouse seem to have extended to Eugene's country residence. Kate feels as though she has taken the place of an older and more cultured woman, and this gradually erodes her confidence. Once the impartial space of the city is left behind, the grand house emphasizes class distinctions between Kate and Eugene. The house also becomes a site of masculine conflict when Kate's father and fellow countrymen burst in one evening to take her away from this "heathen" outsider. To them, Eugene is from a different class and nationality and his grand house represents something that the Brady family has lost. Greenwood points out that Kate's impoverished family have been unable to live in their ancestral "big house" since it was burned by the "Protestant Black and Tans" and that instead, they live in a smaller farmhouse on the land that their ancestral home once stood on (Greenwood 2003, 32). The forced entry by Kate's male relatives is not only an attempt to maintain patriarchal control, but also to wrest her from the "other" male that Eugene represents. Unlike the city, which at least offers Kate the possibility of living in the present, rural Ireland is irrevocably a historic space, bound by its past, and as revealed here, often a troubled and traumatic one.

The narrative spaces of *Girl with Green Eyes* are clearly delineated. Kate's country roots are ideologically ingrained, despite her taste for romantic literature and her desire to find excitement in Dublin. The old house fails to be a safe haven for Kate, and the specter of Eugene's ex-wife Laura drives her away. Unable to deter her feelings of inadequacy, Kate deserts Eugene in a Dublin hotel, and makes the life-changing decision to travel with Baba to London. The repeated experience of the move between places and the unfulfilled promises that this brings to O'Brien's heroines is palpably felt by the representations of space and character in this film. This is explored further in O'Brien and Davis' next collaboration, *I Was Happy Here*, where the heroine's status as an exile is brought to the fore.

The Western Seaboard and *I Was Happy Here*

I Was Happy Here tells the story of young Irish woman Cass who moves to London hoping that her fisherman boyfriend Colin (Sean Caffrey) will join her there. The narrative framework presents a contrast between the west coastal landscape in County Clare where Cass grew up, and the grey, impersonal space of central London, where she meets her future husband Dr Matthew Langdon (Julian Glover). Trapped in an unhappy suburban marriage she flees back to her hometown where she reminisces about her youth and talks to her confidant, Hogan (Cyril Cusack), the owner of the inn where she used to work. The movement of Cass and the resultant sense of displacement are part of the thread that is common across all three films discussed here. As Murray suggests, "the process of migration … plays an important structural role in O'Brien's work by framing and contextualizing the often dramatic shifts in perspective and identity that take place in her characters' lives between Ireland and elsewhere" (Murray 2013, 86). The narrative takes place in Cass's fishing village after she flees from a dismal Christmas day meal with her abusive husband Matthew. Much of the story is presented in flashback, showing Cass's past and includes several distinct spaces, which help to construct the emotional timbre of her story. The distinctions between the fishing village and London are foregrounded in the film. Cass's unhappy experiences in London tend to make her look upon County Clare with nostalgia, which, in turn, emphasizes the cultural gulf between her and Matthew. Hamid Naficy points out that "[e]xile is inexorably tied to homeland and the possibility of return. However, the frustrating elusiveness of return makes it magically potent" (Naficy 1999, 3). As I discuss here, it is Cass's isolation in London and the feeling of entrapment that her marriage brings that makes her nostalgic remembrance of Ireland ever more forceful.

Having an affinity with the sea is a motif that signals the compatibility or incompatibility of the partners in the film. Colin is nomadic by nature. His livelihood comes from the sea, and his eyes represent the romance and mystery of the ocean. Cass remarks that he has "sea eyes – they're changeable." After Colin and Cass have separated, he tells her about his job on an oil tanker saying that he likes working at sea because he gets lost in it, enabling him to forget the past. This conversation is conducted with a fishing net hanging between the two former lovers, signifying their separation, but also, perhaps their connection with the sea. Unlike Colin, Matthew is a city person. As Cass says:

> I don't think he likes the country. We went to the sea once – he sat in the car, I walked up and down for hours, couldn't get enough air. He thought I was mad …

The seaside scenes (filmed at Lahinch beach) are idyllic and represent the heroine's freedom from restraint. In one of the film's most visually striking moments, Cass is shown cycling with carefree abandon along the sands. The seaside setting constructs a feeling of youthful vitality – the liminal space at the edge of the tide, between the permanence of the land and the ever-changing sea indicating Cass's freedom prior to marriage. Later in London, Cass tries to recapture some of this vivacity when she finds a bicycle in a narrow lane beneath the silhouette of the Post Office Tower. Freedom is expressed here via movement. The pull of her rural Irish roots is too intense for Cass to ignore, and as she circles around on the bike, she is ideologically transported back to County Clare, momentarily becoming the girl on the beach once more (Figures 7.1 and 7.2).

Figure 7.1 Cass riding her bike on Lahinch Beach in *I Was Happy Here* (Dir. Desmond Davis; Prod. Partisan Productions, The Rank Organisation; 1966).

Figure 7.2 Cass in her London bedsit in *I Was Happy Here* (Dir. Desmond Davis; Prod. Partisan Productions, The Rank Organisation; 1966).

Alone and Stranded in London

Cass's move to London shares similarities with Kate Brady's move to the same city at the coda of *Girl with Green Eyes*, and like Kate's life in the novel *Girls in Their Married Bliss* (O'Brien 2007b), Cass's hopes for adventure soon begin to unravel. As Murray argues, the "degree of personal transformation achieved by escaping to London in these novels is undeniably limited. Rather than offering a means of liberation for O'Brien's protagonists, the city threatens to be the site of their emotional exile or nemesis" (Murray 2012, 66). As Weston suggests, "the psychological battles of the individual are inseparable from the cultural context in which they are fought … engagements with a wounded past problematize the future, calling into question the possibility of moving forward" (Weston 2010, 88). Cass's Irish roots and the "restrictive roles for women" that are inherent in this make it impossible for her to assimilate fully to London life (Weston 2010, 88). Matthew and Cass's incompatibility is marked out from the start. On their second meeting in a noisy pub, Matthew asks Cass to join him with his rugger-loving friends. Although Cass is at home in the pubs of her village – she worked in a seaside inn with Hogan, after all – the London pub is evidently a masculine space. She looks lost in the crowd of men as they gather around her in the cramped space of the bar singing a bawdy, raucous song. This is contrasted with another musical scene when Cass returns to Ireland and skips joyfully down the middle of the village high street as she imagines hearing the sea shanty "Shoals of Herring" coming from one of the local pubs.

The pivotal scene in which Cass and her husband have Christmas dinner takes place in the impersonal space of a hotel dining room. This might be considered as the type of "non-place" or "temporary abode" that Marc Augé refers to. In this instance, the hotel is a "transit point" somewhere between Matthew's idea of home in the suburbs of London, and Cass's remembrance of home in the fishing village. The hotel provides Cass with a transitional space and escape route from her marriage (Augé 2008, 63). When Matthew wonders why there are so few diners in the hotel, Cass explains to him that they are all "at home next to fires, warm" – a veiled complaint about their far-from-cozy circumstances. When Cass takes issue with the way that Matthew speaks to the waiter, her husband asks her how it feels to "identify with the downtrodden." He then delivers a misogynistic diatribe that is directed at both Cass and her country. To him, Cass and Mother Ireland are one and the same:

> I was not dragged up in an Irish bog. Why don't you go back to those country cousins of yours? Mother Earth!

This exchange directs Cass back home. The film concludes with the heroine staring out to sea. The ever-changing tides emphasize the pervasive theme of movement and migration that runs throughout O'Brien's work. Greenwood argues that in the context of postwar Ireland and Britain, O'Brien was "remarkable" for "anticipating the zeitgeist" and "disillusionment" that came with the "permissive society" of the 1960s (Greenwood 2003, 22–23). This sentiment is clearly foregrounded in *I Was Happy Here*. As Danny Powell suggests, 1960s' films such as *The Knack* (Richard Lester, 1965) and *Darling* "dispel the myth of a sexual revolution" that treats men and women equally (Powell 2009, 178). Similarly, Murphy states that "*Georgie Girl* (Silvio Narizzano, 1966), *Alfie* (Lewis Gilbert, 1966) and *Smashing Time* (Desmond Davis, 1967) all look for thrills in the big city but end up endorsing homely virtues like sincerity, loyalty, friendship" (Murphy 1992, 146). What makes O'Brien's and Davis's work in *I Was Happy Here* unique, however, is that the subjective view of London is experienced through the eyes of an Irish female exile who realizes how much she misses home. As Naficy argues, "[m]ost of us take for granted our place in the world and come face-to-face with it only when we are threatened with displacement" (Naficy 2001, 152). It is this sense of displacement that makes Cass feel so lonely and isolated in the big city.

The Country Girls

Almost twenty years after their previous collaboration, Desmond Davis and Edna O'Brien returned to the author's first novel for a production of the Channel 4 TV movie *The Country Girls*. After a notoriously unstable decade of British film production in the 1970s, Channel 4 helped to revitalize the industry in the 1980s with a series of low-budget made-for-television films, some of which were successful enough to warrant a cinema release. Neil Jordan's first feature, *Angel* (1982), for instance, was financed by both the Irish Film Board and Channel 4, and was the first of Channel 4's films to receive theatrical exhibition (Rockett 2005, 209). Although *The Country Girls* was produced by London Films and was therefore arguably a British production, it was the first of the O'Brien/Davis collaborations that had assistance from Bord Scannán na hÉireann, the Irish Film Board. This would lead one to expect a more authentic representation of Ireland on screen, but, at times, *The Country Girls* tends to present "Irish land as scenery" that sometimes deviates from the construction of place in O'Brien's novel, as I will explain later (Meaney 1998, 238).

The narrative explores Kate's (Maeve Germaine) life in the period in which she and her friend Baba (Jill Doyle) lived in the country before moving to Dublin. Kate is infatuated with an older man in her village, Mr Gentleman (Sam Neill), but is estranged from him during her and Baba's time in the convent. The girls hatch a plot to escape from there by being expelled, and eventually move to Dublin, bringing us to the point in which the audience was introduced to Kate and Baba in *Girl with Green Eyes*.

The opening of the film establishes the rural setting and the two main characters, as they skip down a country lane framed by green hills. In the following scene, they act out a confession. Kate informs Baba (as the priest) that she has thought about boys touching her "under me frock." To which the worldlier Baba exclaims "don't tell him about boys ever, he's fanatical, he'll have you whipped!" The confession takes place outdoors in a sun-dappled coppice with smoke from a smoldering bon-fire drifting across the scene. The romantic setting is disrupted by the scandalous conversation of the two girls. Meaney's observation about gendered Irish landscapes is appropriate to these two opening scenes:

> [L]andscape is simultaneously gendered (as feminine) *and* politicized in films set in Ireland. Panoramic introductions to Ireland as scenic location are often concluded by a scene of political confrontation or a first view of a heroine, sometimes both at once.
>
> (Meaney 1998, 238)

The confrontation here is addressed ideologically against the Church and previous works of Irish fiction. As Ciara Barrett suggests, "[o]ver the history of Irish visual and literary culture... the Irish woman has been denied a basic, earthly embodiment, tending instead to be figured as a de-sexualized religious or political symbol" (Barrett 2015, 61). Although these themes are alluded to in the 1960s films, the 1980s production allows its heroines to talk more frankly about sex within the green Irish countryside, making for a politically symbolic text. Baba sees through the hypocrisy of society and the Church. She "recognizes that the Catholic ideal of womanhood, the Virgin Mary, is unrealistic" (Byron 2002, 457). At the convent she undermines the authority of the Mother Superior in the most transgressive way possible by passing a note around the classroom which she knows will be intercepted. The contents referring to Father Tom having sex with Sister Mary result in the girls' expulsion, giving them the opportunity to move to Dublin. Here they gain an independence that was lacking in the village, and Kate also obtains the opportunity to meet Mr Gentleman away from prying eyes.

Kate and Mr Gentleman, and the Romance of the Landscape

One of the spaces in which Kate and Mr Gentleman meet is noteworthy because of the way that it deviates from the same key scene in O'Brien's novel. Late one night, Mr Gentleman drives Kate to a remote boathouse by a lake where he tells her about his plan to take her away for a weekend in the traditionally romantic city of Vienna. In the novel, this scene takes place in the front room of the Dublin lodging house where Kate and Baba live, and Mr Gentleman asks Kate to undress for him so that he can see her naked body. The scene as written is filled with awkwardness; Kate does not want Mr Gentleman to look as she unclasps her suspenders and brassiere, and she stands in mild embarrassment, not knowing what to do with her hands once she has no clothes on. When Mr Gentleman returns the favor and undresses for her, Kate imagines the "horror" if Joanna (the landlady) "should burst in in her nightdress and find us like two naked fools on the green velveteen couch" (O'Brien 2007a, 211).

The film version tends to favor a more cinematic treatment of the scene by framing the two characters in silhouette against a moonlit lake. This romantic construction of place – due to the media's reinterpretation of the scene – ultimately diminishes Kate's disappointment of the unrealized trip to Vienna and provides her with a romantic memory that the awkward scene in the front parlor would not have done. The breathy voice-over from Kate that accompanies much of the film reinforces her romantic outlook on life, but again, the political intentions of O'Brien in subverting romantic fiction may be lost by the cinematic representation. Kate's voice-over is told in the past tense because she is recalling events that happened before she left for London, but this past tense also gives the film a nostalgic quality, which is reinforced by the period *mise-en-scène*. Even as Kate boards a boat for her new life in England at the film's conclusion, her internal monologue is a reminiscence of events in Ireland. Naficy argues that the process of displacement causes the exile to live out their experiences through a sense of loss. He says it is as though "the experiences of here and now are not sufficient or real enough by themselves unless they are somehow projected as loss or are mediated by memory and nostalgia" (Naficy 2001, 153). Kate's desire to make a new start in London is prompted by the disappointment of her failed relationship with Mr Gentleman, yet the romantic setting of their last encounter and the nostalgic remembrance of her homeland arguably temper the crushing level of disappointment that is represented in the novel.

Conclusion

Representations of place in the O'Brien/Davis films make a key contribution to the audience's understanding of the characters. National boundaries and gendered spaces alike help to construct the identities of Kate, Cass, Eugene, Colin, and Matthew. Murray argues that "rather than being unambiguous and cohesive entities, identities are constructed from contested and sometimes contradictory discourses of nation, gender and generation" (Murray 2013, 90). It is important, therefore, to consider that the identities in the three films discussed here are not fixed – like Colin's eyes, "they're changeable." As I have revealed by analyzing the representation of Kate in a series of narrative spaces such as the Dublin tearoom and Eugene's house, or the Cass of County Clare and London, these women alter with the landscape as well as with the people they share time with.

Exile and displacement play an important part in these films, either as an integral part of the narrative, or as a key feature of a film's conclusion. The move from one space to another is represented not only by a change in location, but also by shifts in the characters' identities. In the case of Cass, this is illustrated in her personal transformation caused by the movement between the western seaboard of Ireland and London. Although jaded and distressed by her experience as an exile, she ultimately seems somewhat stronger, firmly telling husband Matthew that reconciliation is out of the question. In the conclusion of *The Country Girls*, Kate recalls her memories of life in Ireland nostalgically in a voice-over presented in the past tense. Her ties with Mother Ireland ensure that a move to London will not entirely sever her from her rural roots. The significance of the landscape is integral to analyses of the films discussed here. As Conn Holohan argues:

> [I]t is through a shared understanding of belonging that a space becomes one in which we may collectively belong. However, as an examination of Irish cultural discourses over the past decades reveals, that understanding necessarily shifts over time in response to wider social, economic and cultural changes.
>
> (Holohan 2015, 15)

As revealed here, the films of Desmond Davis and Edna O'Brien offer an illuminating insight into the representation of place and the changing identities of Irish women in the mid- to the late twentieth century.

Works Cited

Adams, Steven, and Anna Gruetzner Robins. 2000. "Introduction." In *Gendering Landscape Art*, edited by Steven Adams, and Anna Gruetzner Robins, 1–11. Manchester: Manchester University Press.

Augé, Marc. 2008. *Non-places: An Introduction to Supermodernity*. 2nd ed. Translated by John Howe. London: Verso.

Barrett, Ciara. 2015. "Black and White and Green All Over? Emergent Irish Female Stardom in Contemporary Popular Cinemas." In *Ireland and Cinema, Culture and Contexts*, edited by Barry Monahan, 59–70. Hampshire: Palgrave Macmillan.

Barton, Ruth. 2004. *Irish National Cinema*. London: Routledge.

Byron, Kristine. 2002. "In the Name of the Mother ...: The Epilogue of Edna O'Brien's Country Girls Trilogy." *Women's Studies* 31 (4): 447–65.

Greenwood, Amanda. 2003. *Edna O'Brien, Writers and Their Work*. Tavistock: Northcote House Publishers.

Geraghty, Christine. 2009. "Women and 60s British Cinema: The Development of the 'Darling' Girl'." In *The British Cinema Book*, 3rd ed., edited by Robert Murphy, 313–20. London: BFI.

Harper, Graeme, and Jonathan Rayner. 2010. "Introduction: Cinema and Landscape." In *Cinema and Landscape*, edited by Graeme Harper, and Jonathan Rayner, 13–28. Bristol: Intellect.

Hill, John. 1986. *Sex, Class and Realism, British Cinema 1956–1963*. London: BFI.

Holohan, Conn. 2015. "'Nothin' but a Wee Humble Cottage': At Home in Irish Cinema." In *Ireland and Cinema, Culture and Contexts*, edited by Barry Monahan, 13–23. Basingstoke: Palgrave Macmillan.

Hutchings, Peter. 2009. "Beyond the New Wave: Realism in British Cinema, 1959–63." In *The British Cinema Book*, 3rd ed., edited by Robert Murphy, 304–12. London: BFI.

Meaney, Gerardine. 1998. "Landscapes of Desire: Women and Ireland on Film." *Women a Cultural Review* 9 (3): 237–51.

Morgan, Eileen. 2010. "Mapping Out a Landscape of Female Suffering: Edna O'Brien's Demythologizing Novels." *Women's Studies* 29 (4): 449–76.

Murphy, Robert. 1992. *Sixties British Cinema*. London: BFI.

Murray, Tony. 2012. *London Irish Fictions, Narrative, Identity and Diaspora*. Liverpool: Liverpool University Press.

——— 2013. "Edna O'Brien and Narrative Diaspora Space." *Irish Studies Review* 21 (1): 85–98.

McWilliams, Ellen. 2011. "Making It Up with the Motherland: Revision and Reconciliation in Edna O'Brien's The Light of the Evening." *Women: A Cultural Review* 22 (1): 50–68.

Naficy, Hamid. 1999. "Introduction. Framing Exile: From Homeland to Homepage." In *Home, Exile, Homeland. Film, Media, and the Politics of Place*, edited by Hamid Naficy, 1–13. London: Routledge.

—— 2001. *An Accentuated Cinema, Exilic and Diasporic Filmmaking.* Woodstock, Oxfordshire: Princeton University Press.

Obert, Julia C. 2012. "Mothers and others in Edna O'Brien's The Country Girls." *Irish Studies Review* 20 (3): 283–97.

O'Brien, Edna. 1978. *Mother Ireland.* London: Penguin.

—— 2007a. *The Country Girls.* London: Weidenfield and Nicholson.

—— 2007b. *Girls in Their Married Bliss.* London: Phoenix.

—— 2007c. *Girl with Green Eyes.* London: Phoenix.

Powell, Danny. 2009. *Studying British Cinema: The 1960s.* Bedfordshire: Auteur.

Rockett, Kevin. 2005. "The Miracle." In *The Cinema of Britain and Ireland,* edited by Brian McFarlane, 207–15. London: Wallflower.

Tarr, Carrie. 1985. "Sapphire, Darling and the Boundaries of Permitted Pleasure." *Screen* 26 (1): 50–65.

Weston, Elizabeth. 2010. "Constitutive Trauma in Edna O'Brien's 'The Country Girls Trilogy': The Romance of Reenactment." *Tulsa Studies in Women's Literature* 29 (1): 83–105.

Filmography

Alfie. Dir. Lewis Gilbert, UK, 1966.
Angel. Dir. Neil Jordan, Ireland/UK, 1982.
The Country Girls. Dir. Desmond Davis, Ireland/UK, 1984.
Darling. Dir. John Schlesinger, UK, 1965.
Georgie Girl. Dir. Silvio Narizzano, UK, 1966.
Girl with Green Eyes. Dir. Desmond Davis, UK, 1964.
I Was Happy Here. Dir. Desmond Davis, UK, 1966.
The Knack. Dir. Richard Lester, UK, 1965.
The Loneliness of the Long Distance Runner. Dir. Tony Richardson, UK, 1962.
Look Back in Anger. Dir. Tony Richardson, UK, 1959.
Smashing Time. Dir. Desmond Davis, UK, 1967.
A Taste of Honey. Dir. Tony Richardson, UK, 1961.

8 Singing about the City

Imaginations of the City in Telugu Film Songs

C. Yamini Krishna

Introduction

Cities are not constant formations in time; they are historical entities formed as a part of the social, cultural, political, and economic conditions prevailing at a particular moment. The kinds of cities we live in reflect the social ties, relationship with nature, lifestyle, technologies, and esthetic values of the people (Harvey 2003). The official policies document only the city of the governmental plans; the lived experience often slips through the official registers. It is this gap that the narratives of popular culture can be thought to fill. I specifically argue in this chapter for the case of film songs as archives of the city.

Preben Kaarsholm (2004) writes that films have supplemented the role of literature and print culture as icons of modernity. Ranjani Mazumdar (2007) argues that cinema like several other visual forms documents the change brought by modernity and participates in it. She notes that film functions as an archive of the modern, housing the allegorical images of the city. Mazumdar therefore reads the cinema in a metaphorical mode to argue that (Bombay) cinema gives us access to the urban subjectivities. I dwell on this idea of film as an archive of the urban. While there is a certain imagination of the city which a particular film presents, there are glimpses of the real city which also peep through these imaginations. Mazumdar (2007) uses Rahul Mehrotra's (2002) concept of kinetic city in talking about cinematic representations. She notes that each city comprises two cities: the static city or the permanent city which is the city of the monuments, the city which can be depicted on the maps; and the other city is the kinetic city, which marks the city's relationship with the people. Hawkers, festival processions, webs of electric cable, and street dwellers are all a part of this city. I use these ideas of static city and kinetic city to conceptualize what I simply call the tangible city. The tangible city is the city at that particular moment, and it comprises both the monuments and the relationship of the people with them. The tangible city is thus the city in the images of the traffic, pedestrians, the hawkers, along with the monuments. Through the tangible city, I read the static city and the kinetic city in relation to each other. For example, the plot and the treatment of the film might construct a certain imagination of the city life; individual elements of the film like the songs often present the images of the traffic or city dwellers. They give us some flavor of the tangible city at that time. The city which is then realized on the screen is a negotiation between the imagined city of the narrative and the tangible city of some of the images. The film songs sung about the city particularly present rich repositories of visions of the city in their lyrics and the visual images of the city.

When placed in historical and cultural contexts of a particular time, films tell complex stories of the city and its everyday life. This also ties in with the idea of popular culture presented by Stuart Hall (1981). He argues that popular culture is not to be understood either purely as resistance or completely as subjugation to the ideology of capital, but as a ground on which negotiations happen. He calls this dialectic of cultural struggle the struggle between points of resistance and moments of supersession (228). In this chapter, I read film songs as these grounds on which negotiation between the tangible and the imagined city happens. The imagined city is the city of the dominant discourse and the tangible city is that of the several contesting narratives. The film song unearths the multiplicity of visions of the city. These alternative voices are memorialized by the film songs. They become the repositories to access the lived experience of the city of a particular time. A discerning spectator can get a glimpse of what it meant to live in the city in an earlier era through these songs.

It is with this understanding of film as an archive that I attempt to trace the changing narrative of the city of Hyderabad through the study of film songs. I examine city songs from Telugu films in their social, political, and cultural context to read the specific stories of the city. This helps us understand what stories, facts, myths, and discourses the songs are drawing from to construct the city, and, in turn, what this reveals about the lived experience of the city. As a result, we get a glimpse of the dominant and contesting discourses of the city in that moment.

Film Songs

Sangita Gopal and Sujata Moorti (2008) have argued that songs are one of the distinct features of Bollywood. Like Bollywood, Telugu (the state language of the South Indian states of Andhra Pradesh and Telangana) cinema[1] particularly places high focus on its song and dance sequences. Film songs in Telugu cinema (and also other Indian cinemas) come at several junctures of the narrative; sometimes they are a device to travel through time and space, sometimes a celebration of the protagonists being in love, sometimes singing the angst of the characters, sometimes as a comic interlude, in short, the situations for songs are infinite. Songs are also distinct in form; unlike other cinematic elements they do not attempt to form a continuous narrative, rather they have the liberty to work with flashes of images. Songs use montages to weave several locations, instances, and images together. In particular, city songs are filmed to present the city to the audience. I use film songs as palpable material for capturing the fleeting experience of the city, across time.

Songs also get wide circulation through media platforms such as radio, television, and digital media, which are independent of the film. Sudipta Kaviraj (2004) argues that because songs are repeated several times in different situations outside the immediate context of the film, they take a permanent seat in aural or visual memories of the people. He notes that most popular songs are capable of achieving a "freestanding meaningfulness as a literary, musical object, as a rhetorical comment on life" (65). He argues that songs have a special capability of capturing the texture of the city. He writes

> It is through these songs, forming an aesthetic series or combinatory, that the inhabitant of the modern city formed an expressive language of his emotions and moods, and his ultimate reception of this life-world.
>
> (66)

Kaviraj points out that the songs in Bombay films were written by progressive Urdu poets and several times reflected their own musings on the city. This point is also valid in the case of Telugu films, particularly in the early two to three decades post-independence, the 1950s–1970s. Telugu cinema had several progressive poets like Sri Sri (Srirangam Srinivasa Rao)[2], C. Narayana Reddy[3], Arudra,[4] and others who wrote film songs. These poets have often used film songs as vehicles to communicate their reflections on life to the large film audience. Their songs are adorned with rich metaphors and idioms. Film songs thus can be argued to stand independently as literary and cultural objects outside the immediate context of the films.

Kaviraj's arguments emphasize the significance of songs as creative objects to study the city. In the closely knit structure of commercial films, where all the different narrative threads have to culminate toward a particular ending, songs can be present without the purpose of leading up to a conclusion. They can be thought of as defiant parts in the structure of the film. They allow for certain poetic freedom. Visually also city songs are distinct; while the films' narrative scenes might be shot completely in studios, city songs are shot in real locations and present rich visual documentation of the sights and experiences of the city. The historical negotiations of the city can be unearthed through the study of songs as archives of the city.

In what follows I examine film songs as archives of the city at two levels: first, as literary objects which narrativize the imaginary of the city, and second, as visual archives of the city which present the glimpses of the tangible city. The interaction between the lyrical and the visual aspects present the negotiations between the tangible and the imagined city.

Singing about Hyderabad

The Telugu film industry is currently set in Hyderabad; it moved to the city from Madras[5] in the early 1970s. Telugu cinema has produced quite a few songs about the city or about particular locations of the city. Among the wide repertoire of songs, I will examine three songs dispersed across time that sing about the city life. The songs serve as examples; the argument that city songs constitute an archive of the city and present an esthetic of the city can be illustrated by the study of any city songs. I will analyze *Idenandi Idenandi Bhagyanagaram* from *MLA* (1957), *Rim jhim rim jhim Hyderabad* from *Mattilo Manikyam* (1971), and *Chal chal re chal mere sathi* from *Happy* (2006). I examine songs as independent creative objects outside cinema and hence focus on the lyrics and the visuals; their significance in the plot of the film is irrelevant to the current context.

A brief history of Hyderabad will help us better understand the changing imaginations of the city in the songs. The city of Hyderabad has undergone several historic changes, which can be broadly divided into four periods based on the sociopolitical context: (a) before 1948, (b) from 1948 to 1956, (c) from 1956 to 2014, and (d) after 2014.

Until 1948, Hyderabad was the capital city of the Asaf Jahi Dynasty. The last ruler Mir Osman Ali Khan Bahadur ruled the princely state of Hyderabad from 1911 to 1948. It was a modern city well connected, via the railways and telephone networks, to the rest of India. Eric Beverley (2015) characterizes the culture of the Hyderabad state under the Asaf Jahi rule as "globally mediated, polyglot, multi-religious, cosmopolitan" (293). Scholars like Karen Leonard (1973), Vasant Kumar Bawa (1992), Omar Khalidi (1988), and A.G. Noorani (2014) have argued that Hyderabad was a religiously tolerant and pluralistic society. Hyderabad was annexed by the Indian union in 1948 with the help of police action.

Hyderabad functioned as the capital city of Hyderabad state, which was a part of the Indian union from 1948 to 1956. The linguistic state of Andhra (based on Telugu language) was formed in 1953 and was reorganized to include Hyderabad state in 1956, with Hyderabad city as its capital. From 1956 to 2014, Hyderabad operated as the capital of Andhra Pradesh state. In 2014, Andhra Pradesh was bifurcated into two states and Hyderabad currently is the capital of Telangana[6] state. The history of Hyderabad has been the case of shifting boundaries and changing identities.

With these changes, the social and cultural life of the city has also undergone several changes. The position of Muslims has altered from being the ruling class during the Nizam period to becoming a powerless minority after 1948. The linguistic identity of the city has changed from being a polyglot city with Urdu and Persian as official languages and Marathi, Telugu, and Kannada as spoken languages to being identified as a Telugu city. The history of the Nizam period is hugely contentious in the context of rising right-wing nationalism in India. On the eve of departure of the British from India, the Nizam (and other princely states) were given a choice to join India or Pakistan or remain independent and the Nizam chose to remain independent. This is often interpreted as an anti-India move. The Nizam being a Muslim ruler is often painted by nationalist historians as an autocratic ruler who discriminated against the Hindu subjects.

Another significant event which changed the fate of the city was the implementation of neoliberal reforms in 1990s–2000s under the leadership of then chief minister N. Chandrababu Naidu. Hyderabad was reimagined as a global Information Technology hub with partnerships with international technology giants like Google, Microsoft, and Infosys who set up their India offices in Hyderabad. The city was also physically transformed to suit the new needs: Hyderabad Information Technology Engineering Consultancy City was built with wide roads and flyovers. These newly developed areas are called Cyberabad. Like several global cities, Hyderabad was imagined as a servicing city.[7]

The changes Hyderabad city has undergone intersect with the paradigms of religious identity (the change of the position of the Muslims from one of dominance to being a minority), linguistic identity (the change of Hyderabad from being a polyglot city to a Telugu city), and economic identity (the change of Hyderabad from being a city in the local economy to becoming a global Information Technology hub). Each of these changes has social and political context and consequences attached to it. The cultural identity of the city is negotiated on these axes in the film songs.

In the next section, I give brief descriptions of the lyrics of the songs, present the analysis of the songs, and discuss the esthetic of the city as constituted by these songs. The city's shift from the Nizamian city to the capital city of a Telugu speaking state and then as a global city is marked by these songs. These songs present the changes in the city life brought by each of these historical shifts.

The first song I examine is *Idenandi Idenandi Bhagyanagaram* (*This is Bhagyanagaram*)[8] from the film *MLA* (K.B. Tilak, 1957); the song was written by Arudra and sung by Ghantasala and S. Janaki. The song is in Telugu language and describes the city of Hyderabad through a series of adjectives. It is described as the capital city of 30 million Andhras, as the city built by Quli Qutb Shah, the ruler of Golkonda for his lover Bhagmati, as the city housing the famous Charminar, and as the city of museums, wide roads, university buildings, and gardens. The lyrics associate the city with the glorious history of Andhras when *Telugu Talli* (Telugu mother) flourished in Golkonda, and sing about its capture by Aurangazeb from the Qutb Shahis; the stories of Tana Shah and Ramadasu also feature prominently.

No copy of the film is available today, so I examine only the lyrics. Each Indian film has several songs and all the songs of a particular film are compiled and released as an album. These songs were mostly released as cassette tapes until the 1990s and are now released on CDs. The MP3 versions of the old songs are also available for download at various music sites. Radio and television programs curate and present several songs in their thematic programs. For example, a particular song can be featured in a theme around the director of the film, music director of the film, star of the film, or the topic of the film. The above song continues to be circulated through radio, MP3, and other formats. It often gets featured on radio and television programs curated on the theme of the city of Hyderabad.

The song uses popular legends about the city to construct a certain historicity to the city. The legend of Bhagmati[9] is the love story between the emperor Quli Qutb Shah and the village girl Bhagmati. It is a widely circulated story that the emperor built the city and named it after her as Bhagyanagar. The legend of Ramadasu[10] is the story of Kancherla Gopanna (also known as Ramadasu), a devotional poet who was imprisoned by Abul Hasan Qutb Shah (also known as Tana Shah) and was released when Tana Shah saw Lord Ram in his dream and asked him to release Ramadasu. The origin story of Charminar is that the monument was built to commemorate the victory over plague. Charminar is the iconic four-pillared monument in the old city built in 1591. It is the most recognizable symbol of the city across the world. The song narrativizes the plague story saying, "the disease got cured by the grace of Allah" (*Allah daya valla a peeda poinadi*) also pointing to the Islamic culture of the city at that time. All three legends are used to build a mythology for the city. The song from 1957 comes immediately after the formation of the linguistic state of Andhra Pradesh. This can be seen as an introduction song to the new capital city of Hyderabad to the 30 million Andhras[11] (then the population of the state). The song is sung in chorus by male and female voices, which is a common practice in street theater. Oral narration of legends is a historical tradition in India and continues in theatre today. The use of a local mode of history telling bestows a certain authenticity to the legends told through the song. Film song draws from folklore (oral history); this affirms Hall's (1981) argument that popular culture is a ground of negotiation, not just in content but also at a formal level.

The inclusions and exclusions of the song make the historical contentions visible. While the song mentions the wide roads, museums, modern buildings, and gardens, it does not mention the rule of Mir Osman Ali Khan Bahadur, the last Nizam under whose rule the city was modernized. The song claims the city as "a jewel that adorns mother India" (*bharatamaatha jadaloni pasidinaagaram*). This has to be understood as the nationalist claim over the Hyderabad state in the context of the annexation of the state in 1948. The question of modernity represented in the modern buildings and roads is particularly significant in the context of Hyderabad as the British often painted the princely states as backward and autocratic to justify their rule, and it is this legacy that the postcolonial history also takes on (Beverley 2015). The disregard for the Nizamian history also serves the purpose of justifying the annexation of Hyderabad by the Indian nation. The Telugu capital city of Hyderabad thus is not comfortable acknowledging the Nizamian past. The reference to Telugu mother[12] (*Telugu talli*) is that the citizens of the state are imagined as the sons of the linguistic mother. The Telugu connection to the city of Hyderabad is thus established using the Andhra history.

The second song I examine is *Rim jhim rim jhim Hyderabad*[13] from the film *Mattilo Manikyam* (B.V. Prasad, 1971); the song was written by C. Narayana Reddy and sung by S.P. Balasubramanyam. The song presents Hyderabad as a working-class city, the city of the rickshaw wallah (rickshaw puller); the visuals of the song supplement the lyrics with the protagonist driving the rickshaw through all the important landmarks of the city. Through the travels of the rickshaw, the viewer gets a tour of Charminar, Jumma Masjid, Assembly Hall, Jubilee Hall, Hussain Sagar, and Secunderabad, leaving behind the motor cars. Singing about the power of the rickshaw, the song also pledges its support to the labor class as opposed to the rich and powerful, as symbolized by the motor car. From the description of the monumental city, the song then goes on to describe the lived city. We see the view of the city from the eyes of the working-class man; the use of the monumental city serves the purpose of presenting the city as a historic city with diverse modern influences. It celebrates the city's multi-religious and multi-lingual culture and sings about Gandhi cap and Rumi cap. We see images of a man in a Rumi cap and another in a Gandhi cap embracing each other, as the lyrics go on to talk about the Urdu (*Kya bhai*) and Telugu (*emoi*) languages. The linguistic and sartorial differences here are used as symbols of religious differences, that is, Urdu is associated with the Muslim and Telugu with the Hindu. It has been widely argued that the association of Urdu with Muslims is a recent phenomenon, which has been forged in the postcolonial India (Datla 2013); the song is evidently concerned with making these linguistic-religious connections. The traces of the Nizamian city are represented as the fraternal culture of the city.

We see a significant critique of the income disparities in the city in the song; it sings that "the rich cannot digest food and the poor cannot find food to eat" (*unnavadiki tinte aragadu lenivadiki tindi dorakadu*); the images of a footpath and bungalows are used to present the contrast between the rich and the poor. It is the working class which has the legitimate claim on the city. The rickshaw wallah operationalizes his claim by traversing the labyrinthine lanes which the car can never access. The song's comment on the economic disparities has to be understood in the context of the dominant economic discourse in the early decades of post-independent India, of the influence of M.K. Gandhi and Jawaharlal Nehru. Gandhi professed a simple lifestyle, symbolized by his loin cloth; he placed the poor on a higher moral pedestal as compared to the rich. According to him, the rich could only redeem themselves by serving the poor. Jawaharlal Nehru, the first prime minister of India, emphasized the industrial and scientific development of the nation to bridge the gap between the rich and the poor. Gandhi was assassinated in 1948 and Nehru died in 1964. By the 1970s, the nation had moved into the next generation of leaders, but the song, from 1971, reviews the promises of the nation. The poet reflects the Gandhian discourse by presenting the life of the poor as peaceful and that of the rich as chaotic. He poses questions on the unrealized pledge of social justice. The poet expresses his despair, pondering if the promises will ever be realized, "I wonder when one would see the day when there are no disparities" (*hecchu taggulu tolige roju epudostundo emo*). Rendered in the voice of a working-class man, it questions the state of Indian democracy.

In the film, the song is a mix of the protagonist riding the rickshaw on the busy streets and the images of the rickshaw being superimposed on the footage of the city. The images are pan shots which show the expanse of the city; these shots cut occasionally to close-ups of the rickshaw. In some cases, the rickshaw is added, post-production, to the footage of the city. The filming arrangement is a practical one, because the city could not be managed according to the needs of the shooting. The existing city is therefore shot without stopping the traffic, adjusting the street dwellers, and so on, but beyond such pragmatism, this approach to shooting also allows the tangible city to encroach into the imagined city. While the majority of the film was shot in the studio, this song alone was shot on location and has real images of the city; hence, it becomes an archive of the city of the 1970s. The city song also marks a disjuncture in the film via two modes: (a) the song functions outside the narrative structure of the film and hence is able to concern itself with the city life and (b) it steps outside the constraints of the studio space and hence becomes the visual archive of the living city. It is this song that actually marks the location of the narrative of the film, through its visuals and lyrics. While the problems of the city might be common across different cities, it is the song which makes the plot a story of Hyderabad and not any other city.

The third song I examine is *Chal chal re chal mere sathi*[14] (*Come My Friend*) from the film *Happy* (A. Karunakaran, 2006), and sung by Clinton. Interestingly, this Telugu song has some parts in Hindi and a considerable portion in English rendered with an American accent. It presents an interesting case for comparison with the earlier songs. It is written by Viswa (Vemuri Visweswar), an upcoming lyricist in the Telugu film industry; unlike the other lyricists discussed in this chapter, he is professionally engaged as a lyricist by the film industry and is not known to participate in any other literary pursuits.

The protagonist sings about him becoming a Hyderabadi (citizen of Hyderabad) and embracing the city. This is a song of the global city of Hyderabad, a city which revels in its fast-paced life and its position in the world market. It is the song of Cyberabad, the hub which houses all the major servicing corporations. The song describes the city as a place of opportunities, which embraces migrants like none other. The city is a place where migrants can leave their past identities and choose "what they wanna be." The embodiment of the culture of the city is a global citizen, symbolized by an Information Technology professional, who "works hard, parties harder." This global citizen is an interesting amalgamation of the global and the local: she/he aspires for a place in the world market, but also has to maintain the local connection. Saskia Sassen (2000) characterizes a global city by global capital and immigrant workers. She argues that cities are the sites where global and local spatialities and temporalities intersect. Cities simultaneously operate as a part of global networks and local environments. The song reflects this idea of the global city, pointing to the immigrant economy of globalization; the lyrics state "There is no other place like Hyderabad in embracing people" (thanavodilo choticheyi Hyderabaduki satinkedi), "People come to Hyderabad from several different places with a lot of aspirations" (ekkadekkadi nuncho yuvathe entho asalathoti ee Hyderabad kikadilostaru). The role of the history and culture of the city is to provide a distinction to attract the attention of global capital. The depiction of the linguistic diversity in the song also reflects this shift in the governmental aspirations for the city. The earlier songs emphasized Urdu and Telugu, but in this case more than half of the song is rendered in English, which has to be understood via its position as the language of global capital. It enables the Hyderabadi to access global opportunities and acts as a bridge between the global and the local. The vision of the city presented by the lyrics goes hand in hand with the governmental propaganda of the official plan for the city. As argued by Sassen (2000), the global world is pegged on financial hubs like New York, London, Tokyo, Singapore, etc. The government intends to model Hyderabad on these global centers. The representation of the "new" culture of the city is akin to this.

I read the contentions between the official vision and the tangible city through the slippages between the lyrics and the visuals. The song begins with the protagonist, an immigrant to the city, being welcomed to the city. He belongs to the working class (a pizza delivery boy), but has no markers of his class; he now wears the corporate uniform. Outside work he wears jeans[15] and jackets and does not display any identification of his class status. As he sings of Hyderabad, the camera shows images of the protagonist in different locations, he sometimes sings in a pub, sometimes delivers pizza to an IMAX cinema, sometimes we see him dancing in front of Charminar followed by a quick succession of the images of the monuments. As he sings about history, we see him dancing with Muslim children depicted wearing skull caps, and we see glimpses of images of women in *hijab* and the *irani* cafes of old Hyderabad. The lyrics acknowledge the history, but invite us to look toward the future. This kind of interaction between the lyrics and images serves to present Muslims as a part of the history, but does not give any space for them in the imaginary of the global future. In the song, we see Muslims only in the old city and while singing about the history. Furthermore, the new city becomes the symbol of progress and the old city a space of the past. The song as a visual archive cannot hide these contentions between the new city and the old city though the lyrics themselves do not explicitly emphasize such tensions. The Islamic influence on culture becomes visible on the streets. The visual archive of the song documents all these contentions.

When read in conjunction with the 1971 song, the 2006 song presents an interesting contrast on the idea of the working class. The working-class man in 1971 was a rickshaw puller; in 2006, it is the white-collar Information Technology worker. Blue-collar workers and unorganized laborers find no mention in the 2006 song, since there is a certain invisibility rendered to the markers of the working class. Though the protagonist himself is a pizza delivery boy, his actions are indistinguishable from the middle and upper classes: he dances in the pubs and rides sports bikes. While the labyrinthine lanes were accessed using the rickshaw, a public vehicle in 1971 song, in 2006 it is the sports bike, a private vehicle, which traverses the city. In the earlier song, the poet laments socioeconomic inequalities, but in the latter song they are accepted as a part of the system, for the song sings that, if the migrants do not make effort to keep up the pace with the city, they are bound to falter, as the city stops for nobody. This shift in the working-class imaginary of the city has to be understood in the neoliberal turn of the cities focused on individualism. The gospel of individualism discredits and discourages solidarity of the working class. It places the burden of success or failure completely on the individual's abilities. The question of social justice itself does not find much resonance in the parlance of "income" and "progress." The song constructs the individualism discourse through the working-class man's disassociation with class markers. He does not demand social justice because he thinks he is on a par with the upper classes: he wears the same clothes and inhabits the same social spaces. The song thus becomes a unique space where these multiple contestations of the city are allowed to engage with each other. The distinct form of the song makes it attuned to communicate these facets of the city.

The Esthetic of the City

The three songs discussed from different time periods present distinct narratives of the city. The city of *Idenandi Iidenandi Bhagyanagaram* can be broadly described as a narrative of a historical city embracing modernity, the historicity itself invoked by the monuments and legends.

The city of *Rim jhim rim jhim Hyderabad* is a working-class city with glaring inequalities; the influences of the history of the city itself is now depicted as a culture of fraternity among religions. The city of *Chal chal re chal mere sathi* is the global city, where history and culture are pedestals to attract global capital. The negotiations between the lyrics and the visuals present the different contestations of the city. They help us to find the historical traces of the city we see, live in, and experience today.

It is significant to note that these three songs as independent creative objects continue to circulate in the contemporary time, showing that all the different ideas of the city exist, overlapping each other. The esthetic of the city is thus that of these overlapping narratives. The Information Technology city does not erase the inequalities of the city or the Nizamian history but overlaps it; the traces of different sociocultural milieus are etched into the city spaces and are archived in the songs. Though historical time periods might have passed, the contemporary period echoes the past in very tangible ways. The existence of these overlapping narratives does not let one vision of the city to be fixed. The old songs become the gaping holes through which the jubilant mode of the present and visions of development and progress can be questioned. The songs give us a wide range of words and ideas to construct our own narrative of the city. While the film texts might resolve the conflicts toward a certain ending, the beauty of the songs as independent creative objects is that they leave the city in the making, not forcing finality.

Notes

1 The Telugu film industry is one of the largest film-producing industries in the world. It addresses the Telugu-speaking population across the world.
2 Sri Sri received the Sahitya Academy Award in 1972 and was also a prominent member of Viplava Rachaitala Sangham (Revolutionary Writers Association), a Marxist writers' association.
3 C. Narayana Reddy is a Jnanpith and Padma Bhushan award-winner for his literary contribution to Telugu language.
4 Arudra has received the Sahitya Academy Award for Telugu literature in 1987.
5 Telugu, Tamil, and Malayalam films were produced from Madras from 1930s to 1970s. After the formation of linguistic states in 1956, these language film industries moved to their respective state capitals beginning in the 1970s.
6 The Telangana state was formed in 2014 and the politics of it are unfolding at the moment. For the current chapter, I limit my analysis until the early 2000s.
7 In a servicing city, the major economic activity happens through varied services like the financial sector, hospitality, retail, entertainment, etc. See Nigel Harris (1997) for more details.
8 All the translations of the songs are by the author.
9 The legend is also circulated in other media, including book: *Hyderabad: A Biography* by Narendra Luther (2006); play: *Quli: Dilon ka Shahzada* (*Quli: The King of Hearts*) (2015); and film: *Bhagmati* (2005).

10 This legend is also found in films like *Ramadasu* (1964) and *Sri Ramadasu* (2006).
11 The term Andhras (*Andhrulu* in Telugu) refers to Telugu-speaking people.
12 The language is imagined as the mother and its speakers as the children, thereby forging a particular brotherhood among the Telugu speakers. We may regard it as a cultural phenomenon of linguistic nationalism. See Mitchell (2009) for a discussion of the rise of linguistic nationalism in South India.
13 *Rim Jhim* is just used as a rhythmic sound that does not have any specific meaning.
14 *Chal chal re chal mere sathi* is used as a colloquial way of addressing a friend.
15 Jeans in India are seen as an identification of urban middle and upper classes. For more discussion on meanings of jeans in Bollywood, see Wilkinson-Weber (2011).

Works Cited

Baig, Mohammed Ali. Dir. *Quli: Dilon ka Shahzada*. 2015. Play.
Bawa, Vasant Kumar. 1992. *The Last Nizam: The Life and Times of Mir Osman Ali Khan*. New Delhi: Viking.
Beverley, Eric Lewis. 2015. *Hyderabad, British India, and the World: Muslim Networks and Minor Sovereignty, c. 1850–1950*. New Delhi: Cambridge University Press.
Datla, Kavita Saraswathi. 2013. *The Language of Secular Islam: Urdu Nationalism and Colonial India*. New Delhi: Orient BlackSwan.
Gopal, Sangita, and Sujata Moorti. 2008. "Introduction: Travels of Hindi Song and Dance." In *Global Bollywood: Travels of Hindi Song and Dance*, edited by Sangita Gopal and Sujata Moorti, 1–59. Minneapolis: University of Minnesota Press.
Hall, Stuart. 1981. "Notes on Deconstructing 'the Popular'." In *People's History and Socialist Theory*, edited by Raphael Samuel, 227–40. London: Routledge.
Harris, Nigel. 1997. "Cities in a Global Economy: Structural Change and Policy Reactions." *Urban Studies* 34 (10): 1693–703.
Harvey, David. 2003. "The Right to the City." *International Journal of Urban and Regional Research* 27 (4): 939–41.
Kaarsholm, Preben. 2004. "Introduction: Unreal City: Cinematic Representation, Globalization and the Ambiguities of Metropolitan Life." In *City Flicks: Indian Cinema and Urban Experience*, edited by Preben Kaarsholm, 1–25. London: Seagull Books.
Kaviraj, Sudipta. 2004. "Reading a Song of the City: Images of the City in Literature and Films." In *City Flicks: Indian Cinema and Urban Experience*, edited by Preben Kaarsholm, 60–82. London: Seagull Books.
Khalidi, Omar. 1988. *Hyderabad, After the Fall*. Wichita, KS: Hyderabad Historical Society.
Leonard, Karen. 1973. "The Deccani Synthesis in Old Hyderabad: An Historiographic Essay." *Journal of the Pakistan Historical Society* 21 (4): 205.
Luther, Narendra. 2006. *Hyderabad: A Biography*. New Delhi: Oxford University Press.

Mazumdar, Ranjani. 2007. *Bombay Cinema: An Archive of the City*. Minneapolis, London: University of Minnesota Press.

Mehrotra, Rahul. 2002. "Bazaar City: A Metaphor for South Asian Urbanism." In *Kapital and Karma: Recent Positions in Indian Art,* edited by Angelika Fitz, Gerald Matt and Michael Wörgötter, 95–110. Vienna: Hatje Cantz Verlag.

Mitchell, Lisa. 2009. *Language, Emotion and Politics in South India: The Making of a Mother Tongue*. Bloomington: Indiana University Press.

Noorani, Abdul Gafoor Abdul Majeed. 2014. *The Destruction of Hyderabad*. London: Hurst.

Sassen, Saskia. 2000. "The Global City: Strategic Site/New Frontier." *American Studies* 41 (2/3): 79–95.

Wilkinson-Weber, Clare M. 2011 "Diverting Denim: Screening Jeans in Bollywood." In *Global Denim*, edited by Daniel Miller and Sophie Woodward, 51–68. Oxford: Berg Publishers.

Filmography

Bhagmati, Dir. Ashok Kaul, India, 2005.
Happy, Dir. Karunakaran, India, 2006.
Mattilo Manikyam, Dir. B.V. Prasad, India, 1971.
MLA, Dir. K.B. Tilak, India, 1957.
Ramadasu, Dir. V Chittoor Nagaiah, India, 1964.
Sri Ramadasu, Dir. K. Raghavendra Rao, India, 2006.

9 The Dao of the East-West City

Globalizing Identities and Urban Harmonies in Xiaolu Guo's Literature

Michael P. Moreno

The Chinese Post-cultural Revolution has ushered in an epoch of varied interconnections between Eastern and Western identities and ideologies. This, in turn, has generated important narrative productions of resistance and concord through which twenty-first-century urban geographies are being articulated. Within this narrative space, urban locations, in particular, function as cross-cultural terrains, which interconnect and potentially harmonize East-West epistemologies. This physical and philosophical transmigration between the urban East and West can be articulated through Chinese-British writer and filmmaker Xiaolu Guo's novels *A Concise Chinese-English Dictionary for Lovers* (2007) and *Twenty Fragments of a Ravenous Youth* (2008).

Guo's novels situate urban spaces in a yin-yang of identities, which attempt to create balance and harmony through their fragmented odysseys. *Dictionary* demonstrates how a young Chinese woman's yearlong English grammar education in London pits her Confucian/post-Maoist sensibilities against her older British boyfriend's Western mores of individuality, sexuality, and humanism. Likewise, *Fragments* shows how Westernization collides with twenty-first-century Beijing as a young female film-extra/would-be-screenwriter struggles to capture the morphing of East-West culture taking shape around her. The characters' urban odysseys and sojourns offer interstices that provide moments of harmony between traditionally contested cultural and ideological loci. Attempting to create meaning between the worlds they inhabit, even if for a fleeting moment, Guo's literary characters continuously struggle to formulate a relationship between the East and the West into a fluid alignment of transformations and interconnections from the fragments of their respective lives. As such, these characters enter a "third space," which is one "of extraordinary openness, [and] critical exchange where the geographical imagination can be expanded to encompass a multiplicity of perspectives" (Soja 1996, 5), thus allowing for a globalized agency and literacy that is mutable and always-becoming. However, cultivating this identity is predicated on the body's fluidity and ability to occupy multiple spaces at once, for the "body is not *in* space like things; it inhabits or haunts space" (Merleau-Ponty 1963, 5, italics mine). This *haunting* of space, then, means that one is no longer moored to a precise location, but is free to be a part of a broader matrix of sites.

Guo's literary and cinematic writing-style is indicative of how East-West cities transform their identities rapidly and fluidly while redefining and repositioning their inhabitants via globalization. Crisscrossing between literature and cinematic writing demonstrates interchanges between real and imagined spaces that move literary characters beyond their geopolitical positions and into a third space "where issues of race, class, and gender can be addressed simultaneously without privileging one over the other" (Soja 1996, 5) across a global stage. Guo's writing not only reveals a yin-yang process in keeping with Eastern cultural tradition, but also demonstrates this in the universal application of narrating the East-West urban phenomenon through the production of literature.

Since the fourteenth century BCE, yin-yang has functioned as a philosophical practice and organizing principle through which to articulate and address the complex processes of order and chaos in the universe. Seemingly disparate elements and features in the world and universe meet and assume aspects of the other in order to sustain this balanced, fluid relationship. Robin Wang (2012) suggests, "harmony and disorder are conceived through contiguity and distance, and finding harmony depends on combining contrasting elements into relations of contiguity. Harmony is ultimately a matter of integration, and this is the main function of yinyang thinking" (16). Guo's *Dictionary* and *Fragments* articulate this yin-yang dynamic by showing how London and Beijing, respectively, have become literary instruments of a twenty-first-century East-West zeitgeist and a broader, global ethos. An East-West identity can equally be applied to the city as much as to the inhabitants of the city, and both protagonists' odysseys underscore this movement toward translating an historical binary (East/West) into the yin-yang principle (East-West) of interconnectivity, fluidity, and innovation.

Part Chinese-English dictionary and part fictional journal entries, *Dictionary* charts the wanderings of impressionable twenty-three-year-old Zhuang Xiao Qiao, from China. The protagonist goes to London at her parents' insistence to improve her English communication skills, which is reflected in the novel's form: English vernacular writing that slowly evolves into a more polished narrative as the protagonist matures and becomes more adept at translating her East-West experiences. During her one-year sojourn abroad, "Z" – as she calls herself in order to accommodate the British who are unable, or unwilling, to pronounce her name – is absorbed into Western culture. The experiences of studying English with other foreigners, spontaneously moving in with a London sculptor, and exploring cultural and ideological taboos expose Z to Western values of sexuality, individuality, and self-expression. London transforms Z from the Eastern and Western fragments of her journeys into a global subject, one which is "a slippery and paradoxical signifier of liberation and entrapment, self-sufficiency and deficiency, as well as communication and non-communication" (Poon 2013, 2). Throughout the interstices of contested public and private spaces, fleeting moments of love and loneliness, and intermingling Chinese words and English phrases, *Dictionary* reveals how the East-West city translates, and is translated by, its inhabitants who, in turn, become newly defined beings that transcend time and place in their mutability and multiplicity.

Z's introduction to London is, at first, a complicated one. Already, the exhausting flight from Beijing and the disorientation from crossing multiple time zones have confused her. Being unmoored or ungrounded, however, does not necessarily mean being unbalanced; an East-West identity attempts to assemble disparate parts into a whole to articulate and sustain moments of concord, albeit fleeting ones. Indeed, this identity that Z generates throughout the novel is "oriented to imagining and creating a world which is 'singularplural', and holds sameness and difference together in creative tension" (Oboe 2013, 278). The crucible of such "creative tension" then is the East-West city itself. Just as East and West have been historically and epistemologically constructed as a binary, the East-West city deconstructs this into a fluid totality, a "contact zone" whereby various texts (cultural, linguistic, spatial, etc.) are "systematically received in radically heterogeneous ways" (Pratt 1991, 39) and transcribed into cross-cultural connections, which have the potential to coalesce into a balanced whole, yet one that is not necessarily absolute, utopic, or static.

London becomes this third space for Z, but at first, her impressions of an alternate site are informed by paradoxes and juxtapositions of what she expects from London and what she eventually discovers. On her own and alone for the first time, Z begins to fear her surroundings and her uncertainty in navigating her way: "I think unsafe feeling come from I knowing nothing about this country" (Guo 2007, 11). Cars that move in opposite directions, a homeless man who watches her "like an angry cat," a black man she imagines "beating [her] up just like in films" (11), all feed into her Western urban-phobia and distance her from the city. "London should be like emperor's city. But I cannot feel it" (11). Despite the absoluteness of her small, concise Chinese-English dictionary, she is shocked by how she is still unable to translate her impressions of London through an Easterner's register. While the city seems to confirm the media-manufactured misunderstandings Z brings from the East, there is also a breakdown of syntax and cultural literacy for her that further generates mistranslations between the East and the West. What Z previously "knows" of the West contradicts what she now sees:

I worry I getting lost and nobody in China can find me anymore. How I finding important places including Buckingham Palace, or Big Stupid Clock? I looking everywhere but not seeing big posters of David Beckham, Spicy Girls or President Margaret Thatcher. In China we hanging them everywhere. English person not respect their heroes or what?

(11)

Z's stereotypes and visual registers of the West impact her ability to chart these Western spaces with any accuracy or confidence since they do not resemble the mythos of the West from the Easterner's perspective. As such, this creates a different experience from other visitors to the city in terms of articulating London's identity. In Z's encounter, a disjunction occurs between spaces/places and mediated spatial zones.

Z's fear and confusion over the East-West correlation comes from a feeling of spatial distance and exile from her homeland of familiar associations; and yet, her confusion underscores how lived and imagined spaces are also blurred as a result of global-technology. Film, television programs, and a multitude of black-market images of the West, which have filtered through Chinese cities can result in a disjuncture between manufactured images and actual experiences. This state of psycho-spatial exile, however, only induces a yearning in Z to explore what surrounds her. Her exile creates an opening for a dual perspective, a cross-translation of East and West. More precisely,

> [b]ecause the [person in] exile sees things both in terms of what has been left behind and what is actual here and now there is a double perspective that never sees things in isolation. Every scene or situation in the new country necessarily draws on its counterpart in the old country
>
> (Said 2000, 378)

As such, Z's displacement moves her closer to seeking balance within a new consciousness that still comprises fragments from an immediate Eastern past and Western present:

> Am I writing in Chinese or English? ... I see other little me try expressing me in other language. Is like seeing my two pieces of lips speaking in two languages at same time. Yes, I not lonely, because I with another me
>
> (Guo 2007, 33)

The sudden absence of a communally based environment forces Z to produce a new method for reading the paradoxical signs whirling all around her. "To learn a language means to acquire a body" (Poon 2013, 3); Z recognizes that, if she has no community, then she will have to rely on herself to translate the foreign experience of an East-West state of mind.

Guo's work demonstrates that an East-West subjectivity is not either/ or, and Z is still in a state of exile and not completely cognizant of how the East and the West are intermingling in her mind. As a geopolitical and cultural exile, she

> exists in a median state, neither completely at one with the new setting nor fully disencumbered of the old, beset with half involvements and half-detachments, nostalgic and sentimental on one level, an adept mimic or a secret outcast on another
>
> (Said 2000, 370–1)

In this third space, Z begins to produce an East-West narrative that allows her a broader lexicon from which to draw in a city that has already become a cultural and linguistic contact zone.

Z's East-West subjectivity takes on greater resonance when she meets a British man, twice her age, while watching a German film in South Kensington. The man, who remains nameless throughout the novel, makes a connection with Z when she notices him periodically smiling at her during the film. Z notes, "Nobody smile to me before like you in this cold country. In the darkness, I am thinking you must be kind man" (Guo 2007, 39). Here, Guo shifts her novel from first person point of view to second. The narrative alteration is significant because although the novel maintains the format of an annotated journal-like dictionary, this is where the novel becomes less confessional and more epistolary directing Z's attention toward "you," her soon-to-become British lover. This change in point of view also functions as a kind of literary voice-over, where we hear Z's intimate desires and perspectives as she narrates her new experiences and struggles to connect with the West. The novel itself, consequently, generates an East-West language by rescripting a conventional Chinese-English dictionary into an East-West one.

Despite the fact that Guo never reveals the actual name of the British man who suddenly appears in Z's life, he is the one who forms the connection and initiates a more intimate East-West exchange between them. Just as Z has resigned herself to a simple Latinate letter, the British boyfriend has no precise identification beyond Z's immediate sensory experience: "You tell me your name, but how I remember English name? Western name are un-rememberable, like all Western look the same. But I want remember you, want remember the difference you with others" (Guo 2007, 40). The British man has entered Z's world of cultural, ideological, and linguistic translation. To her, he is a creature of safety and comfort in a whirling sea of endless definitions and referents that is London. She has already become the signifier "Z" in London, a stand-in for an identity in flux. Likewise, the British man is now immersed in this East-West exchange, which impacts his own identity. Together, Z and the British man explore London and one another's bodies in an effort to define themselves, each other, and inevitably one another's cultures. It is, ultimately, the tension and differences from this intimacy that brings about the yin-yang dynamics in their interchange.

This rescripting of London into an East-West contact zone is especially made through the public and private locations of British gardens. Guo uses the garden, a long-time esthetic symbol of British imperialism and civilization, to showcase expressions of Western containment, definition, and orderings of the broader, (post)colonized world. "The garden provides an image of the world," according to Siri Meyer, "a space of simulation for paradise-like conditions, a place of otherness where dreams are realized in an expression of a better world" (cited in Johnson 2012, 1); and yet, this "better world" is one borne from a Western/colonizing perspective, something of which Z is quite aware. Moreover, Kew Gardens serves as monument where the West conquers not only nature, but also the East in a narrative that is retold each time a visitor wanders its bucolic pathways.

However, the public garden becomes an opportunity to critique remnants of former British colonial power. As her personal guide, the British man invites Z to tour Kew Gardens, encouraging her to navigate the Underground, whose map has always looked "like plate of noodles" (Guo 2007, 16) to her. "'Queue Gardens?'" she asks, mistranslating the location for a homonym. "'Meet me at Richmond tube station,' you say. 'R-i-c-h-m-o-n-d'" in their telephone exchange (43). Although unintentional, the British man's subtle, paternalistic instructions can be read as molding and shaping the Eastern subject into a Westernized one, which plays into "a common enough Eurocentric historical narrative that it is the West which inaugurates China into modernity" (Poon 2013, 3). However, Z dismantles this notion later in the garden by pointing out its cultural mistranslation of organizing vegetation and trees into a Eurocentric narrative of power and epistemology:

> We see there is different small gardens with different theme. Africa garden are palm trees. North America garden are rocks. South America garden are cactus. And there is too Asian gardens. I so happy Manager not forgetting Asia gardens. But I so disappointing after we walk in [to the Asian gardens]. Lotuses and bamboos is growing in India garden. Where is my Chinese garden? "Doesn't look like they've made a Chinese garden," you say to me. "But that very unfair," I say in angry voice. "Bamboos belongs to China. Panda eats bamboos leafs in China, you must hear, no?"
> (Guo 2007, 43)

Westerners, like the British man, would not necessarily pay much attention to the fact that a Chinese garden is absent from the Asian section, so it is significant that Z points this out and educates the man to this taxonomical discrepancy, thus ensuring the inclusion of an Eastern perspective in a Westernized reconstruction of nature.

Like Kew Gardens, the British man's private garden at his East London home becomes a vibrant space for further articulating the fluctuations of the East-West contact zone and fostering the couple's intimate relationship. In the chapter entitled "fertilise," lists are organized in columns with English vegetative terminology beside their equivalents in Chinese characters, establishing a yin-yang lexicon that bonds the lovers' language together. This lexicon underscores how "[y]inyang thought appeals to integrated processes rather than divided dualisms" (Wang 2012, 14). The private garden is also a showcase for the British man's original art sculptures of abstract masculine bodies and plaster phalluses twisting in various shapes and poses in the dirt, not only an intimate expression of the man's professed bisexuality and Western liberties, but also an extension of his desire "to feel the weight of the life" (Guo 2007, 126). However, after months of conversations, lovemaking, and a host of cultural mistranslations, the boyfriend's sense of heaviness and intensity creates greater distance between them as they grapple to maintain balance in their individual lives and their experience.

While the East London home provides Z with a sense of comfort and sanctuary from "[t]he grey city kept away by this garden" (56), it slowly grows into a place of loneliness and solitude for Z as the year progresses and the relationship deteriorates, taking on the molting colors of the autumnal garden. There is now a growing awareness that in order to cultivate harmony in their East-West world, they will have to focus on themselves and abandon a shared destiny with one another. The British man begins to feel as though he has lost his "own space to think about [his] sculptures, [his] things, and [his] own words" (141). Likewise, Z eventually discovers that they "live in such different cultures," realizing that it is "very difficult for both [of them] to find the right way to communicate" (141). The lovers discover that articulating the East-West city and their place within it is no longer predicated on maintaining their relationship. Z recognizes she can cultivate an East-West subjectivity all on her own, with the knowledge that she possesses the yin-yang principle within herself. Through *Dictionary,*

> Z uses language as mediator, as facilitator and as bridge. She uses language to make sense of who the other is and who she herself is. She uses language to fashion herself as an adult, and to make sense of both Chinese and English culture
>
> (Rahbek 2012, 7–8)

With an unrenewable visa and this newfound knowledge, Z returns to China but, against her parents' wishes, settles in Beijing to begin a new life on her own terms.

Nevertheless, Beijing – itself now transformed with great velocity and purpose – challenges Z to yet again find her place within another urban crossroads, for this capital city has morphed into its own East-West network of spaces. She returns to China with new eyes: "The whole city is dusty and messy. Unfinished skeletons of skyscrapers and naked construction sites fill the horizon....It is unrecognizable....I feel out of place in China" (Guo 2007, 280–1). The city is awash in a frenetic energy that sparkles and glows with communist cultural relics repurposed into shiny capitalist opportunities, where "everybody talks about buying cars and houses, investing in new products," but it is also where Z finds that she "can't join in their conversations" (282). While she is now in Beijing and prepared to begin a new life in this city, she uses this newly acquired lexicon that allows her to crisscross between the East and the West. Living between cultures and languages, nevertheless, requires that Z continue crafting an East-West subjectivity and agency by translating the lessons of London into the "web of interlocutions" (Oboe 2013, 271) that has become Beijing.

Just as Xiaolu Guo's protagonist in *Dictionary* must learn to reconcile and balance the East-West fragments of her life in London, Guo's protagonist, Fenfang, in *Twenty Fragments of a Ravenous Youth*, struggles to articulate her own conflicted identity and a transforming Beijing into an East-West cultural narrative as a screenwriter. As such, analyzing these two novels together demonstrates what transpires when the West is Easternized and the East is Westernized. Ultimately, Guo's works reveal how urban landscapes complicate the notion of place as monolithic in its identity and generate multiple narratives of power and consciousness, which form the Post-cultural Revolution lexicon of her characters and contribute to the city's ever-evolving global identity.

Abandoning her village is young Fenfang's only option if she wants to cultivate an existence all her own far away from "a nothing place that won't be found on any map of China" (Guo 2008, 51). Fenfang longs for an existence beyond this static space, where the women were always "[sitting] and [weaving] never-ending baskets out of dried sweet-potato stalks....hook[ing] [them] together for eternity" (52). Following the inexorable current of millions of nameless, rural migrant workers, Fenfang sets her prospects on Beijing and enters a life that pits her against traditional Confucian/Maoist collectivism and a growing ahistorical zeitgeist of contemporary, technological, and capitalistic opportunism, now flowing through the burgeoning streets of the capital city. Who she is and what she becomes on her journey both challenges and inspires Fenfang to narrativize an East-West agency culled from the fragments of deferred dreams and class/gender exclusion throughout Beijing's transcultural spaces.

Like the Chinese sojourners from previous centuries who traversed to new lands, Beijing, itself, now becomes the new destination of hope and possibility. Interestingly, Fenfang's twenty-first-century odyssey shows the internal flows of migration from the rural provinces to the city. She narrates that this "was a brave new world for me, bright even at night. I wanted to rub up against it" (Guo 2008, 8–9). After roaming the streets looking for a cheap hotel and being rejected by doormen who conspicuously loathe her peasant's status, Fenfang finds herself in East Beijing, overwhelmed by "thin alleys bordered by low, grey houses surrounding noisy, crammed courtyards. Countless alleys packed with countless homes where countless families lived" (9). The crush of humanity in this urban vortex seems in great contrast to her silent village. Along with this hope of possibility and agency in the Westernizing spaces of a historically Eastern city comes the struggle to create this new identity, one no longer fashioned and determined by the traditional, Confucian-based family system.

Having drifted now through an assortment of odd-jobs around the city – hotel toilet scrubber, factory worker, cinema custodian – Fenfang considers the opportunities for generating a narrative voice from an unseen source of creativity that could reach many places, much like her village's river from childhood memory:

> I used to imagine the source of the river.... From there, the water flowed through our world to yet another magical world, a magical place close to heaven where lucky people lived....Wherever it was, it was not a place the people from my village could ever enter
>
> (51)

Finding this metaphorical fountainhead in the whirling urban flow seems impossible, for the chasm between village and the city is extreme:

> No matter if it was morning or afternoon or the middle of the night, you would always find a sea of trucks and vans and cars....But not only was Beijing flooded with cars, it was a city of smoke....the city was in a permanent fog
>
> (64)

of noise, pollution, construction, relocation, and demolition. China was hard at work building an East-West city as "a new urban mosaic that did not exist" in Mao's lifetime (Ma and Xiang 1998, 546). While Guo's *Dictionary* posits Beijing as an Eastern city moving toward the Western horizon of transformation and innovation, *Fragments* demonstrates how Beijing fully embodies an industrialized identity that is "reinscribed as a site of confrontation and remaking, without the possibility of closure" (Oboe 2013, 271). This, in turn, contributes to the city's role as an intersection between Eastern and Western – rural and urban – cross-cultural discourses.

As stated in Guo's documentary film *The Concrete Revolution: The Other Side of the "Chinese Miracle"* (2004), for all those of the floating population who came to Beijing from the rural districts, like Fenfang, and who believed they would find this Chinese urban miracle amidst the cacophony of images, sounds, and simulations, the city is a bittersweet "stage for hope and disappointment... a gateway into the new world." Beijing's landscape is alive with possibility but only at the cost of "increased social polarization and spatial segregation" (Chao-lin 2001, 18). Surprisingly, Fenfang finds consistent work in the Chinese film industry even if it is only nondescript, faceless parts in films: "Woman Waiting on the Platform, Lady in Waiting, Bored Waitress" (Guo 2008, 74). However, she wants to believe that there is more for her in Beijing, that she can find that metaphorical fountainhead before it is too late. The transformations going on throughout the urban sectors are breathless, for it seems everything around her is "being demolished and rebuilt every hour" (*The Concrete Revolution* 2004), and this is all the more reason she is ravenous to make a place for herself here.

This frenzy is further emphasized by the way in which Guo constructs *Fragments*. Replete with narrative jump cuts, film stills from her documentary *The Concrete Revolution,* and intimate, cinematic descriptions of urban scenes, the novel conveys a new Chinese narrative broadcast beyond the walls of the city and out to the world. "Everything around me was changing so fast – my apartment block, the local shops, the alleys, the roads, the subway lines...I had to do something, ask my brain to start working, so I could match this fast-moving city" (Guo 2008, 74). To harness the acceleration all around and construct the East-West narrative of Beijing, Fenfang follows the advice of her close friend Huizi, screenwriter and advocate of the minor role actor, to write her own narrative and become her own person.

With the directness of Confucian honesty, something that characterized Z as "'that rude one'" among her Londoner peers (Guo 2007, 32), Fenfang begins to think of herself as a film writer and views the frenetic energy swirling about through a metaphorical camera lens. "Inspired by Huizi, I started to watch nameless men and women in the street. We were alike: none of us heroes, just ordinary people – extras – drifting through messy streets in a vast, messy Beijing" (Guo 2008, 74). While walking along the disheveled roads in her neighborhood, Fenfang notices – with flâneuse-like precision and "the obsessive-compulsive process of reading the city" (Nesci 2014, 72) – how the interstices are being reinvented, streets reconfigured, and old residential structures morphed into shiny apartment buildings that soar into the sky among the clouds: "In just one night all the food stalls had disappeared, along with the men from the countryside who used to run them" (Guo 2008, 75). So many people had disappeared, and the city was transforming at a panicking rate as though behind schedule. From the rubble and empty streets around her, she suddenly realizes that the city, in its rush to become the center of the twenty-first century in a new and improved China, is the source of her own inspiration. Like Guo herself, Fenfang realizes that the growing "disenfranchised groups living in the margins of China's cities" (Costanzo 2014, 81) were giving her a filmic voice and a vision. Her contentious relationship with Beijing, then, actually exposes her to a city on the threshold of change, where the rawness and fragments of blurring scenes and sounds inspire her and seem to speak directly to her from a third space.

In this whirlpool of film-extras, leftovers, estranged lovers, and forgotten lives – "past street food vendors, past Beijing University students wearing thick glasses and the same Eastpak rucksacks... going to McDonald's to enjoy its complimentary cold air" (101, 102) – Fenfang harnesses an energy from the endless, fluid exchanges of cruelty and ambition into an East-West city, one which provides a language for her to articulate the phenomenon all around her. Beijing, this "city that never showed its gentle side," a city one had to fight with or else "[y]ou'd die if you didn't" (157) has become her muse, allowing her to sense the quotidian human rhythms throughout its pulsing arteries. Hao An, her protagonist, now embodies the city: "The moment I thought of him, I felt like I'd heard about him before. I was sure he'd been mentioned in the scraps of gossip I picked up as I wandered around the neighbourhood. I started to write" (75). A fragmented mirror of her own life experiences, Fenfang's screenplay *The Seven Reincarnations of Hao An* charts the world of an aging Beijinger who comes to the city in the final months of the millennium (or the end of the world, as her protagonist maintains) and drifts from job to job, interweaving with faces and places looking for a sense of home. Hao An's sense of placelessness reveals Fenfang's own peregrination through Beijing, a mobility that paradoxically provides both agency and loneliness. Indeed, the difficulty in balancing her "peasant" identity with her newly formed "urban" one within the yin-yang constellation still proves to be an obstacle.

Despite this narrative premise for her screenplay, Fenfang feels unable to write in the city itself, and so, much like her literary counterpart in *Dictionary* who is encouraged by her lover to go to continental Europe for a few weeks on her own, Fenfang embarks upon her own sojourn to contextualize the fragments from the East-West city by staying in China's various villages, looking for a sense of lost history: "I wanted to create a completely new world, inventing everyone and everything" (106–7). She believes that perhaps by returning home – to her past memories – she will better understand how to read Beijing as a contemporary site of cultural evolution. Persistent in this search for the symbolic East-West fountainhead, she mistakenly believes nostalgia will recover her inspiration. Indeed, her return offers little, for she feels like an observer watching a distant world frame by frame.

> It felt like a scene from a film, a typical Chinese family scene. I could almost feel the Director hovering in the background, overseeing the set-up....I worried that [my village] would pull me back, that it would not let me go again....I suddenly missed the cruel Beijing life. I missed my insecurity. I missed my unknown and dangerous future....I missed the sharp edges of my life.
>
> (115, 117)

The return home only confirms that the rural village and her family would never satisfy her desire to direct her own destiny and locate her own place within a rapidly transforming existence.

For Fenfang, revisiting her village only recreates the "same rhythm, same movement, same speed" (116–17) from which she had once escaped. Returning to Beijing, then, becomes the solution, for, ironically, Beijing provides the contrasts, the tensions, and the lure to actually produce Fenfang's fragmented sense of balance. This frenetic and harried relationship between Fenfang and Beijing actually "allows for the dynamic energy that comes through their interactions. It is also this difference that enables yinyang as a strategy – to act successfully, we must sometimes be more yin and sometimes more yang, depending on the context" (Wang 2012, 8). Indeed, this is the same interior yin-yang that Z experiences in *Dictionary* when she too finds herself immersed in the East-West currents of twenty-first-century Beijing.

While the process is slow, Fenfang's return only confirms that complex relationship with her East-West identity. Her screenplay is twice rejected, and a sexist producer says, "women can't write" (141). And yet, while these "sharp edges" (117) of Fenfang's Beijing life bring her not only a heavy sense of displacement and loneliness, they also generate a sense of clarity and ravenousness, feeding her ability to make interconnections between the fragments of Beijing's urban matrix and her own movements through the city. This is what first drew her to the capital and its energy. Eventually, on the night of a ferocious sandstorm, Fenfang feverishly crosses through the city to find the "Underground Director," who is impressed with her work and purchases her screenplay for ¥5,000. Fenfang, "a new-generation woman" (70) in a new China and one who possesses a "migrant's double vision" (Bhabha 1994, 5) of the two worlds of which she is a part, has grown adept at navigating and narrating the city streets ebbing and flowing with vendors and an array of pirated products: Western fruits, banned books and music, foreign films; here, "you could find whatever you were looking for" (Guo 2008, 99). This ever-emerging, nongovernment-sanctioned marketplace "was our university and our only path to the foreign world" (100), where West crosses into the East in a yin-yang paradigm of possibility and opportunity. Here was the fountainhead she had sought since childhood. The agency created in this intersection and site of fluid exchange becomes a spatiotemporal and sociocultural paradigm – and *dao* – for a twenty-first-century relationship to place.

Xiaolu Guo's novels demonstrate how drifting across geo-ideological borders can disrupt epistemological systems of power and associations with place. It is within this disruption, then, where narratives of trans-migrational exchanges between people and places are made possible. In a yin-yang strategy, both Z in *A Concise Chinese-English Dictionary* and Fenfang in *Twenty Fragments of a Ravenous Youth* seek a conjunction and agency in cities that have become contact zones for East-West identities and subjectivities. As such, the transcultural production of an East-West narrative draws upon an intimate and global experience of fragmentation generated not so much by a singular universal phenomenon, but by "multiverses" which illustrate the "different dimensions" (Guo 2008, 94) that comprise ways in which urban space is articulated. While Guo's literary and filmic oeuvre invokes, while displacing, conventional narratives of selfhood and place, generating a lexicon for articulating these phenomena requires the acquisition of a new language, one imbued with mutable and mobile meanings. Guo's literary London and Beijing offer us a view into how subjects attempt to navigate the transcultural odysseys across East-West landscapes of the twenty-first century.

The literary East-West city becomes more than a crucible for generating a third-space consciousness; it becomes a fountainhead where fluid spatialities are continuously narrativized through a critical balance of coalescing and colliding fragments of new selfhoods and global cultures. Moreover, the third space of East-West cities creates a flow between east and west in a ceaseless confluence that dissolves the conventional binary construction of the East/West dichotomy. Guo's works offer new ways of viewing, presenting, and understanding the global phenomenon of city spaces overlapping through a constant flow of nonbinary realms. While ultimately it may be utopic to think that urban harmonies are lasting, what is significant is Guo's ability to intersect literary and visual narratives within her writing and present competing understandings of East and West discourses. Her narrative form only underscores that fluidity between spaces and worlds – both actual and imaginative, linguistic and cultural – to demonstrate the globalized subjectivity of her characters and the locations they encounter and transform.

Works Cited

Bhabha, Homi K. 1994. *The Location of Culture.* Abingdon: Routledge.
Chao-lin, Gu. 2001. "Social Polarization and Segregation in Beijing." *Chinese Geographical Science* 11 (1): 17–26.
The Concrete Revolution: The Other Side of the "Chinese Miracle." 2004. Directed by Xiaolu Guo, Xiaolu Guo, Ltd., Toby Eady Associates.

Costanzo, William V. 2014. *World Cinema through Global Genres*. Hoboken, NJ: Wiley Blackwell.

Guo, Xiaolu. 2007. *A Concise Chinese-English Dictionary*. New York: Anchor Books.

——— 2008. *Twenty Fragments of a Ravenous Youth*. New York: Anchor Books.

Johnson, Peter. 2012. "The Eden Project—Gardens, Utopia and Heterotopia" *Heterotopian Studies*. Accessed 10 November 2017. www.heterotopiastudies. com/wp-content/uploads/2012/05/4.2-The-Eden-Project-pdf.pdf.

Ma, J.C. Laurence and Biao Xiang. 1998. "Native Place, Migration and the Emergence of Peasant Enclaves in Beijing." *The China Quarterly* 155: 546–81.

Merleau-Ponty, Maurice. 1963. *The Primacy of Perception*. Evanston, IL: Northwestern University Press.

Nesci, Catherine. 2014. "Memory, Desire, Lyric: The Flâneur." In *The Cambridge Companion to the City in Literature*, edited by Kevin R. McNamara, 69–84. Cambridge: Cambridge University Press.

Oboe, Annalisa. 2013. "Language, Eros and Culture in Xiaolu Guo's *A Concise Chinese-English Dictionary*." In *The Tapestry of the Creative Word in the Literatures in English*, edited by Maria Renata Natale et al., 267–79. Udine: Forum Editrice, http://www.academia.edu/17876879/ Language_Eros_and_Culture_in_Xiaolu_Guo_s_A_Concise_Chinese-English_Dictionary_for_Lovers_in_The_Tapestry_of_the_Creative_Word_ in_the_Literatures_in_English._Forum_Editrice_Udine_2013_.

Poon, Angelina. 2013. "Becoming a Global Subject: Language and the Body in Xiaolu Guo's *A Concise Chinese-English Dictionary*." *Transnational Literature* 6 (1): 1–9.

Pratt, Mary Louise. 1991. "Arts of the Contact Zone." *Profession*: 33–40.

Rahbek, Ulla. 2012. "When Z Lost Her Reference: Language, Culture and Identity in Xiaolu Guo's *A Concise Chinese-English Dictionary*." *Otherness: Essays and Studies* 3 (1): 1–12.

Said, Edward. 2000. "Intellectual Exile: Expatriates and Marginals (1993)." In *The Edward Said Reader*, edited by Moustafa Bayoumi and Andrew Rubin, 368–81. New York: Vintage.

Soja, Edward. 1996. *Thirdspace: Journeys to Los Angeles and Other Real-and-Imagined Places*. Hoboken, NJ: Blackwell.

Wang, Robin R. 2012. *Yinyang: The Way of Heaven and Earth in Chinese Thought and Culture*. Cambridge: Cambridge University Press.

Filmography

The Concrete Revolution: The Other Side of the "Chinese Miracle." Dir. Xiaolu Guo, UK, 2004.

Part IV

The Social Construction of Place: Meaningful Imaginaries

Introduction

Steven Allen and Kirsten Møllegaard

As suggested in the previous section, crossing borders and moving to new places add a range of perspectives to the social construction of place. New places are infused with hopes and dreams, fears, and anxieties. The chapters in Part IV investigate literary and cinematic representations of belonging through the imaginary connections people form with certain places. Distance between places in time and space plays an important role as well in the way place and space are configured as homelands, heartlands, or safe havens. The social construction of place is inherently dialogic and thus frequently contested. How do meaningful imaginaries about other places emerge? How do people form attachments to certain places? As Setha M. Low and Irwin Altman observe, places are "repositories and contexts within which interpersonal, community, and cultural relationships occur, and it is to those social relationships, not just the place qua place, to which people are attached" (1992, 7). The centrality of human relationships is thus a primary concern in the social construction of place.

Millions of people worldwide live in between cultures as expatriates or in marginalized diasporas away from what once were their homelands. Stuti Govil's chapter "Contested Spaces: Adichie, Lahiri and the Politics of Belonging" investigates how gendered spaces structure the experience of living in a new and unfamiliar place. She questions assumptions about yearning for the homeland and the idea of fixed origin in her analysis of the ways in which the process of identity formation (particularly the intersection between gender and nationality) unfolds within, outside, and because of a new locality. Govil focuses on the works of two novelists who have personal experience as immigrants and with life in diasporic communities, and whose global-local perspectives position diasporic experience in relation to the concept of homeland. Govil compares Jhumpa Lahiri's novel *The Namesake* (2003) and second short story anthology

Unaccustomed Earth (2007) to Chimamanda Ngozi Adichie's novel *Americanah* (2013) and collection of short stories *The Thing Around Your Neck* (2009). Govil analyzes Lahiri and Adichie's works as reflections on the processes of globalization and argues that identity formation is crucially tied to attachment to place, even if that place may be imaginary rather than experienced. By focusing on the literary representation of women's migration from countries in the Global South to the West, Govil provides an important perspective on how gender filters the experience of place, and how diasporic identities are multivarious and unique.

Even within the same country, migration can have an alienating effect. In the chapter "Vertical Heterotopias: Territories and Power Hierarchies in Tosh Gitonga's *Nairobi Half Life*," Addamms Songe Mututa focuses on cinematic representations of the way unequal urban spaces function in Kenya's capital Nairobi, Africa's fifth largest city. *Nairobi Half Life* (Tosh Gitonga, 2012) follows the protagonist Mwas, who arrives in Nairobi from the country with high hopes of an acting career in the big city. However, lacking the right connections and social network, Mwas soon finds himself on the wrong side of the law and incapable of escaping the criminal network of gangs that roam affluent uptown neighborhoods like Westlands at night and retreat to downtown Kirinyaga road during the day. Mututa carefully analyzes the film's *mise-en-scène* and camera angles and discusses how Gitonga's cinematography constructs vertical heterotopias and power hierarchies in its portrayal of Nairobi's cityscape. The social tensions and social inequalities between uptown and downtown are symbolically reflected in the city's architecture, with the massive high-rise buildings of uptown towering over downtown's shantytown. Mututa argues that the film reflects postmillennial imaginaries about the sprawling African city with its focus on unemployment, police corruption, crime, and Mwas' broken dreams.

Kylo-Patrick Hart's chapter "Ideologically Charged Urban and Rural Places in American Movies about HIV/AIDS: Social Constructionism and the Cultural Imaginary in the Late Twentieth Century" examines the binary construction of the city versus the country and its function in American HIV/AIDS films. Hart argues that the city/country dichotomy is ideologically charged with a discourse that portrays the city as a place of plague, disease, and death, whereas the country is cinematically rendered as a place of health, healing, and life. Such stereotypes permeate the cultural imaginary via the powerful medium of cinema, thus bringing into question how place is not only socially, but also ideologically constructed along a binary of disease/health. Hart analyzes the social construction of the city versus the country in four American movies about HIV/AIDS that were released during the first two decades of the AIDS pandemic: *Chocolate Babies* (Stephen Winter, 1997), *An Early Frost* (John Erman, 1985), *In the Gloaming* (Christopher Reeve, 1997), and *Jeffrey* (Christopher Ashley, 1995). Hart discusses how the city in these movies is represented as the place of "deviant" people and HIV/ AIDS, in dramatic contrast to the country, which is represented as all that is good and moral in American society. The representational distinctions between city and country exemplify the construction of otherness in AIDS movies of the late twentieth century. As Hart points out, such representations dangerously reinforced outdated culturally shared notions of HIV/AIDS as a plague of the city and a threatening phenomenon of concern almost exclusively to residents there, concealing much-needed, more accurate social information about the true nature of AIDS during the influential period when the pandemic was continuing to be socially constructed for audience members of all kinds.

The social construction of place is an on-going and often contested process. This section's chapters highlight three distinct examples of the way places are constructed by way of fictional and cinematic narratives that imbue them with specific cultural desires, anxieties, and imaginaries.

Work Cited

Low, Setha M. and Irwin Altman. 1992. "Place Attachment: A Conceptual Inquiry." In *Place Attachment*, edited by Setha M. Low and Irwin Altman, 1–12. New York: Plenum Press.

10 Contested Spaces
Adichie, Lahiri, and the Politics of Belonging

Stuti Govil

Introduction

I found the works of Pulitzer Prize-winning author Jhumpa Lahiri when I was sixteen years old and had not yet processed the many movements I had made across unfamiliar towns in India. Her works spoke of migrating to foreign lands and her protagonists' longing; I saw glimpses of my own lived experiences. This chapter is inspired by the journeys we all undertake, for work, for love, and for families.

I will analyze the writings of Jhumpa Lahiri and Commonwealth Prize-winning author Chimamanda Ngozi Adichie and develop a contextual understanding of narratives of place as evident in both authors' works. The two are considered canonical in their own right and, through their wide-reaching work, are able to represent specific contemporary lived experiences, whether in India, Nigeria, or in transit. I focus on these two because they engage with place, diaspora, and gender and have very similar writing styles, centering on the internal monologues and struggles that men and women have. It is important to note that both Adichie and Lahiri have lived in diaspora, away from their respective homelands in Nigeria and India. While Adichie is a first-generation expat living between Nigeria and the United States, Lahiri's parents left their home in Calcutta,[1] West Bengal, for England before she was born. I will argue that these personal narratives feed into the authors' bodies of work and inform their relationship with the homes they left behind. This is based on the assertion that lived experiences are contingent on sociocultural and geographical environs.

While Lahiri's and Adichie's works may not be entirely autobiographical, the complex associations with the home and the world, the country of their birth, and the country of their residence are most delicately inspired by their personal experiences of having lived in diaspora. I will explore the ways in which the two authors place their protagonists and the ways in which they negotiate various movements. I will also unpack notions of home in specific contexts. For the purpose of this chapter, I will critically analyze Adichie's novel *Americanah* (2013), a coming-of-age story about a young Nigerian woman, Ifemelu, who moves to the

United States hoping to achieve an American education and an American career, which nobody in her family has achieved before, while she navigates American racism, the politics of defining herself through the racial lens, and falling in and out of love. I will also focus on Adichie's anthology of short stories, *The Thing Around Your Neck* (2009), which offers a glimpse into contemporary Nigeria, in which Adichie defiantly proffers alternative narratives about the representation of Africa and African stories.

An analysis of Jhumpa Lahiri's first novel, *The Namesake* (2003), and relevant stories from her second short story anthology, *Unaccustomed Earth* (2007), reveals the importance of place in her work. *The Namesake* chronicles a family that moves to the United States from Calcutta. It is the story of Ashoke Ganguly, who left his home in Bengal after a unique personal tragedy. He is a professor at the Massachusetts Institute of Technology in Boston and represents the beacon of achievement for his family. He and his wife, Ashima, never truly feel at home in the land of promise and remain homesick for what they left behind. They raise two children, Gogol and Sonia, who identify as American. This dichotomous relationship and the notion of finding a voice and identity for children of first-generation migrants are at the helm of the narrative. *Unaccustomed Earth* is a collection of several short stories, and, as the title suggests, it focuses on second-generation immigrants in lands they are not quite accustomed to. These are therefore tales of those that are in the process of making new homes and identities.

Both authors have a similar awareness of living in diaspora; consequently, the disparate notions of home and nation-state are closely linked and problematized in their respective writings. The nation-state is a polarizing concept with the nation-state being conceptualized as an "imagined community" (Anderson 1991, 6). Nations are defined as independent, distinctive, and unique imagined communities. They are imagined as a collective, in order to be embedded into a collective memory and experience (Anderson 1991, 53). The people that form this collective, or community, often do not have more than their national identity in common with each other. Each citizen of the nation is conferred a national identity, which becomes in some senses a primary identity and often supersedes more primordial identities like tribe, ethnicity, religion, race, and gender (Appadurai 1996, 15). This national identity thus becomes an important marker of one's attachment to the nation, one's nationalism, and the allure of the nation-state is ever-present in cultural texts and remains a complicated entity. I also argue that the process of identity formation is influenced by the absence of a fixed locus of home.

It is no coincidence that I choose two women authors. Adopting a gender lens adds to the structural complexity of the argument because women in diaspora often have to navigate spaces that are considered inherently male. In the journeys of women across oceans, existing patriarchal structures are broken down into newer, but similarly intricate patterns. How different does the home and world of a woman look when she moves from Calcutta, India, to Boston, USA, or from Abuja, Nigeria, to Philadelphia, USA, or from New York back to Lagos? In this chapter, through relevant instances present in their works, I analyze the world of Lahiri and Adichie's women who live in diaspora. Doreen Massey, feminist geographer and theorist, stresses that space and place are differently interpreted by those holding different positions (Massey 2001, 12). In this particular case, both the positions of agency held by Adichie and Lahiri and the spaces that their protagonists (usually female) occupy are relevant and interpreted differently. I assert the importance of their personal experiences in this relationship.

An interesting characteristic of diasporas was suggested by William Safran (1991) in "Diasporas in Modern Societies: Myths of Homeland and Return" in the first issue of *Diaspora: A Journal of Transnational Studies*. Safran asserts that people living in diaspora retain a collective memory and vision about the original home and still believe that the host society will never fully accept them (83). I will challenge the notion of acceptability and argue that even those that feel accepted by the host society have a relationship with it that is based on conflict. I employ Avtar Brah's concepts of "homing desire" and "desiring the homeland" (Brah 1996, 180) and will elaborate on them in the next section. She writes that people living in diaspora sustain an ideology for return (180). The works of Lahiri and Adichie generate questions about the ways in which their protagonists navigate and think through their movements across the globe. I explore the relationships that their diasporic characters have with the place they live in and with their home countries. In the last section, I will deconstruct these relationships via the gender lens. Through analyzing their bodies of work across the intersecting rubrics of space, place, diaspora, homelands, and gender theory, I consider the ways in which their work addresses the social construction of space, place, and movements.

Space, Place, and Diaspora

The migration of communities of people has a long history. At this particular point, in the space-time continuum, more people are moving across borders than ever before. According to research conducted by the United Nations, 244 million international immigrants are living abroad, an increase of 41 percent from the year 2000 (United Nations 2016). The globalization rhetoric focuses on the movements of capital and labor across the boundaries created by nation-states. These movements of ideas, people, labor, and technology may be considered to be "flows"

(Appadurai 1990, 297). In this context, the movement of people, the "ethnoscape," is of utmost importance because diasporas are intrinsic and salient features of globalization. Often, the Greek etymology of the word "diaspora" is invoked, meaning the scattering of seeds, and people living in diaspora are said to be scattered entities. Brah's concept "diaspora space" (1996, 181) elaborates on the intersectionality of those living in diaspora, for whom border and dislocation are sites of cultural and sociopolitical interrogation. While the ethnoscape refers to the movements of people, I use Brah's conceptualization of diaspora space as it accounts for what happens after the movement of people has taken place and they have found new roots.

I make a distinction between the terms "space" and "place." "Any search for space in literary texts will find it everywhere and in every guise: enclosed, described, projected, dreamt of, speculated about" (Lefebvre 2007, 15). David Harvey's approach stems from Henri Lefebvre's seminal writings and he asserts that space is composed of interactions (Harvey 2004, 1). Space has been conceived as unbounded, while place gets defined as "bounded, fixed, static and unproblematic" (Massey 2001, 5). I contend that this is a simplistic binary because geographical place is received differently by the varied agents who stake claim to it, based on their privilege. Homeland is a contextual idea and can be analyzed through the memories and interactions of people who inhabit and recall the homeland. In Adichie and Lahiri's texts, the geographical place (represented largely by the United States) is conceived of as unbounded, with limitless potential. The original homeland, thus, becomes fixed and static.

Diaspora space emerges as an alternative to the conventional binary of the homeland versus host country. The homeland thus becomes a specific place bounded in history and geography that functions as a marker for identity and as a site for political engagement and contestation. The literature of writers living in diaspora becomes particularly relevant. The authors voice their own lived experiences and, in the process, capture unique experiences of a distinctive set of people living in diaspora. I will examine the four texts mentioned in the previous section and analyze the representation of space and place for the protagonists as those belonging to specific diasporas.

Diasporas and Leaving Homelands

"In America, anything is possible. Do as you wish," Ashoke Ganguly regretfully chides his teenage son Gogol in Lahiri's *The Namesake* (Lahiri 2003, 100). Much of Ashoke's relationship with the country that became his escape from the memories of a near-fatal train accident is depicted through this wistful sentence. America is the place that offered him a new life, away from the traumatic memories of the past.

Like Ashoke, people in diaspora are placed in a distinct position, within the overwhelming and overbearing presence of nation-states: one nation-state that they leave and one that becomes their host. The nation-state, as a hyphenated entity, has always enjoyed preeminence in discussions of international, transnational, or global importance. The discussions around globalization continuously evoke national actors (Sreberny 2002, 293). If at all, the local appears as an antithesis to the idea of the all-encompassing nation-state, without due credence to the dynamism and multiplicity of the local (301). What remains perpetually missing is the individual, who is a part of the nation-state, but considered undifferentiated from other citizens. With the opening up of economic and physical borders, migrants encounter others who have traveled from their homelands. It is often in this interaction that national identities get inquired upon and thereby get concretized as imagined communities (Anderson 1991).

Ashoke has made a home for himself and his family in this new place, in America, but struggles to place himself at the helm of events. To him, America represents all that signifies promise, even if it means uprooting yourself from familial bonds and memories. Lahiri's first-generation migrant protagonists, that is, those who have themselves undertaken the physical journeys of migration, are akin to Ashoke. They remain awed and skeptical, sometimes owing largely to their skewed cultural imagining of the West. Their children go through identity crises typical of having had a childhood marked by the despondency of the parents' longing for the homeland and the struggle of growing up, looking, and feeling noticeably different. Ashoke's children, Gogol and Sonia, think of India as an alien land when they visit, and long to go back to their American home on Pemberton Street.

Like Lahiri, Adichie's protagonists travel to the United States for the prospect of a better future. In *Americanah* and several stories in *The Thing Around Your Neck*, the narrative to leave Nigeria is centered around the longing to escape university strikes, communal riots between Igbo and Hausa[2] people, the aftermath of the Biafran Civil War (1967–1970), looming abject poverty, and the military dictatorship during most of the 1970s and late 1980s that made hundreds of Nigerians leave their country. Thus, Adichie's protagonists go through a different trajectory of self-discovery as their everyday lived experience is not governed by the loss of the homeland. They are, instead, hopeful and wish to begin a new life in the new social contexts. Ifemelu, a writer of a popular blog on contemporary race relations in the United States, may have left the love of her life behind in Nigeria, but instead of pining for Lagos, her struggle to be accepted in the United States takes her onto a path where she discovers the complex reality of race politics.

The very title, *Americanah,* refers to Ifemelu (and others like her) and is a loaded gender-specific Igbo euphemism for women who become

American. To think of Ifemelu as an Americanah (Adichie 2013, 65) is to assert her foreignness and divest her of any sense of Nigerian identity. The place that they emigrate to becomes a marker of identity because those women who leave their homeland for America stand to lose their primary, collective identity as Nigerian women. What remains is what America, as a culturally loaded conceptualization, represents. Here, Brah's (1996, 180) conceptualization of "homing desire" and "desiring the homeland" becomes particularly relevant for a comparative analysis.

Brah argues that the concept of diaspora is a critique of fixed origins, with there being two forces of "homing desire" and the "desire for a homeland" (1996, 180). She writes that all diasporas sustain an ideology for return (180). It is this movement for return that is most indicative of the presence of the nation-state in everyday life. To *return* somewhere implies belonging and an eventual desire to be within that nation-state. However, I believe that Brah's assertion that all diasporas sustain an ideology for return is a somewhat simplistic conception of the ways in which different people living in diaspora authentically live their lives. One of the central attributes of people living in diaspora is their journey *to* somewhere, after having left home. Being physically away from their homeland and their countries of origin, they are never seen as the mainstream populace of their homelands. The place they move to is constructed as a foreign land that needs to be explored and made their own. The feeling remains of being the Other in a country that is not theirs to claim birthright over.

Reading Adichie and Lahiri's texts corroborates the two forces of homing desire and desiring the homeland. While Lahiri's protagonists exhibit many strains of desiring the homeland, Adichie's writing displays a strong "homing desire" within the characters. Lahiri's protagonists, like the author and her family, are predominantly Bengali and have left the East Indian state of West Bengal shortly after the Independence of India in 1947, when borders started seeming slightly more porous. Her characters display a familiar strain of longing for the homeland, where memory about the cities and towns and homes they have left concretizes and causes hurt and pain. This is Brah's imagining of desiring the homeland. In Brah's thesis, the homeland is represented largely by the nation-state as an "imagined community" (Anderson 1991), while Lahiri's protagonists desire a homeland and an imagined community that they are immediately familiar with – Bengal. In *The Namesake* and many stories of *Unaccustomed Earth*, the characters long not for India's capital New Delhi, but for the Bengali capital of Calcutta. Gogol Ganguly even feels distanced from his other Indian classmates in the United States because they are culturally different from him. At one point in the novel, the children admonish their parents for being unable to come to terms with the changes that the city of Calcutta has gone through. Like Ashima and Ashoke, Lahiri's other first-generation migrant characters are rooted in the places they have left behind, and their locus of identity is defined by them.

In direct contrast to this, Ifemelu (Adichie 2013) breaks off all contact with her family, friends, and lover once she feels she has committed a sexual transgression by cheating on her long-term boyfriend, an error in judgment done to be able to afford rent. For her, the locale and balmy heat of Nigeria soon start to wither away in memory, to be replaced by an active reimagining of her identity as being a young Black woman in Philadelphia. For Ifemelu, this imagining of an alternative reality is relevant. She made her escape from her home because of the strife and poverty brought by the military dictatorship in Nigeria. It is also worth noting that unlike her other friends and lover, Obinze, she has no plans to leave Nigeria until the university strikes and her parents' sense of despair urge her to apply for a partial scholarship in America. For her, home becomes dotted with memories of conflict and suffering, such as everyday rioting between Hausas and Igbos, striking professors, and abject poverty (Adichie 2013, 25, 47). "Home" does not offer Ifemelu a future or any prospects. America does. In contrast, for Obinze, the path to escape Nigeria is made significantly more difficult because of his gender and aspirations to contribute to the workforce. He leaves Nigeria as a professor's son but ends up cleaning toilets in England and being deported – a much less privileged experience than the ones his friends or classmates go through.

The New Place: Contested Identities, Contested Realities

In the previous section, I delineated the journeys that Adichie's and Lahiri's protagonists undertake toward their eventual displacement and what their movements signify in terms of the relationship that they have with the new place. In this section, I will unpack the interactions with the new geographical and sociocultural spatialities that Adichie and Lahiri write into their characters' new lives.

A telling passage that sets the tone for how Gogol starts to view his parents as outsiders is when the Ganguly porch is vandalized (the -uly is replaced by -rene, rendering it as "gangrene," an infectious disease that causes healthy tissues to die) by children not much older than himself (Lahiri 2003, 67). Instead of feeling the outrage that Gogol does, Ashoke dismisses the racist attack with casual disregard. In contrast to this meek reaction, when the Ganguly's return to Calcutta on holiday and meet those that have seen them grow up, blood relatives, and close family friends, they boisterously speak in Bengali, a language they otherwise relegate only to the domestic, indoor space in America. Lahiri tells her readers that Ashoke and Ashima slip into "bolder, less complicated versions of themselves ... revealing a confidence that Gogol and Sonia never see on Pemberton Road" (81). This signifies an easy point of departure for Ashoke's and Ashima's identities. They seem to live out a performance on Pemberton Road, shelving their authentic selves to be able to integrate into a small town in a much larger country among citizens with different cultural and linguistic backgrounds. That their identities reflect specific geographical contexts is evident. It also speaks to their status as outsiders in America where they have built successful careers and a safe haven for their children, but what they are never able to share with America is their authentic expression and being. They do not really seem to "live" in the here and now. They may have a life in America, but it is undercut by the experience of having lost something tangible in order to achieve the kind of success they did.

Since Lahiri often writes from her experience of growing up in Boston in a Bengali family to parents who had immigrated to America (Lahiri 2016), common scenes in her books are the parties that are attended almost exclusively by Bengalis. The hosts labor over foods that evoke the sights, smells, and mustiness of a Bengali kitchen. As in *The Namesake,* in "Hell-Heaven" (2007b), "Only Goodness" (2007c), and "Once in a Lifetime" (2007a) from *Unaccustomed Earth* (Lahiri, 2007), much of the plot is centered within the confines of these parties.

> What I remember most clearly are the hours before the party, which my mother spent preparing for everyone to arrive: the furniture was polished, the paper plates and napkins set out on the table, the rooms filled with the smell of lamb curry and pulao

Hema, the protagonist from "Once in a Lifetime" quips (Lahiri 2007a, 223). The memories of food are strong and they denote the presence of the homeland, in the new place. In Lahiri's universe, the guests are drawn to each other in an unknown, uninhabited space in the search of familial comfort.

By contrast, Adichie's protagonists leave Nigeria and remain isolated from those that they had known in another life. In "Imitation," from *The Thing Around Your Neck* (Adichie, 2009a), Nkem is a young Nigerian housewife living in America. Through the story, the reader is reminded that she is indeed very fortunate to have married and moved to America, even if her husband is unfaithful. She makes no acquaintances besides an African-American house-help and is constantly aware of the power imbalance between them. She thinks ruefully of the house and family in Nigeria that she has not seen in over a year. The longing for home makes her commit her first indiscretion against a cheating husband and an unfulfilling life in a foreign place. Similarly, in "The Arrangers of Marriage" (Adichie 2009b), the young woman leaves Nigeria to live with her husband in the United States. In a dissatisfying marriage, she seeks out the friendship of a mixed-race woman, but does not make any friends outside the cluster of apartments she lives in. This compounds her ennui of living in a country where nobody quite recognizes her as an individual with talent and ambition.

From the same anthology, "A Private Experience" (Adichie 2009c) is a haunting account of two women who have to seek refuge in the back of a dilapidated shop following the eruption of communal riots between the Igbo and Hausa people in Lagos. The reader is introduced to only one of the two women, Chika, who is concerned with having dropped her expensive necklace and ruining the bag she bought while away in London. The reader learns very quickly of the difference between the two women. They are separated not only by several rungs of the class ladder, but are also very different in their mobility. While Chika is well traveled and thinks of Nigeria as a temporary place, the other woman sees no escape from her life and her poverty. It is to Adichie's credit as a master storyteller that she forces the two to spend a night in close quarters, an experience that leaves Chika with a lingering melancholy and an awareness of the ways in which grief, too, becomes unequal.

Specific political conditions in the geographical place inform the relationships that the protagonists share with their home countries. In Adichie's work, the home country is represented, like Brah theorized, as a site for both safety and terror (Brah 1996, 180). This is a combination of the military strife and the distinctive reasons for leaving. In *Americanah*, Ifemelu starts to forget the nuances of the homeland in a span of a couple of years and sustains no desire for returning due to the memories of poverty and grief. In "A Private Experience" (Adichie 2009c), Chika loses her sister in a moment of chaos and confusion. This enhances her desire to leave Nigeria for the safer havens of England or Canada. In contrast, for Lahiri, the home epitomizes a site of safety and her protagonists create lives similar to the ones they have left behind.

A common thread of empathetic knowledge about not really fitting in a foreign place runs through the works of both authors. This immediately brings to mind Marc Augé's notion of "non-places" (Augé 1995). For Augé, the space and place debate (Massey 2001; Harvey 2004) is complicated by the theoretical distinction he makes between an anthropological place and a non-place. Anthropological places are places that "can be defined as historical, relational and concerned with identity" (Augé 1995, 77). Those that lack history and are not relational or concerned with identity are non-places (Augé 1995). While Augé also defines these places as contractual and identifies them in modern-day shopping malls and airports, in the writings of Lahiri and Adichie, the host societies seem like non-places. In the writings of Lahiri and Adichie, the host country is represented as a contractual space where their protagonists earn livelihoods and procure opportunities, but which also limits their authentic expression owing to the unspoken, unsaid contractual obligations. Instead of rightfully expressing anger when his front porch is vandalized, Ashoke Ganguly merely shrugs. Similarly, Nkem (Adichie 2009a) performs the wifely duties expected of her in exchange for the better standard of living in the West that her husband has promised her, even in the face of his infidelity.

In their state of being displaced, both authors' protagonists occupy what Homi Bhabha delineated as the third space; they are at the threshold, never fully belonging on either side (Bhabha 1994, 37). It bears mentioning, thus, that diasporic subjectivity is double and acknowledges the elsewhere in relation to the cultural context of the current home (Radhakrishnan 1996, 13). For people living in diaspora, home becomes a kind of in-betweenness, a liminal space where they interact with others like them. Ifemelu meets other African women from Ghana, South Africa, Kenya, and Ethiopia in Black salons and while she is enrolled at university. The people she meets may have nothing at all in common, but for an American populace, they can all be defined as "Black" or "African-American." This shared, imposed identity brings them closer.

Gendered Places

A specific cultural trope that is repeated in Adichie's *The Thing Around Your Neck* and *Americanah* is the dissatisfied wife who moves across oceans for the husband who is building a career in the West. Interestingly, Lahiri's body of work also centers on women who left their homes to support the livelihood of husbands they have been arranged to marry and hence do not know very well. The intersection of place, gender, and diaspora is a crucial site for investigation.

The works of Adichie and Lahiri express the authors' feminist political beliefs. Adichie subverts conventional narratives of Nigerian womanhood and changes the locale that the woman is placed in. Typically, patriarchal structures outline rigid structures of control of women and often implement them through enforcing what is called a "woman's place" (Massey 2001, 192). The domestic space is thus relegated to the woman for cooking and rearing children, and feminized labor is unaccounted for. Lahiri and Adichie both accord the complexity of character and breadth to the woman thus consigned. In this section, I will delineate specific instances that further the intersection of place, gender, and diaspora.

The narrator of "Hell-Heaven" (Lahiri 2007b) is a young daughter who recounts her early childhood memories and realizes that her mother was unhappily married to her father and in love with a young colleague of his. This, in itself, would be considered an act of insubordination in patriarchal structures, but not to the narrator. She understands that her mother was in a place she did not quite consider hers and that did not offer her much. The children in Lahiri's works have not regarded their parents' journeys to America as something tangible. They have heard the ruminations of loss, but to them growing up as Americans superseded concerns about their parents' homeland. The children of immigrants have visited these homelands as outsiders, but have never lived in them. For them, the anxieties of the place they grow up in become more overwhelming than a retelling of their parents' childhood.

Ashima Ganguly, a finely etched character in *The Namesake,* spends most of her days cooking for her husband. As she has no concrete plans nor anywhere to be through the day, she fills the vast expanses of days by walking around her husband's university. She had never previously traveled away from Calcutta and finds it unnerving to build a new life. Her relationship with her present city is fleeting and anchored to her husband, Ashoke. The Gangulys travel to India annually, trips that the children scorn. Gogol remembers that his mother never stepped into the kitchen during all these visits and would visit the city, barely staying contained indoors. She knows the city of Calcutta intimately and has grown up navigating its many nooks. She does not quite feel weightless in the same way in Boston – there is a certain heaviness that living in diaspora places on the woman in Lahiri's texts. A telling point is when Ashima finally returns to her homeland, to her brother's residence in Calcutta a few years after her husband's death. She feels she is finally able to be free; there she feels the joys of independent living that she and Ashoke worked so hard to provide for their children. America could never become Ashima's permanent abode. She tried to come to know it, but always with the assurance that one day, she would leave.

Interestingly, the world of the daughters of these first-generation women looks very different. The daughters, whether in "Hell-Heaven" or in "Only Goodness" or in *The Namesake* grow up to be American, and they long for American food and beverages and wish to date American men. Their rebellion extends to their immediate place. All of Lahiri's younger women feel the desire to be *elsewhere*. While Ashima wants to run toward the familiar and the familial, her daughter Sonia moves to the West Coast, and Moushumi (her daughter-in-law) seeks to escape America and her family and move to Paris. In "Only Goodness," the protagonist Sudha grows to distance herself from her parents and alcoholic brother and finds a home in London. She feels suppressed by her mother's fixed imaginings of what good Indian girls look, behave, and dress like. She flees Wayland and America for London to assert her authentic self. The search for a unique identity takes these young women to different places, almost as if discarding the old self would become easier with a change in locale.

It is of note that in a hybrid setting in the diaspora space, even the hitherto sacrosanct line between the madam of the house and the hired help is blurred. The house girl becomes a close confidante, pontificating on cheating husbands, American visas, returning to Nigeria or treating hair burnt from the chemicals in a relaxer. This has been made possible, as evident in Adichie's works, because each woman is from somewhere else and is united in her gendered identity and experience in the new place. In their interactions, a space of equality is created based on the gendered experiences of women living away from home.

Lahiri places the inner struggles of men and women at the helm of the narrative. The physicality of the external world is almost a byproduct of her writing, conspicuously and consciously absent (Reddy 2011, 31). By contrast, Adichie writes about women who actively engage with the political struggles that come with being in their external places – strikes, communal riots, and racism. The men in her books and short stories are presented as seen and witnessed by the women. Her female characters negotiate issues ranging from war, university strikes, the loss of innocence, the making and breaking of relationships, to complex race relations. For Ifemelu, the realization that she was considered Black (not African) in America and was expected to feel the same trajectory of emotions as someone who has ancestors who were sold into slavery spoke about the danger of a single story, as Adichie elaborated on in her Technology, Entertainment, and Design (TED) Talk many years later (Adichie 2009d). While Adichie's female characters bear some superficial resemblance to her in terms of foreign education, city of birth, age, and family background, each is varied and intricately layered to represent the specific situations she writes them into. She forces the reader to notice how women are first told to remain indoors as soon as violence breaks out (Sharobeem 2015). In Ifemelu's relationships with white and African-American men, Adichie places Ifemelu at the center of the power dynamic. Emboldened with the new life she has built for herself in an unfamiliar place, she calls the shots in her romantic life, subverting conventional Nigerian advice on the right age to get married. In her day-to-day life, Ifemelu negotiates the disjuncture caused by the difference in place and fights the cultural restraints from her home country.

Conclusion

In this chapter, I have asserted that Adichie and Lahiri draw from their personal experiences as women writers living in diaspora. I have also argued that their protagonists develop and display a relationship with their immediate environs while still mythologizing an unattainable homeland that they left, either in the search of better opportunities (Lahiri's protagonists in particular), or while escaping trauma caused by political factors (as essayed by Adichie and her narratives). The search for identity is rife and complicated by the process of leaving the original homeland and finding new homes.

Adichie and Lahiri's lived experience of losing their homeland and the crisis of belonging feed into their writing. Whether it is Ifemelu's initial years in America or Ashima Ganguly's bewilderment with the new city, the authors' process of discovering a new place and finding a home in it is evident. For both Adichie and Lahiri, the countries of origin are more layered than a monolithic and fixed conception. They problematize even the household and in the process, their characters negotiate this crucial dilemma as they are embroiled in complex race relations, disintegrating families, and blossoming relationships.

I stress the importance of critical reflexivity when consuming cultural texts. Popular literary fiction speaks to a shared ethos of belonging and often examines those spaces that are considered foreign. In this chapter, I have engaged with literature on space and place and interwoven it with Brah's seminal theory on diaspora space. In a globalized world, the migration and movements of people inform us about the fluidity of borders and cultural experience across the imagined communities of nation-states (Anderson 1991). People living in diaspora undergo unique, yet shared experiences and portraying these is as much a challenge as it is crucial to chronicle. Adichie and Lahiri place the agency of representation firmly on their protagonists as they move from cities and towns in the Global South in search of a home in the West. Even as they do so, the original homeland is not wiped away from memory but remains present, producing a diverse conceptualization of the authors' respective countries. Finally, as we all bear witness to the hundreds of thousands of people leaving their homes every day, it is worth asking: how often does identity get formulated and reformulated based on place?

Notes

1 In January 2001, the city of Calcutta was renamed Kolkata, in an attempt to rid the city's name of its Anglicized past.
2 There are three distinct communities in Nigeria – Igbo, Hausa, and Yoruba. There have been many clashes of the Hausa and Igbo people, and much of it goes unreported for being too commonplace (Handley 2010). Nigeria has many other ethnic groups.

Works Cited

Adichie, Chimamanda Ngozi. 2009. *The Thing Around Your Neck*. London: Harper Collins.

————— 2009a. "Imitation." In *The Thing Around Your Neck*, 33–61. London: Harper Collins

————— 2009b. "The Arrangers of Marriage." In *The Thing Around Your Neck*, 242–68. London: Harper Collins

————— 2009c. "A Private Experience." In *The Thing Around Your Neck*, 62–81. London: Harper Collins

————— 2009d. "Danger of a Single Story." Accessed 31 May 2017. https://www.ted.com/talks/chimamanda_adichie_the_danger_of_a_single_story/transcript?language=en.

————— 2013. *Americanah*. New York: Alfred A. Knopf.

Anderson, Benedict. 1991. *Imagined Communities: Reflections on the Origin and Spread of Nationalism.* London: Verso.

Appadurai, Arjun. 1990. *Disjuncture and Difference in the Global Cultural Economy.* London: Sage.

———— 1996. *Modernity at Large.* Minneapolis: University Press Minnesota.

Augé, Marc. 1995. *Non-Places: Introduction to an Anthropology of Supermodernity.* London: Verso.

Bhabha, Homi. 1994. *The Location of Culture.* London: Routledge.

Brah, Avtar. 1996. *Cartographies of Diaspora: Contesting Identities.* London: Routledge.

Handley, Meg. 2010. "The Violence in Nigeria: What's Behind the Conflict." *Time.* Web. Accessed 10 April 2018. http://content.time.com/time/world/article/0,8599,1971010,00.html

Harvey, David. 2004. "Space as a Key Word." Paper for Marx and Philosophy Conference. Institute of Education, London. Accessed 17 April 2018. http://frontdeskapparatus.com/files/harvey2004.pdf.

Lahiri, Jhumpa. 2003. *The Namesake.* New York: Harper Collins.

———— 2007. *Unaccustomed Earth.* New Delhi: Random House India.

———— 2007a. "Once in a Lifetime." In *Unaccustomed Earth*, 223–51. New Delhi: Random House India.

———— 2007b. "Hell-Heaven." In *Unaccustomed Earth*, 60–83. New Delhi: Random House India.

———— 2007c. "Only Goodness." In *Unaccustomed Earth*, 128–73. New Delhi: Random House India.

———— 2016. *In Other Words.* Translated by Ann Goldstein. New York: Alfred A. Knopf.

Lefebvre, Henri. 2007. *The Production of Space.* Translated by Donald Nicholson-Smith. London: Blackwell Publishing.

Massey, Doreen. 2001. *Space, Place, and Gender.* London: Blackwell Publishing.

Radhakrishnan, Rajagopalan. 1996. *Diasporic Mediations: Between Home and Location.* Minneapolis, MN: University of Minnesota Press.

Reddy, Vanita. 2011. "Jhumpa Lahiri's Feminist Cosmopolitics and the Transnational Beauty Assemblage." *Meridians* 11 (2): 29–59.

Safran, William. 1991. "Diasporas in Modern Societies: Myths of Homeland and Return." *Diaspora: A Journal of Transnational Studies* 1(1): 83–99.

Sharobeem, Heba M. 2015. "Space as the Representation of Cultural Conflict and Gender Relations in Chimamada Ngozi Adichie's 'The Thing Around Your Neck'." *Rocky Mountain Review* 69 (1): 18–36.

Sreberny, Annabelle. 2002. "Globalization and Me: Thinking at the Boundary." In *In Search of Boundaries: Communication, Nation-States, and Cultural Identities*, edited by Joseph M. Chan and Bryce T. McIntyre, 293–307. Westport, CT: Ablex Publishing.

United Nations. 2016. "244 Million International Migrants Living Abroad Worldwide, New UN Statistics Reveal." UN SDG. Accessed 16 Feb, 2018. http://www.un.org/sustainabledevelopment/blog/2016/01/244-million-international-migrants-living-abroad-worldwide-new-un-statistics-reveal/.

11 Vertical Heterotopias

Territories and Power Hierarchies in Tosh Gitonga's *Nairobi Half Life*

Addamms Songe Mututa

In Nairobi, the familiar street tussle between hawkers and city council officers is a vignette of the city's unstable spatial territories that separate the formal city from the informal and enforce an uptown-downtown disconnection. For many city residents, and the government, this is not a trivial issue. The Kenya National Assembly (1997, 691) debated hawking as an intolerable disruption of the city, suggesting that informal street vendors move to Ngara Open Air Market located past Kirinyaga Road, the furthest downtown street in the city, and across the Nairobi River. A later parliamentary session criticized this move, arguing that the hawkers' relocation will disconnect them from uptown residents, their main customers (Kenya National Assembly 2005, 750). Over a decade later, current Nairobi Governor, Mike Sonko, rephrased this eviction plan as a "progressive and humane relocation of hawkers to designated streets and lanes" (2017). He promised to build a hawkers' market in Kariokor, historically an informal trading space adjacent to Ngara.

While Sonko's gesture may signal a desire to incorporate the informal city within the formal, in practice, many hawkers have developed deviant mechanisms to negotiate such spatial restrictions. They occupy downtown streets during the day and move to uptown during the evening to meet the crowds that rush through the city to go home. This nocturnal migration follows a well-calculated conjecture that the city council officers who patrol uptown leave the city in the evening. It construes a gamble that has become a template for a seesaw power arrangement between the council officers who control the city during the daytime and the hawkers who control it during the evening. In retrospect, the tussle exemplifies the strategies that make it possible for the city's uptown and downtown spaces to coexist yet stay "alien to one another" (Foucault 2008, 19), a tapestry that maps out, on the one hand, the practice of power within the city's horizontal territories marked by downtown and uptown, and on the other hand, the hierarchies of power between these enclaves. This contentious relationship between downtown and uptown is the focus of my analysis of David "Tosh" Gitonga's film *Nairobi Half Life* (2012).

Gitonga's film is a collaborative training project between novice filmmakers in Nairobi and experienced film production trainers from

Germany. It is an initiative by One Fine Day Films, DW Akademie, and Ginger Ink, and was backed by Film und Medienstiftung NRW, Bundesministerium für Wirtschaftliche Zusammenarbeit und Entwicklung, DW Akademie, ARRI Film & TV Services in Germany, and Goethe-Institut Nairobi. The film tells the story of Mwas (Joseph Wairimu), who comes to Nairobi to start an acting career but, after a tumultuous entry into the city, finds himself in a life of crime.

In the initial scenes of the city, Mwas is robbed of all his belongings by a street gang as multitudes watch the spectacle. Subsequently, we see him moving around the city, ending in uptown where he is arrested next to the Hilton Hotel on Moi Avenue by city council officers who mistake him for a fleeing hawker. Later, he is incarcerated overnight without trial at the Central Police Station where he meets Oti (Olwenya Maina), a gang leader who recruits him to his gang. Oti directs him to Gaza, a downtown area from where the gangs operate, to find Dingo (Abubakar Mwenda), the leader of another gang, as he awaits Oti's release. Much of the narrative revolves around Mwas surviving as a criminal in downtown while trying to establish himself as an actor in uptown. I argue that this double life is a key narrative model of how Nairobi youths encountering the city's divided space and its spatial wrangles may ingenuously pursue their dreams. Through Mwas' narrative, the film demonstrates how crime and policing render the city's discourse of power, as well as the confrontation between downtown and uptown characters, which is heightened in the play at the end of the film.

By passing these incidents as normal events, the film hints to the viewer about mechanisms of city (streets) control, setting the stage to understand Mwas' movement as a potential mapping of the city space imaginary, which is anchored, on the one hand, in spatial restrictions which reinforce socioeconomic enclaves, and on the other hand, by the horizontal and vertical functioning of power that exists between the enclaves. In the discussions that follow, I will explore how the film uses these spatial imaginaries as markers of power hierarchies within the city, arguing that the film's narrative utilizes Mwas' routine movements between downtown and uptown to build an exposé of corruption and oppression while also incorporating urban youth issues including poverty, crime, police brutality, prostitution, drug dealing, and access to opportunities. These issues are mediated through spatial and infrastructural symbols of inclusion and exclusion, which are at the center of my discussion.

Many Nairobians easily recognize the familiar image of street hawking in *Nairobi Half Life*, where hawkers are fleeing city council officers. Setting the scene during the daytime, in uptown, posits the downtown hawkers' daring intrusion as an illustration of the difficulty faced by the city's marginal characters when accessing uptown. The hawkers' hasty retreat and Mwas' subsequent arrest on suspicion of being a hawker signal the strictness with which city council officers control the streets, and re-enact Nairobi's street realism of unequal power, which relegates hawkers to backstreets. In turn, this control suggests the territories that demarcate the formal uptown and the informal downtown. Through the character of Mwas who straddles these two versions of the city – the harsh life of downtown and the professional career life of uptown – the film creates opposed spatial narratives. It mobilizes his experiences into horizontal and vertical signifiers of power hierarchies, showing downtown as an exceptional space where the city's contrasting ideals of formality and informality coexist. Consequently, we can read this representation of downtown through Michel Foucault's (2008) theory of space heterotopias.

Foucault's inventive theory of space heterotopia features in his "Des Espaces Autres" (Foucault 1984), translated as "Of Other Spaces" (Foucault 2008). In this article, he describes heterotopias as "a sort of counter-emplacements, a sort of effectively realized utopias in which the real emplacements, all the other real emplacements … are simultaneously represented, contested and inverted" (Foucault 2008, 17). This concept provides a framework to understand how the film depicts power structures through transposals and conflicts within spaces. I also use Hilde Heynen's (2008) suggestion that heterotopias can "easily be presented as marginal spaces where social experimentations are going on, aiming at the empowerment and emancipation of oppressed and minority groups" and, at the same time, can be "presented as instruments that support the existing mechanisms of exclusion and domination, thus helping to foreclose any real possibility for change" (322). Arguably, Gitonga's film is enamored by Heynen's idea of how contradictory power concretizes antipodes and hierarchies which, in Nairobi city, are marked by, first, the streets and infrastructure functioning as spatial texts of enclaves; second, horizontal practices of controlling these enclaves; and third, practices of vertical hierarchic power which accompany such control. In the rest of this chapter, an argument is made that representations of contemporaneous enclaves, horizontal power, and vertical hierarchies are concrete portraits of vertical heterotopias in Nairobi city. I set off with a discussion of spatial enclaves.

Spatial Enclaves

Nairobi is historically a divided city. It started in the 1900s as a midway terminus for the British colonial Uganda railway connecting Mombasa to Lake Victoria. At the time, British colonialists settled on the western side of the depot, which includes today's high-end neighborhoods of Westlands, Lavington, Runda, and Kileleshwa. In as early as 1911, the British colonial government established a native zone for the Sudanese (Nubian) soldiers returning after fighting for the British King's African Rifles (KAR) in World War I. Melissa Wangui Wanjiru and Kosuke

Matsubara (2017) describe the then forested zone as the "KAR training ground a few kilometers south west of Nairobi city center," mainly settled by "survivors and widows of Sudanese soldiers fighting for the British KAR" (28). The settled zone was later renamed "'Kibra', a Nubian word for jungle" (28), alluding to its seclusion from the city, and perhaps the harsh survival conditions associated with it. Kibra has grown to become today's Kibera slum, described by Rosamond Hutt (2016), and Amélie Desgroppes and Sophie Taupin (2011) as one of the largest slums in the world, while Westlands is now a hub of high-end businesses, corporate entities, international organizations, and expatriates.

Nairobi Half Life reopens this history of spatial enclaves using composition, simultaneity, spatial practices, and neighboring. The scene of the minibus, in which Mwas travels to the city, arriving at the main countryside terminal uses high-angle long shots, composed to give a general view of the city. Its *mise-en-scène* contrasts two materially different spaces: the rusted shacks in the foreground and the modern city in the background. This filmic image of material binary positions the squalid foreground space, framed in the lower vertical part of the screen, as beneath the horizontal bar of the modern city skyline in the background. Composed of adjacent but different vertical portions of the screen, the image configures, almost geometrically, the relationships of power hierarchies the film seeks to explore and which are developed through subsequent shots. On the one hand, a *mise-en-scène* of dilapidated shacks, informal businesses, filthy streets, and dingy spaces shows downtown as a pauperized zone. We see this disrepair as a microcosm of the city's poor areas and thus as an index of Kibera, the biggest of several slums that dot Nairobi. On the other hand, the skyscrapers of uptown signify affluence associated with wealthy suburbs such as today's Westlands. The film repeatedly uses this visual contrast to construct a spatial split. Through the contrast produced by such composition and *mise-en-scène*, the film acquaints the viewer with the different perspectives of the city; the pessimistic one filled with squalor and the optimistic one with a promise of success. *Nairobi Half Life* pursues the realism of a contiguous yet differentiated city as a strategy to illustrate that Nairobi is not a fixed space, but a place to experiment with different social spaces marked by enclaves characterized as social groups (Lefebvre 1991, 33) that overturn each other through the possibilities that they offer.

Mwas' quest is about locating his position within these versions of the city. There is the pessimistic city where he is robbed, arrested, and incarcerated in jail just for being in uptown, and where Jose (Bernard Safari) proves to be a con. This space replaces Mwas' optimistic, unified vision of the city with the reality of a cohesively disempowering city. Then there is the seemingly more affable downtown, where Dingo's gang facilitates for Mwas a meager job in a drab downtown eatery, a gesture that gives him hope of survival. Foucault (2008) uses the terms "simultaneity," "side by side" (14), and "counter-emplacements" (17) to describe such coexistence. In relation to Gitonga's film, these terms are sustained through a spatial contiguity between uptown and downtown, which supports rather than nullifies power difference.

We can also read the enclaves through Manuel Castells' (1976) "system of neighbouring," where "activities relative to neighbouring" and "social relations in the strict sense" (97) comprise ways of dividing urban space and enjoining individuals to specific groups. Going to uptown is, for the gangs, an expedition to steal car parts and hijack cars, while coming to downtown for the police is a trip to receive bribes. Gangs need their downtown affiliation to befriend the police, and the police need their uptown affiliation to subdue the gangs. Such an ephemeral network relies on established hierarchies and serves only to amplify a sense of territory. Through Mwas' character, *Nairobi Half Life* incorporates this discourse of spatial hierarchies in a way that preempts the power play between these two spaces, reenacting the quintessential strictures that sustain enclaves. In the next section, I discuss how the film uses enclaves to concretize horizontal power differences.

Horizontal Power

In this section, I use the term horizontal power to mean the way characters relate to and exploit what appears as nonhierarchical spatial relations to exert influence in city spaces. In Nairobi city, horizontal power is often exercised in the form of intrusion into restricted spaces. The August 7, 1998, bombing of the American Embassy is a remarkable incident of such spatial intrusion. The location is significant because the embassy was in a highly policed area, adjacent to a major bank and nearby government offices. By penetrating such a secured area, this terrorist attack represented a deviant intrusion into the city's uptown, challenging the power associated with this space. While the embassy has since relocated to the western part of the city, recent narratives still retell the tragedy in relation to the streets. Wanuri Kahiu's *From a Whisper* (2008), a film about the embassy bombing, shows that laxity in controlling the streets permitted the incident. The film tells the story of Tamani (Corrine Onyango), a teen girl whose mother died in the bomb blast; Abu (Ken Ambani), a security officer in charge of street surveillance; and Fareed (Abubakar Mwenda), a terrorist who bombs the embassy. Fareed's incursion into the city with a truckload of explosives (despite Abu's knowledge) signifies his ability to access and use the street without prohibition, hence his challenge to the horizontal power represented by uptown streets.

Gavin Hood's *Eye in the Sky* (2015) is in a way a sequel to Wanuri's film, using a comparable motif of terrorism in the city and character interrelations to enable access to restricted streets. In this film, the militias' control of the predominantly Somali estate of Eastleigh located a short distance from the city center is emphasized with images of militias inspecting family compounds and others patrolling the streets in pickup trucks mounted with machine guns. Street conflict is retold through Jama Farah (Barkhad Abdi), a Kenyan Somali military undercover agent assigned to infiltrate the al Shabab base in Eastleigh and deploy remote-controlled video micro-surveillance devices; Alia Mo'Allim (Aisha Takow), a Muslim girl selling bread on the side of the street adjacent to the targeted al Shabab base; and the terrorists preparing to bomb the city. By juxtaposing the images of the undercover agent with those of the armed terrorists, Hood associates the control of the streets with a discourse of power as terrorism and counterterrorism rely on spatial exclusion and intrusion respectively to assert this power. (The counter insurgency operation involving armed drones is a response to such horizontal restrictions.) Kahiu's and Hood's films therefore use streets to establish characters' unequal ability to access and control the streets, mark insider/outsider splits, and assign different power levels (Heynen 2008, 322).

In *Nairobi Half Life*, Mwas' act of walking around the city is simultaneously a process of generating attributes that operationalize differences between what constitutes downtown and uptown and forming his identity as a city misfit, which seems tied to where he can survive. His movements to different spaces within the city guide the viewer to identify the working of boundaries and power between the various spaces in the city. Mwas' interactions with different characters as he traverses the city can thus be read as him decoding how the city's different spaces are structured to exist side by side yet offer different possibilities. Indeed, one notices that his initial experience of the city configures it as a deathtrap, one that plunges him from uptown to downtown and embeds him among criminals, a view that is gradually reversed when we begin to see the police, and not the gangs, as the real brokers of violence and crime in the city.

Many critics of this film seem to miss the significance of the mundane occurrences that Mwas encounters in the streets; such events are the raw materials of the film's depiction of the underlying power tussle in the streets. James Hodapp (2014), for instance, adopts a superficial view, dwelling heavily on the film's technical and thematic semblance to Hollywood genres, thus overlooking crucial creative gestures, which mark the film as a unique narrative of Nairobi as a specific place, and not just another crime genre film. In what appears to be a hasty review guided by stereotypes, Hodapp not only compares the film's cinematography and themes to Hollywood conventions, and in particular those of crime genres, but also fails to recognize the emphasis that Gitonga puts on minute actions which point toward the complex system of relationships between downtown and uptown played out in the streets. The medium shot of Mwas looking at the gangs stealing car parts in the city center in broad daylight, for instance, stands out as a beacon of two versions of Nairobi at work in the streets: namely the survivalist downtown and the opulent uptown. Equally important is the choice of specific symbolic locations which designate various inherent practices within the city. By setting the film in Kirinyaga Road, the furthest downtown street in Nairobi city, the director primes the characters for conflict with those from uptown as this street is seen as a place for hustlers making a living from opportunistic, informal, and at times illegal trade. Additionally, the long shot of the gang crossing Nairobi River from Ngara Market toward Gaza with stolen car parts mimics the hawker's daily journey to the city that brings the informal city (with its aberrant practices) into contact with the formal (and thus signals their encroachment onto the city). The contribution of such details to the discourse of power cannot be ignored as they identify crucial markers of horizontal power within Nairobi city. For this reason, the film should not be reduced to a Hollywood-style crime narrative as it makes serious commentaries about power play in Nairobi city, for it is a narrative of a precise place not a generic city.

Consequently, the spatial conflicts between social formations residing in downtown and uptown mark the negotiation of power that is essential for surviving at the city's edge, Gaza. In referring to downtown as Gaza, Gitonga assigns it a status of what Foucault (2008, 18) calls "crisis heterotopia," that is, a space "reserved for individuals who are, in relation to society and to the human environment in which they live, in a state of crisis." While Foucault identified the natural category of crisis, this reference still befits the visual esthetics of Gaza as a place where those deemed unfit to mingle in the city converge. In this film, the name plays two distinct roles. First, given that, in Nairobi, Gaza refers to a cult-like brutal teen gang operating from the city's poor neighborhood of Kayole (Gumbihi 2015), assigning this name to downtown adds to the realism of crisis among the characters residing there. Downtown acquires the signification of a sanctioned zone and Mwas is seen as a character embroiled in crisis. Second, if we consider the etymology of the name Gaza, the blockaded Palestine territory associated with policed life and constant surveillance (Feldman 2015), the act of situating Mwas in Gaza assigns him these unfavorable life conditions and produces an anticipation of oppression. Yet, if we dismiss his lawlessness as a mere reproduction of "shantytown life, gangs, police corruption, [and] violent lifestyles" as Todd McCarthy (2012) does in his review of *Nairobi Half Life*, we miss out essential signals of how Gaza, the furthest downtown space in Nairobi's street geography, designates power differences and generates heterotopias. While this film fits well into the popular stereotypical narrative of a chaotic, crime-laden postcolonial African city, it does not merely expose a malignant downtown ostracized from uptown or validate a shantytown mentality as Mwas' actions are poised as strategies to mitigate his crisis. The social realism of atrophied citizens embodied by his struggles to access horizontal space, namely the streets, conveys this latent power difference.

McCarthy's reading, like that of Hodapp, overlooks the forked discourse of power that is revealed through the process of attaining membership in downtown. Foremost, the vetting that precedes inclusion into social networks and spaces is a key part of the internal spatial control. Mwas needs "certain permission" and must complete "a certain number of gestures" (Foucault 2008, 21) to attain membership in Gaza. When he first arrives, a member of Dingo's gang asks him who is looking for Dingo. The question creates a nebulous identity around the gang, suggesting vetting so that Dingo is not accessible before certain initial conditions are fulfilled. Mentioning Oti's name and explaining that they met in jail at the Central Police Station affords Mwas partial admission and work in a shabby restaurant. It benefits the narrative of inclusion/exclusion to see this job as a way to keep him outside the gang's network until Oti can personally vouch for him, a routine that underlies the intricate "system of opening and closing" that keeps Gaza both isolated and penetrable (Foucault 2008, 21), and which constitutes its territorial power.

Additionally, this vetting process also reveals mechanisms of external spatial power. Because the police do not require permission to scrutinize the activities of the gangs in Gaza, this generates a new schema of unequal power between uptown and downtown residents. Yet, the aura of camaraderie that the police show when they subsequently come for their "tax," meaning bribe, introduces their imposed de facto membership. This is significant in the discourse of horizontal power in the film, which relies on such hegemonic relationships between social and economic groupings. Arguably, vetting activates the means of regulating social power and interaction (Heynen 2008, 314).

One may ask: if there were no downtown, how would Mwas' character arc develop? Of course, this is speculative, but such conjecture informs us about the role of downtown in integrating individuals with deviant behavior (Foucault 2008, 18) into the city. By situating the film in this space, *Nairobi Half Life* does not merely justify the narrative of slum life or the chaos of so-called Third World cities, but uses the ghetto as a template of a meticulous system of representing urban splintering and unequal horizontal power by mimicking what Michiel Dehaene and Lieven De Cauter (2008, 8) call the "reproduction of the asymmetrical power relations and social dualism." In other words, the process of showing downtown and its inhabitants as being of lesser socioeconomic standing is simultaneously a process of rendering the asymmetrical power between downtown and uptown. The next section focuses on vertical hierarchies which are concurrently embedded in this asymmetry.

Vertical Hierarchies

Verticality is not new in urban studies as cities have been built upward for a long time. However, recent interest in vertical allegories by urban space theorists points toward novel thinking about city space. Influential works include Stephen Graham and Lucy Hewitt (2013), Hewitt and Graham (2015), and Elden Stuart (2013) who have shifted focus from horizontal to the vertical analysis of urban space. In this section, I base my discussions on Graham (2016) who notes: "boundaries and relations between layers and levels within volumes of geographic space ... [are] as important as those that horizontally demarcate traditional flat notions of boundaries and territory" (13). His suggestion that the relationship between horizontal and vertical territories commands equal importance in modern spatial theory marks a turning point in how we should think of urban verticality, which has been overlooked in favor of horizontal space. This guides my analysis of how *Nairobi Half Life* uses composition and placement of characters in spaces to suggest disconnected territories and vertical power hierarchies within the city.

The choice of uptown as the setting for the scene of Mwas' undignified arrest best exemplifies the way street activities actuate vertical borders and generate a sense of hierarchic territories. In this film, the Hilton Hotel is shown with camera angles that highlight its (uptown) higher status. We first see the hotel when Mwas halts to admire Jimmy Gathu, a renowned media personality. In the initial shot, the camera is placed low looking up the towering hotel and then it tilts down the building to emphasize its vertical elevation. The shot invokes the symbolic power associated with verticality in modern metropolises (Graham 2016, 152) where higher vertical elevation connotes higher power, and lower level, lower power. Including Mwas at a lower level in relation to the towering Hilton Hotel dwarfs him, alluding to his powerlessness and insignificance. Such composition hints at his anxiety as he seems out of place compared to the normal angle shots showing Jimmy Gathu at the hotel entrance. This style of cinematography invokes power difference between Mwas and uptown space and marks him as an intruder. The scene, a culmination of earlier high-angle shots of Mwas walking around the city where the camera, hovering above him, mimics rooftops or imaginary skyscrapers, visually annotates how vertical elevation (shown by the two antipodal camera positions) is incorporated into the visual landscape of the city in relation to the protagonist. At one point, the camera zooms out to increase the vertical distance simulating increasing elevation of the buildings around him. This surveillance gaze, a passable reference to Foucault's concept of the panopticon where constant surveillance configures power hierarchies (Foucault 1995, 200) and hence subjugation, uses verticality to signify Mwas' estrangement, disorientation, and instability in the city.

This composition style is contrasted in a later shot of his arrival in downtown. The scene starts with a high-angle shot that cranes down to the street level, mimicking a vertical descent from uptown to downtown by changing the camera's vertical elevation and generating an aura of ease. The descent is accompanied by changing material structures from the skyscrapers of uptown to the dilapidated low-lying shacks of downtown. If we see the opulent uptown structures in contrast to squalid downtown as "dialectics of power" (Dovey 1999, 15), then the different materials and vertical difference between the structures designate different social and economic groups in the city. This division of the city, horizontally into uptown and downtown, and vertically into higher and lower social tiers, teases out a familiar vertical and material contrast which various filmmakers have used to represent vertical hierarchies in Nairobi city. Nathan Collett's *Kibera Kid* (2006), for instance, opens with a panoramic long shot panning across the city's skyline of skyscrapers, using the wide angle and composition as an inventory of how the city's vertical power is envisioned in the high-rise buildings. The westwards camera panning is also significant because Westlands is the most affluent section of Nairobi and has been the domain of the elite class since the founding of the city. Yet, the panning ends with an abrupt swish pan to the opposite direction, stopping with a high-angle shot of rusted shacks of the Kibera slums. Not only do the images of the slums' vast rusty shacks contrast those of the towering skyscrapers indicating material affluence of the city, but also their low elevation, emphasized by the high-angle framing, indicates a vertical difference. Closer shots of the slum show a *mise-en-scène* of heaps of garbage, rusty tin shacks, and muddy lanes, which hint of the protagonist's grotesque survival in this space. This vertical and material contrast underpins the narrative of inequality that Collett pursues in this film and establishes a hegemonic hierarchy that becomes the template of verticality in Gitonga's film. The question that I will explore here is how *Nairobi Half Life* addresses the city's vertical hierarchies and possibilities for survival.

On the one hand, the squalid downtown shacks where Mwas first meets Dingo's gang indicate a tenuous claim to space in the city (Graham 2016, 116). Marie Huchzermeyer's (2008) and Emmanuel Mutisya and Masaru Yarime's (2011) assertion that squalid spaces designate an unbuilt city can be applied to Dingo's shack, which is assembled from and furnished with a collection of leftover junk. Yet, the gangs capitalize on this image, which they adapt by posing as scrap metal dealers, to camouflage their criminal life. On the other hand, the skyscrapers are the "material embodiment of hubris and ego in the material 'race' upward" (Graham 2014, 239–40), denoting the unrelenting upward socioeconomic mobility of uptown. This contrast establishes a vertical binary, which, in turn, inscribes vertical signifiers of power within horizontal spaces, so that we associate going to uptown with being elevated to a higher social level. Downtown characters' trips to uptown are deviant intrusions driven by necessity to bypass schemas of socioeconomic inequality that they encounter in their space. Making money from cars depends on hurriedly ripping parts off automobiles or hijacking and reselling them. These acts represent a well-established street aphorism that deviant actions mitigate constraints imposed upon characters by the city's socioeconomic (vertical) hierarchies. Considering that Mwas' endeavor to succeed as an actor is beleaguered by widespread bottlenecks that tie him to the city's periphery, his experiences constantly question how he may rise above his status as belonging to the city's underclass and connect with the upper tiers.

This "how" of social progression can be understood through Graham's (2016, 129) idea of an "elevator" which is inseparable from the tiered city's corporate culture that places juniors on the lower floors and the seniors on higher levels. Elevators then can be simultaneously seen as symbols of intricate notions of vertical territories, boundaries, and power. In *Nairobi Half Life*, the quest to find out what really is the protagonist's elevator is not straightforward. For a while, we see Mwas' criminal activity as a necessary way of uplifting himself, yet it results in oppression by the police. Subsequently, he is elevated from Gaza to uptown through his acting at the Phoenix Theater, which is incorporated in the film as a *mise en abyme* play. In the play, Mwas and Cedric (Mugambi Nthiga) intrude into a wealthy home. Addressing the homeowners, Cedric says: "we have come to remind you of our existence ... to give you a message." By deploying the metaphor of being forgotten, he suggests the rigidity of territories. Mwas teases out this rigidity with a question: "Have we decided to be the way we are or have we looked away from everything that is around us to protect the island that we live upon?" The question tasks both the theater's and the film's audiences to see the fragmentation of space into "islands" as a mechanism that keeps those in higher tiers secluded from those in lower tiers. The metaphor of islands is further engaged by use of English language in the play, contrary to downtown where characters use Sheng, a popular street dialect in Nairobi. By abandoning his informal street language and adopting the language of the elite, Mwas is construing what Frantz Fanon (1967, 14) calls "a dislocation, a separation," so that even though it seems like this code-switching enables him to transition between spaces and achieve a form of "vertical" mobility, it is indeed a marker of his alienation. One could thus argue that by availing the spatial infrastructure necessary for overcoming his spatial restrictions, this play provides a platform to achieve vertical mobility. It, however, still supplants horizontal boundaries to exhibit the city's fetishism of cartographic hierarchies. The film's thesis is that vertical mobility, when not accompanied by material accouterments, continually maintains inequality and power hierarchies in the city as it amplifies the vertical gap between downtown and uptown.

Conclusion

In *Nairobi Half Life*, the use of material esthetics and symbolic infrastructures recasts Nairobi's well-known history of enclaves. The protagonist's movement between these enclaves is set against this realism of tussle between various power groups in Nairobi. This, in turn, recalls the synchronous spatial metaphors in Nairobi as a way of connecting audiences with the city's discourse of hierarchic power and the streets as frontiers of this spectacle. This chapter argues that such spatial configurations are integral to the way the film engages with the narrative of horizontal power and vertical hierarchies in Nairobi city, which are conceptualized through Foucault's notion of heterotopias. For this reason, the protagonist's ability to tap into spaces beyond his enclave and intercept opportunities cannot be underrated as it represents an ingenuous disruption of Nairobi's systems of inclusion-exclusion beyond the formal-informal, bourgeoisie-proletariat enclaves. The key argument made here is that the conflict between downtown and uptown which the film pursues creates opposed spatial narratives. It mobilizes the two versions of the city into horizontal and vertical signifiers of power hierarchies, showing downtown as an exceptional space where the city's contrasting ideals of formality and informality coexist. This interpretation of place is Gitonga's greatest contribution to contemporary narratives of Nairobi city.

Works Cited

Castells, Manuel. 1976. *The Urban Question: A Marxist Approach.* Translated by Alan Sheridan. London: Edward Arnold.

Dehaene, Michiel, and Lieven De Cauter. 2008. "Heterotopia in a Postcivil Society." In *Heterotopia and the City: Public Space in a Postcivil Society*, edited by Lieven De Cauter, and Michiel Dehaene, translated by Lieven De Cauter, and Michiel Dehaene, 3–9. London and New York: Routledge.

Desgroppes, Amélie, and Sophie Taupin. 2011. "Kibera: The Biggest Slum in Africa?" *Les Cahiers de l'Afrique de l'Est* 44: 23–34.

Dovey, Kim. 1999. *Framing Places: Mediating Power in Built Form.* London and New York: Routledge.

Fanon, Frantz. 1967. *Black Skin, White Masks.* Translated by Charles Lam Markmann. London: Pluto Press.

Feldman, Ilana. 2015. *Police Encounters: Security and Surveillance in Gaza under Egyptian Rule.* Palo Alto, CA: Stanford University Press.

Foucault, Michel. 1984. "Des espaces autres. Une conférence inédite de Michel Foucault." *(Architecture, Mouvement, Continuité)* 5: 46–49.

——— 1995. *Discipline and Punish: The Birth of The Nation.* Translated by Alan Sheridan. New York: Vintage Books.

——— 2008. "Of other spaces* (1967)." In *Heterotopia and the City: Public Space in a Postcivil Society*, edited by Lieven De Cauter, and Michiel Dehaene, translated by Lieven De Cauter, and Michiel Dehaene, 13–29. London and New York: Routledge.

Graham, Stephen. 2014. "Super-tall and Ultra-deep: The Cultural Politics of the Elevator." *Theory, Culture and Society* 31 (7/8): 239–65.

——— 2016. *Vertical: The City from Satellites to Bunkers.* London and New York: Verso.

Graham, Stephen, and Lucy Hewitt. 2013. "Getting off the ground: On the politics of urban verticality." *Progress in Human Geography* 37 (1): 72–92.

Gumbihi, Hudson. 2015. *"Is dreaded Gaza in Kayole a criminal gang or cult worshipping Jamaican artist?"* www.sde.co.ke/thenairobian/article/2000176721/is-dreaded-gaza-in-kayole-a-criminal-gang-or-cult-worshipping-jamaican-artist.

Hewitt, Lucy, and Stephen Graham. 2015. "Vertical cities: Representations of Urban Verticality in 20th-Century Science Fiction Literature." *Urban Studies* 52 (5): 923–37.

Heynen, Hilde. 2008. "Heterotopia unfolded?" In *Heterotopia and the City: Public Space in a Postcivil Society*, edited by Lieven De Cauter, and Michiel Dehaene, translated by Lieven De Cauter, and Michiel Dehaene, 311–24. London and New York: Routledge.

Hodapp, James. 2014. "Nairobi Half Life by David Gritonga (review)." *African Studies Review* 57 (1): 231–33.

Huchzermeyer, Marie. 2008. "Slum Upgrading in Nairobi within the Housing and Basic Services Market: A Housing Rights Concern." *Journal of Asian and African Studies* 43 (1): 19–39.

Hutt, Rosamond. 2016. *These are the world's five biggest slums* 19 October. www.weforum.org/agenda/2016/10/these-are-the-worlds-five-biggest-slums/.

Kenya National Assembly. 1997. *Kenya National Assembly Official Record (Hansard) 14*. May 1997. Official Report, Nairobi: Kenya National Assembly, 691.

———— 2005. *Kenya National Assembly Official Record (Hansard) 194*. April 2005. *Official Report*, Nairobi: Kenya National Assembly, 750.

Lefebvre, Henri. 1991. *The Production of Space*. Translated by Donald Nicholson-Smith. Oxford and Cambridge: Blackwell.

McCarthy, Todd. 2012. *"Nairobi Half Life: AFI Fest Review"*. www.hollywoodreporter.com/review/nairobi-life-afi-fest-review-391847.

Mutisya, Emmanuel, and Masaru Yarime. 2011. "Understanding the Grassroots Dynamics of Slums in Nairobi: The Dilemma of Kibera Informal Settlements." *International Transaction Journal of Engineering, Management, & Applied Sciences & Technologies* 2 (2): 197–213.

Sonko, Mike. 2017. *Facebook Page*. www.facebook.com/Mikesonkoforgovernor/posts/1616879645017044.

Stuart, Elden. 2013. "Secure the Volume: Vertical Geopolitics and the Depth of Power." *Political Geography* 34: 35–51. doi:10.1016/j.polgeo.2012.12.009.

Wanjiru, Melissa Wangui, and Kosuke Matsubara. 2017. "Slum toponymy in Nairobi, Kenya: A case study analysis of Kibera, Mathare and Mukuru." *Urban and Regional Planning* 4: 21–44.

Filmography

Eye in The Sky. Dir. Gavin Hood, UK, 2015.
From a Whisper. Dir. Wanuri Kahiu, Kenya, 2008.
Kibera Kid. Dir. Nathan Collett, Kenya, 2006.
Nairobi Half Life. Dir. Tosh Gitonga, Kenya /Germany, 2012.

12 Ideologically Charged Urban and Rural Places in American Movies about HIV/AIDS

Social Constructionism and the Cultural Imaginary in the Late Twentieth Century

Kylo-Patrick R. Hart

Acquired immune deficiency syndrome (AIDS) appeared in the American consciousness in 1981 and as a primary subject of American movies four years later. Over the last two decades of the twentieth century, feature-length narrative movies about the human immunodeficiency virus (HIV) and AIDS created and released in the United States contributed substantially to audience member perceptions of the AIDS pandemic, even though they frequently presented somewhat limited social information about its complex and changing realities. Such media offerings were typically quite influential in socially constructing HIV/AIDS in the cultural imaginary during that period, as the majority of Americans at the time did not (knowingly at least) interact with people with HIV/AIDS on a regular basis and, as a result, ended up relying on media images for much of their social knowledge of the AIDS pandemic (Baker 1994; Fee and Fox 1992; Griffin 2000; Kinsella 1989; Patton 1990; Rushing 1995).

Stemming from the representational approaches and patterns contained in nearly four dozen American movies about HIV/AIDS created during the first two decades of the pandemic, this chapter explores the social construction of ideologically charged places of the urban and rural varieties as contained in the following four representative AIDS movies of that era: *Chocolate Babies* (Stephen Winter, 1997), *An Early Frost* (John Erman, 1985), *In the Gloaming* (Christopher Reeve, 1997), and *Jeffrey* (Christopher Ashley, 1995). In doing so, it demonstrates how urban areas in such movies are socially constructed as the places of AIDS dystopia, in dramatic contrast to rural areas, which have historically been socially constructed as the places of moral utopia in United States society.

In the pages that follow, I will invoke the concept I have termed the "anti-queer patrolling eye" to distinguish between the conditions that gay (and/or otherwise queer) males typically experience within these urban versus rural places in their story worlds. As in all types of cinematic fare, acts of looking (or non-looking, as the case may be) by characters in the story world are significant in American movies about HIV/ AIDS. Accordingly, in this chapter, I utilize the concept of the anti-queer patrolling eye to identify and comment upon significant instances when particular characters in a film appear intentionally to be on the lookout for male queerness in its various forms, perceive some, and then react negatively (through dialogue and/or their subsequent actions) to what they have perceived. This concept is employed to provide insights into the lived realities and discriminatory phenomena experienced by queer males with HIV/AIDS in the urban and rural environs of the four AIDS movies being analyzed. Incorporating relevant insights from sources including David B. Clarke's edited collection *The Cinematic City* (1997) and Catherine Fowler and Gillian Helfield's edited collection *Representing the Rural: Space, Place, and Identity in Films about the Land* (2006), this analysis demonstrates how gay men with AIDS are treated remarkably differently in urban versus rural places in their cinematic story worlds, with the resulting on-screen representations both reflecting and socially constructing related conditions for such individuals in the real world during the pandemic's first two decades.

Urban Places in American Movies about HIV/AIDS: Socially Constructing an AIDS Dystopia

As David Clarke writes in his introduction to *The Cinematic City*, "So central is the city to film that, paradoxically, the widespread *implicit* acceptance of its importance has mitigated against an explicit consideration of its actual significance" (1997, 1). By this he means, in far too many instances, inadequate theoretical attention has been devoted to identifying and articulating the relationship between cinematic and urban space. In relation to AIDS movies specifically, what has long been clear is that the vast majority of all such offerings that were created and released during the first two decades of the AIDS pandemic feature one or more United States cities as a noteworthy component of their narratives. What has been less clear over time, however, is the ideological messages that the regular inclusion of these urban places communicate to the viewers of such works. This chapter endeavors to expand the scholarly attention paid to this topic.

From the earliest days of motion pictures to the present, typical representations of urban places have focused alternately on both their attractive and repulsive attributes; while countless films have long revealed their continual fascination with the "distinctive spaces, lifestyles, and human conditions of the city" (Shiel 2001, 2), it has nevertheless also become apparent that so many of these same cinematic representations have tended to valorize rural places over urban ones (McArthur 1997). Perhaps unsurprisingly, therefore, common representations of urban places in AIDS movies have followed the same pattern, with cities simultaneously being socially constructed as welcoming spaces for gay men (and otherwise queer individuals) and, as a direct result, as places of AIDS dystopia. This is certainly the case in the first two AIDS movies under consideration in this chapter: *Jeffrey*, about a young gay man in New York City whose HIV/AIDS fears lead him to become celibate; and *Chocolate Babies*, about the actions and interactions of a small group of radical AIDS activists in New York City during the pandemic's second decade.

As William Rushing notes in his book *The AIDS Epidemic: Social Dimensions of an Infectious Disease*, by the time the earliest cases of AIDS were identified, gay ghettos were quite common in urban areas across the United States as places where homosexual subcultures occupied distinct physical and social spaces that kept them "figuratively walled off from the rest of the city and hence out of sight" of most disapproving outsiders (1995, 20). For gay male residents and visitors, these embracing spaces offered enhanced opportunities for identity formation and community building, on their own terms, to individuals who were often regarded as outcasts in other settings as they simultaneously challenged widely shared notions of conventional masculinity, family, and reproductive sexuality (López-Vicuña 2010). Although long-standing fears of cities have stemmed from the large numbers of individuals they bring together in concentrated areas, in the case of gay men living in gay ghettos, this sense of the collective has been regarded as a very positive and empowering feature of urban life.

During the early years of the AIDS crisis in the United States, it was often believed that such safe spaces required ongoing protection from disapproving others. At least in part, that is because many gay ghettos tend initially to be established in neighborhoods with poorer housing quality and higher crime rates (Hanhardt 2008). A common approach to protecting these special urban spaces, therefore, has involved the formation of gay safe streets patrols, in which the residents of the gay ghettos themselves establish volunteer patrols to help keep their neighborhoods safe from homophobic and other sorts of undesirable acts (Hanhardt 2008).

All of these attributes of life in a gay ghetto are communicated in the AIDS movies *Jeffrey* and *Chocolate Babies*. In the former film, Jeffrey (Steven Weber) is an aspiring actor who enjoys continual emotional support from other close gay friends, including the older interior designer Sterling (Patrick Stewart) and that man's younger boyfriend, Darius (Bryan Batt). The movie opens with white fireworks exploding above the New York City skyline (symbolically suggesting the act of orgasm), which are followed by shots of Jeffrey having sex with a series of men. Combined, these opening images reveal that he lives in an urban gay ghetto, where homosexuality is readily accepted and gay male sexual partners are continually available. Such perceptions are confirmed moments later in the film when Jeffrey heads to the gym and meets Steve (Michael T. Weiss), an attractive local bartender, who kisses him passionately in front of the other men. Days later, when Steve approaches Jeffrey with flowers to officially ask him out, a quickly growing group of onlookers encourage Jeffrey to say yes and clap to express their approval when he does. The importance of protecting their gay ghetto from the deleterious actions of disapproving others is communicated in the film by Sterling's and Darius' voluntary participation in the Pink Panthers Patrol, a gay safe streets patrol intended to prevent gaybashing.

In *Chocolate Babies*, the positive aspects of life in a gay ghetto are made evident through various actions and interactions of the film's central characters: Max Mo-Freak (Claude E. Sloan), an HIV-positive black diva with a political agenda; Jamela (Suzanne Gregg Ferguson), Max's heterosexual, HIV-positive sister; Larva (Dudley Findlay Jr.), an overweight, HIV-positive, cross-dressing queen; Lady Marmalade (Michael Lynch), an aging, IV-drug-using, HIV-positive transvestite; and Sam (Jon Kit Lee), Max's younger Asian-American, HIV-negative lover. Together, these five individuals, with Max as their leader, endeavor to improve the lived realities of people of color in their surrounding neighborhood, especially those with HIV/AIDS. Early in the film, Larva speaks quite candidly to his friends about a recent gay sexual encounter, and Max and Sam are shown frolicking and kissing outdoors. Such opening moments reveal that these characters and their friends, like the ones in *Jeffrey*, live in a supportive urban environment for gay individuals. This message is further communicated in scenes during which Max relaxes in the nude on the rooftop of his apartment building, where he also hosts impromptu queer parties and occasionally engages in sexual acts with others for all his high-rise neighbors to see.

What is ideologically intriguing about these cinematic representations of cities as a sort of gay utopia in American AIDS movies is the degree to which they are simultaneously linked to representations of urban places as an AIDS dystopia. In these latter representations, urban places are portrayed as sites of transcendental alienation as a result of the constantly lurking threat of HIV/AIDS (Easthope 1997). Typical representations of the dystopian aspects of cities portray them as places of chaos, disorder, oppression, and suffering that leave their residents at continual risk of harm (Halper and Muzzio 2007) and experiencing a profound "intensification of nervous stimulation" (Simmel 1950, 410). In part, that is because urban areas contain the highest concentrations of human beings, most of whom have differing motivations for their various actions. With regard to AIDS movies of the 1980s and 1990s more specifically, it is also because urban areas are continually portrayed as the places of HIV/AIDS infection, wherein affliction, dying, death, and grieving are continually distressing components of daily life. It must be noted here that the success of United States cities in providing inviting spaces for large numbers of gay

men, which ultimately resulted in the creation of sex-positive norms of po-
lygamous gay sex that encouraged casual sexual encounters with numerous partners, contributed substantially to the rapid spread of HIV/AIDS
throughout the gay community (and beyond) from the pandemic's earliest
days (Rushing 1995). It is perhaps entirely unsurprising, therefore, that
despite their positive representations of gay life in urban environments,
both *Jeffrey* and *Chocolate Babies* also simultaneously explore how such
conditions have ultimately resulted in gay male residents commonly experiencing such urban places as an ongoing AIDS dystopia.

During the opening minutes of *Jeffrey*, as the eponymous character is
having sex with another man, the condom Jeffrey is wearing breaks and his
sexual partner responds with fear. This is the first indication that the film
is simultaneously exploring the social construction of urban areas as the
places of AIDS dystopia. The montage sequence that follows alternates between brief scenes of Jeffrey attempting to successfully engage in sexual relations with additional men who are terrified of contracting HIV/AIDS (e.g.,
one man is covered from head to toe in plastic wrap to protect him from
bodily fluids) with iconic images from the early years of the AIDS crisis (e.g.,
a *Time* magazine cover pertaining to viruses and AIDS, video footage from
an ACT UP demonstration, etc.). The images contained in the montage lead
Jeffrey to have a nightmare pertaining to the ever-present threat of HIV/
AIDS, which then motivates him to swear off sex entirely in order to protect himself. Reinforcing the significance of this latter development, Sterling
soon reveals to Jeffrey the seropositivity of his partner, Darius.

Days later, Steve reveals to Jeffrey that he is HIV positive. As a result, in Jeffrey's mind the prospect of an ordinary date has now become
analogous to an evening of Russian roulette. He feels that gay life in
the big city has suddenly become "radioactive," ideologically reinforcing
notions of urban locations as the places of AIDS dystopia. This message
is further reinforced shortly thereafter when Darius succumbs to AIDS.
Before the film concludes, Jeffrey expresses his intention to leave the
urban area entirely, with the hope of hiding out in rural Wisconsin until
the AIDS crisis is over. But he ends up reversing his plan after Darius
pays him a brief visit from the afterlife, cautioning him to not let the
specter of AIDS prevent him from fully living his life as a gay man.
The message that Darius imparts is significant, as it suggests that the
prospects of gay men achieving fulfillment are remarkably limited (or
perhaps even nonexistent) in rural environs.

In a conceptually related way, *Chocolate Babies* begins with Max and
his associates confronting a closeted gay politician about his indiffer-
ence to the conditions experienced regularly by the residents of his gay
ghetto. Then, to emphasize that the city of opportunity is also a place
of inequality and make it clear that they want to be taken very seriously, these activists slash parts of their bodies with knives and smear
their HIV-infected blood on the politician, Councilman Melvin Freeman

(Bryan Webster), with the hope of motivating him to do more about the negative realities of the ongoing AIDS crisis. As the days progress, the gang's attacks on other politicians become increasingly more violent; in addition, Max takes the even more extreme action of cutting his own hand and inserting his infected blood directly into Melvin Freeman's mouth, revealing that he is feeling increasingly desperate about the conditions he and others like him experience daily. Acknowledging all of the negative aspects of their everyday lives, Freeman explicitly refers to the group's urban environment as an "AIDS ghetto," a distinct sort of urban social space characterized by misery and despair within which infected individuals typically feel there is no way out (Haile et al. 2011). By the time the film concludes, that depressing perception is solidly reinforced by the reality that both Jamela and Lady Marmalade are now dead, and Max is seen lying on his deathbed atop his apartment building, with Sam joining him by his side as he prepares to pass away.

In addition to the various points that have already been made about the form and function of urban spaces in these two films, consideration of the anti-queer patrolling eye contributes further insights. It is particularly noteworthy that although examples of this concept can be found in both works, their existence emerges from the actions of individuals who live outside the gay ghettos rather than within them. In *Jeffrey*, for example, the anti-queer patrolling eye first reveals itself when Jeffrey is listening to the new age guru Debra Moorhouse (Sigourney Weaver), who singles him out as "the homosexual" in her audience and proceeds to tell him that gay men are evil because they represent the absence of (heterosexual) love. Later in the film, it resurfaces as Jeffrey walks back to his apartment alone at night and is spotted by three homophobic thugs who, after expressing their belief that because he is gay he must also have AIDS, proceed to gaybash him. In an effort to alter such inaccurate social perceptions thereafter, Steve embraces the importance of proudly celebrating alternative sexualities in other parts of the city by helping to organize the annual pride parade, which temporarily transforms presumably straight spaces beyond the confines of the gay ghetto into proudly and openly queer ones, if only for a short while.

In *Chocolate Babies*, the anti-queer patrolling eye first reveals itself when Larva ventures outside of his gay ghetto to spend time with his mother and she reveals she is ashamed of her son's flamboyant homosexuality, calling him both a "big sissy" and a "cocksucker." Later, it reveals itself once again when Sam arrives at his mother's home with an injured Max and the rest of their small group of friends. After the woman tends to Max's wounds and visually examines all of the unexpected visitors to her home, she refers to her son as a "faggot" and his queer friends as a bunch of "freaks" and orders them all to leave.

These various developments, coming both from strangers and biological family members, serve to efficiently reinforce the pervasive message that while gay ghettos serve as supportive spaces for their queer residents, those who live in them are nevertheless at constant risk of attack from disapproving outsiders as well as the ravages of HIV/AIDS. To a substantial degree, that is because such urban spaces have continually been socially constructed in United States society as the places where "deviants" (such as gay males) and "deviance" (such as casual sexual relations with numerous, often anonymous partners that contribute substantially to the rapid spread of HIV/AIDS) coalesce and thrive.

Rural Places in American Movies about HIV/AIDS: Socially Constructing a Moral Utopia

In dramatic contrast to the social construction of urban places as an AIDS dystopia, the social construction of rural places in American movies about HIV/AIDS is one that is much more innocent and pure: a moral utopia. As Rushing (1995) notes, rural gay males who contracted HIV/AIDS during the pandemic's first two decades frequently did so in cities, where they moved for employment or to enjoy a more developed gay culture that is typically regarded as problematic in nonurban settings. When they learned that they had become infected, many returned home (at least temporarily) to seek care and comfort from their biological family members, and sometimes even to die in such rural places (Rushing 1995). These realities are represented in a subset of AIDS movies released during the last two decades of the twentieth century, of which *An Early Frost* and *In the Gloaming* are representative examples.

Throughout cinema history, a significant characteristic of rural inhabitants and settings has been their connection with traditional ways of being associated with the values and expectations of the past (Fowler and Helfield 2006). As Catherine Fowler and Gillian Helfield explain, "The rural inhabitant embodies a lineage and way of life that have been sustained for centuries and thus a certain 'purity' and continuity of culture" (2006, 11). In a related way, the rural setting itself – with its emphases on the representationally "innocent" iconography of clotheslines, churches, fields, fishing holes, flowers, gardens, hedges, lakes, lush lawns, mountains, parks, rivers, tree-lined streets, and Victorian homes with porches and their connections to the traditional past, imaged as either a golden age or a conventional childhood – has very strong ties to patriarchal expectations (Fowler and Helfield 2006; Knepper and Lawrence 2006). As such, it is quite common for rural environs in films, as a result of the traditional appeals of small-town life, to function as a "healer of psychological and physical hurts" (Kidd 2006, 213) to individuals of various kinds. It is also quite common for fathers in such films to be ashamed of some noteworthy aspect of their sons, who grew up in such rural environs, but then moved elsewhere to forge an adult identity, once they return to their childhood home, with traditional conceptions of (heterosexual) masculinity and moralism readily coming into play (220).

The importance of a pastoral setting is immediately established in the opening shots of *An Early Frost*, which explores the experiences of a young man from Chicago when he returns home to inform his rural family members that he is gay and has AIDS. The steeple of a small-town church, surrounded by lush mountains, is most visible as the film begins, its phallic imagery immediately calling to mind the expectations of a (heteronormative) patriarchal society. The image then dissolves into the outside of a welcoming home on a quiet street within which an older woman, Katherine Pierson (Gena Rowlands), is giving a piano lesson to a young boy. When her husband, Nick (Ben Gazzara), returns home from his workday at the family-owned lumber company, he and his spouse are seen enjoying a quiet anniversary celebration with familial loved ones in their living room; the occasion is interrupted when an unexpected guest arrives at the front door: the couple's grown son, Michael (Aidan Quinn). During dinner, Michael informs his parents, his grandmother (Sylvia Sidney), his sister (Sydney Walsh), and the other attendees that he has just been made a partner in his law firm, an impressive accomplishment of which his father is particularly proud. Although Michael must return to the city the next day, it is clear during this visit that he is loved and admired by everyone he has interacted with, especially both of his parents.

The scene transforms from a rural shot of a small-town paperboy riding a bicycle to an urban shot of two high-rise buildings. Michael's gay lover back in the city, Peter (D.W. Moffett), has difficulty waking Michael to get ready for work. Days later, Michael has a coughing fit at work that lands him in the hospital, where it is determined he is both suffering from pneumonia and has contracted AIDS. On his next trip to visit his family, Michael informs his parents that he is sick. When he says that he has AIDS, his mother expresses disbelief. When he adds that he is gay, his father raises a fist to physically assault him. This is the first instance when the anti-queer patrolling eye makes an appearance in *An Early Frost*, as the father who has always loved and admired his son now sees him differently and, as a result, instinctively desires to beat his queerness out of him. Although the next day his mother attempts to reassure Michael that "this is still your home," it is evident that things have changed, especially where his father is concerned. When Michael visits his father at work in an attempt to clear the air, the man coldly refers to Michael as a "stranger" and insists that he should simply return to "his own kind" in the city. This second example of the anti-queer patrolling eye in the film concludes with Michael's father telling his offspring, "I never thought the day would come when you'd be in front of me and I wouldn't know who you are." It is clear from Michael's interactions with his father that homosexuality (as well as anything else, such as HIV/AIDS, that may accompany it) is not welcome within their rural area, the place where goodness and morality are automatically presumed to permanently preside.

Although Michael initially intends to return to Chicago immediately, his plans change when he is admitted to the local hospital, where his father refuses to visit him. Once discharged, he returns to his parents' house to find Peter waiting to see him. Peter urges Michael to come back to their city apartment. The idea certainly meets with his father's approval, as the man gives Peter the cold shoulder at dinner that evening and makes it clear that Peter is unwelcome in his home. Here again the patrolling eye makes an appearance in the film, as Michael's father immediately perceives Peter's homosexuality (even though for much of the film Michael suggests that he is simply a friend or his neighbor) and treats him negatively as a result. Peter heads back to Chicago the next day. Still trying to come to terms with the treatment and disappointment he is experiencing from his father, Michael sneaks into the family's garage in the early morning hours to commit suicide via carbon monoxide poisoning. It is only after Michael's father finds him there, unconscious, that the patriarch reluctantly admits he does not actually want to see his son dead. Nevertheless, Michael returns quickly to Chicago thereafter, to resume his life in the city with Peter and their gay friends by his side.

Like *An Early Frost*, *In the Gloaming* begins with comforting rural images of traditional small-town family life (as opposed to the always already presumed deviance of the gay community) in the form of a flashback of a mother playing outdoors with her son and daughter, on a huge green lawn with a tire swing dangling from a tree just behind them. The special bond the woman feels for her young boy becomes readily apparent. The film then cuts to the same pastoral setting in the present day, as the grown son, Danny (Robert Sean Leonard), returns to his family's home from San Francisco in late summer, in order to live out the final days of his life with AIDS. His sister, Anne (Bridget Fonda), arrives to enjoy dinner outdoors with her brother and their parents (David Strathairn and Glenn Close) on the family's beautiful lakefront property. Although his mother is pleased to be reunited with her child, Danny's father soon makes it quite clear that he does not personally welcome his son's newfound presence in their seemingly otherwise wholesome environment. This is the first moment when the anti-queer patrolling eye emerges in the film. Although Danny's family members apparently have known about his homosexuality for some time, it is clear that his father has chosen to ignore that aspect of his son's identity until this point, when he can see the deleterious physical effects that AIDS is wreaking on Danny's body and is no longer able to deny the reality that Danny is a gay man with AIDS. In response to this disturbing observation, the father chooses not to communicate with Danny directly, instead hoping to find out whatever he needs to know from his wife.

As summer transitions into autumn, Danny expresses to his mother his disappointment that his father has no clue who he is and simply wants both his queerness and his compromised medical condition to disappear. The patrolling eye then reemerges in the film as Danny shares some unpleasant holiday memories with her. After his mother awkwardly chooses to refer to Danny's former male lover alternately as his "friend" and his "roommate," Danny points out to her how, until just now, she has intentionally turned a blind eye to the true status of their relationship because she has never been comfortable with it. He proceeds to tell her how much it hurt that his family never invited both him and his gay lover home for Thanksgiving: "I think the image of me and my lover spooning out cranberry sauce at Thanksgiving was just too much [for you] to bear."

As the days progress, both Danny's father and his sister appear jealous of the amount of time the mother spends with her son. The patrolling eye makes a third appearance in the film when Anne grows tired of witnessing the degrees of attention and affection the matron has been lavishing on Danny. After Anne accuses her mother of "making" Danny gay as a result of her extreme devotion to him, she makes it clear that she is not interested in spending time with her brother during the final weeks of his life and storms out.

What emerges from these various developments is the degree to which gay men (and particularly those with HIV/AIDS) are unwelcome in such rural settings, even by their biological family members. The "evil" temptations that lurk around every corner in urban places as well as those who partake in them have no place at all in rural environs, which have been socially constructed in opposition to the immorality of the city and its "deviant" inhabitants. In other words, gay men and their lived realities are widely regarded in American movies about HIV/AIDS as being alien to the "purity" and "natural order" of rural places, even when those same males were born and raised in those same places. From a representational standpoint, therefore, it is to be expected that Danny remains alive at his family's home for only a few weeks before the "deviance" his presence poses is eradicated through his death. Furthermore, it is not surprising that his father shows no interest in getting to know his grown son until after the young man dies, when doing so can no longer pose any real threat to the "purity" of their rural setting and the individuals who continue to live there. To visually reinforce this final point, the film's closing images are in the form of a crane shot that begins with a close-up of the façade of the family's quaint home before rising into the air to showcase a giant tree and the peaceful beauty of the nearby, still lake. Considered together, they signify that the security and wholesomeness of their rural place remain unchanged from the similarly soothing images that begin this film, despite Danny's temporary return.

Without question, the social construction of rural places in American movies about HIV/AIDS characterizes such domains as all that is morally pure and good, which can serve as a much-needed balm – if only for a short while – to the injured minds, bodies, and souls of gay men with AIDS whose lives have seemingly gone astray in urban gay ghettos and are in need of reimmersion in the agrarian, pastoral, and small-town virtues of rural life (McArthur 1997). As in many other kinds of rural films, the message that comes through loud and clear is that, in such small-town environs, straitlaced individuals "work hard, cooperate, and live simply – inspired by religious faith and surrounded by beautiful nature lovingly cultivated" (Knepper and Lawrence 2006, 323), as well as that the traditional purity of such places must be safeguarded at all costs. Accordingly, the primary representational message communicated to the gay male characters is that although rural places are certainly nice to visit, they will never be allowed to live in them permanently.

Concluding Observations

American movies about HIV/AIDS from the pandemic's first two decades provide a unique form of narratives of place. The urban and rural spaces they feature communicate powerful messages about selfhood in relation to otherness, and about comforting borders between "normalcy" and "deviance" that are really not true boundaries at all. Their contents have been heavily influenced by the distinct cultural, historical, political, and related discourses surrounding the discovery and spread of AIDS, and a bit later HIV, during the crucial period when HIV/AIDS was being socially constructed for the American public. The resulting messages they communicate are far from neutral in their contents; for example, the binary oppositions associated with such influential social constructions of urban versus rural places include cash relations/human relations, excess/modesty, gay/straight, depravity/innocence, metropolis/small town, monstrosity/normalcy, pollution/purity, retribution/redemption, sickness/health, and words/deeds (Mahoney 1997; McArthur 1997; Parker 1993). In addition, in a majority of cases, such films failed to truly serve the informational needs of audience members by ignoring the changing demographics of the AIDS pandemic over time and reinforcing culturally influential perceptions of AIDS as a "gay disease" of concern primarily to city dwellers, as if simply self-identifying with a different sexual orientation or choosing to live in a rural area could provide complete protection from the risk of personal infection.

The representational distinctions between urban and rural places that become evident through a comparative analysis of the contents of *Jeffrey*, *Chocolate Babies*, *An Early Frost*, and *In the Gloaming* provide a noteworthy form of otherness encountered in AIDS movies of the late twentieth century, which contributed significantly to the ongoing social construction of the AIDS pandemic during that era. Narrative offerings such as these contributed substantially to culturally shared social meanings about AIDS, as they offered appealing ways for countless individuals to attempt to make "sense" of the uncertain world around them during the early years of the AIDS pandemic and whether or not they were personally at risk of contracting HIV/AIDS (Watney 1993). However, for the most part, their representations continued to (inaccurately) reassure audience members that the urban/gay and rural/heterosexual communities were somehow naturally and entirely distinct as a result of some imaginary representational boundary separating the so-called "deviant" and "normal" populations (Park 1993). As Simon Watney reminds us, these sorts of media offerings may most effectively

> be regarded as a form of macabre entertainment, which provide a limited series of heavily moralized *tableaux* that tell us much about the complex moral management of modern sexuality but little or nothing about the complex, shifting realities of the epidemic as it is lived all around the world.
>
> (1993, 154)

Unfortunately, the end result of these influential representations was the continual reinforcement of inaccurate perceptions of HIV/AIDS as a threat almost exclusively to gay men and other residents of urban environments, which ended up concealing more accurate social information about the reality of the AIDS pandemic and the range of different types of individuals, in all sorts of places, who needed to proactively protect themselves from its spread.

Works Cited

Baker, Rob. 1994. *The Art of AIDS: From Stigma to Conscience.* New York: Continuum.

Clarke, David B., ed. 1997. *The Cinematic City.* New York: Routledge.

Easthope, Antony. 1997. "Cinécities in the Sixties." In *The Cinematic City*, edited by David B. Clarke, 129–39. New York: Routledge.

Fee, Elizabeth, and Daniel M. Fox, eds. 1992. *AIDS: The Making of a Chronic Disease.* Berkeley: University of California Press.

Fowler, Catherine, and Gillian Helfield. 2006. "Introduction." In *Representing the Rural: Space, Place, and Identity in Films about the Land*, edited by Catherine Fowler, and Gillian Helfield, 1–14. Detroit, MI: Wayne State University Press.

Griffin, Gabriele. 2000. *Representations of HIV and AIDS: Visibility Blue/s.* Manchester: Manchester University Press.

Haile, Rahwa, Mark B. Padilla, and Edith A. Parker. 2011. "'Stuck in the Quagmire of an HIV Ghetto': The Meaning of Stigma in the Lives of Older Black Gay and Bisexual Men Living with HIV in New York City." *Culture, Health & Sexuality* 13 (4): 429–42.

Halper, Thomas, and Douglas Muzzio. 2007. "Hobbes in the City: Urban Dystopias in American Movies." *Journal of American Culture* 30 (4): 379–90.

Hanhardt, Christina B. 2008. "Butterflies, Whistles, and Fists: Gay Safe Streets Patrols and the New Gay Ghetto, 1976–1981." *Radical History Review* 100: 60–85.

Kidd, Kerry. 2006. "The Child in the Cinema: Representations of a Rural Dystopia in *Billy Elliot* and *The Color of Paradise.*" In *Representing the Rural: Space, Place, and Identity in Films about the Land*, edited by Catherine Fowler, and Gillian Helfield, 213–23. Detroit, MI: Wayne State University Press.

Kinsella, James. 1989. *Covering the Plague: AIDS and the American Media.* New Brunswick, NJ: Rutgers University Press.

Knepper, Marty S., and John S. Lawrence. 2006. "World War II and Iowa: Hollywood's Pastoral Myth for the Nation." In *Representing the Rural: Space, Place, and Identity in Films about the Land*, edited by Catherine Fowler, and Gillian Helfield, 323–39. Detroit, MI: Wayne State University Press.

López-Vicuña, Ignacio. 2010. "Mapping the 'Gay Ghetto': Perlongher's O *negócio de michê* as Cartography of Desire." *Chasqui* 41 (1): 159–69.

Mahoney, Elisabeth. 1997. "'The People in Parentheses': Space under Pressure in the Postmodern City." In *The Cinematic City*, edited by David B. Clarke, 165–85. New York: Routledge.

McArthur, Colin. 1997. "Chinese Boxes and Russian Dolls: Tracking the Elusive Cinematic City." In *The Cinematic City*, edited by David B. Clarke, 19–45. New York: Routledge.

Park, Katharine. 1993. "Kimberly Bergalis, AIDS, and the Plague Metaphor." In *Media Spectacles*, edited by Marjorie Garber, Jann Matlock, and Rebecca L. Walkowitz, 233–53. New York: Routledge.

Parker, Andrew. 1993. "Grafting David Cronenberg: Monstrosity, AIDS Media, National/Sexual Difference." In *Media Spectacles*, edited by Marjorie Garber, Jann Matlock, and Rebecca L. Walkowitz, 209–31. New York: Routledge.

Patton, Cindy. 1990. *Inventing AIDS.* New York: Routledge.

Rushing, William A. 1995. *The AIDS Epidemic: Social Dimensions of an Infectious Disease.* San Francisco, CA: Westview Press.

Shiel, Mark. 2001. "Cinema and the City in History and Theory." In *Cinema and the City: Film and Urban Societies in a Global Context*, edited by Mark Shiel, and Tony Fitzmaurice, 1–18. Malden, MA: Blackwell Publishers.

Simmel, Georg. 1950. *The Sociology of Georg Simmel.* Translated and edited by Kurt H. Wolff. New York: Free Press.

Watney, Simon. 1993. "Short-Term Companions: AIDS as Popular Entertainment." In *A Leap in the Dark: AIDS, Art, and Contemporary Cultures*, edited by Allan Klusacek, and Ken Morrison, 152–66. Montreal: Véhicule Press.

Filmography

Chocolate Babies. Dir. Stephen Winter, USA, 1997.
An Early Frost. Dir. John Erman, USA, 1985.
In the Gloaming. Dir. Christopher Reeve, USA, 1997.
Jeffrey. Dir. Christopher Ashley, USA, 1995.

Part V

Landscapes of Belonging: Nation and Identity

Introduction

Steven Allen and Kirsten Møllegaard

As Benedict Anderson famously argued in his groundbreaking study, *Imagined Communities: Reflections on the Origin and Spread of Nationalism* (1983), national identity is forged via imaginary processes that situate the individual within the context of the nation, rather than within the narrow confines of personal life. While Anderson explored the political and economic relationships that contributed to these processes, this section examines how nation and identity are represented in place-based cinema and literature that specifically generate feelings of belonging as part of their narrative strategy. Narratives of belonging precipitate concepts of not-belonging, of otherness, and xenophobia. Nostalgia for what is perceived as an idyllic, harmonious, and homogenous past also influences how national and personal identities are constructed in the present, even when agonizing historical trauma suggests otherwise.

The yearning for home and nostalgia for the past are strong narrative features in film and literature that utilize sentient landscapes as part of their narration. The chapters in this part present three divergent perspectives on how nation and personal identity revolve around home, the unhomely (Freud's concept of *das Unheimliche*), and the search for a place to belong. The Oscar-winning Polish film *Ida* (Pawel Pawlikowski, 2013) is the focus of Sarah Casey Benyahia's chapter, which examines versions of the past through the lens of a young Catholic novice, Ida Lebenstein, who embarks on a journey to discover her own origin. *Ida* is set in the 1960s, when Poland was part of the Soviet bloc and when the horrors of World War II were still within living memory. Ida is permitted to go on a trip with her aunt before taking her vows as a nun. The road trip is narrated cinematically through a landscape fraught with painful historical memories contrasted by episodic glimpses of hope. While the past hovers ominously as a dark weight upon Ida's present, the wheels of history relentlessly propel her toward the future. The film's visual esthetics create a rich perspective on how time and place merge in a landscape where national memories intertwine with a search for personal belonging. Casey Benyahia's close reading of the cinematography reveals the film's subtext of memory and postmemory. She discusses how identifying categories like nation, gender, ethnicity, and religion ineffectually address the ambiguities of belonging that Ida encounters on her journey. By analyzing Ida as a character in a state of liminality in relation to the non-place of the road, Casey Benyahia shows how the lingering traumas of World War II persist in questioning the meanings of nationality and the ambiguity of belonging.

Annie Proulx's three-volume Wyoming stories take the relationship between personal belonging and national identity in a different direction. Her short stories take place in one of the driest, most inhospitable landscapes of the American West, where climate and environment challenge human habitation on a spectacular scale of sublime grandeur and national rhetoric. In the chapter "Home and the Range: On the Concept of Home in Annie Proulx's Wyoming Stories," Kirsten Møllegaard discusses how Proulx develops her characters' identity by contrasting home with the open landscapes of range and wilderness in the three volumes comprising Proulx's trilogy of Wyoming stories: *Close Range* (1999), *Bad Dirt* (2004), and *Fine Just the Way It Is* (2008). The American West looms large in American cinema and literature as a mythical place where American destiny is forged; but, as Proulx shows, it is also a place of rapid environmental degradation due to unsustainable ranching practices. The environmental degradation owing to settler culture and settlers' land use practices thus underlies Proulx's portrayal of rural Wyoming, where death is always symbolic of issues beyond individual control. Møllegaard examines how the concept of home, a symbolic space deeply encoded with social, economic, and cultural gender constructions, informs the way Proulx's Wyoming stories represent the American West both historically and currently as a place in flux, constantly moved and destabilized over time by the effects of white settlement, manifest destiny, and unsustainable ranching methods.

Places of disappearance and contested belonging are prominent themes in Scandinavian crime fiction. Joanna Wilson-Scott analyzes water as symbol of transition, social change, and identity in recent Swedish fiction in her chapter "Narratives of Water: Changing Places and Contested Spaces in Swedish Literature." Wilson-Scott examines four best-selling crime novels, which all significantly engage issues of nation and belonging with the symbolism of death by water: Henning Mankell's *Faceless Killers* (1991), Kerstin Ekman's *Blackwater* (1993), Camilla Läckberg's *The Ice Princess* (2003), and Stieg Larsson's *The Girl with the Dragon Tattoo* (2005). Wilson-Scott argues that, depending on its mobility and clarity, water can be interpreted as a metaphor for change as well as for a resistance to change. Lakes and rivers are, of course, distinct features of the Swedish landscape and part of the nation's self-perception as place and its nostalgia for idyllic nature. Wilson-Scott explores the motif of death by water within the context of Swedish national identity and theorizes that the trope of the ocean, as both barrier and threshold, symbolically points toward greater social concerns such as globalization and fluctuating perceptions about national identity under the pressure of immigration.

National identity is produced by a sense of belonging and nostalgia for idyllic stability. The themes discussed in this section situate landscapes and specific landscape features as active elements in national discourses.

Work Cited

Anderson, Benedict. 1983. *Imagined Communities: Reflections on the Origin and Spread of Nationalism*. London: Verso.

13 Between Place and Non-place

Disrupting the Categorizations of the Past in *Ida*

Sarah Casey Benyahia

In its exploration of Polish society during and after the Second World War, *Ida* (Pawel Pawlikowski, 2012) shows the destruction of lives through ethnic categorization and state control. These limiting and divisive categories are national and cultural, evident in the historical desire to confer stable and fixed borders, religious and ethnic identities. The film's setting in time and place, Poland in the early 1960s, is pivotal. The context of historical and political events, specifically the effect of the German occupation and annexation of Poland in the Second World War and its inclusion in the Soviet bloc in 1947, is used in *Ida* as an allegory for the limiting and damaging nature of all forms of categorization on humanity. These historical events are part of the profile of a country whose borders had been redrawn frequently throughout the previous two hundred years. The film contrasts this experience of division and confinement of people and places with the possibility of a future openness which leaves behind rigid definitions.

The plot of the film concerns Ida Lebenstein, a young Jewish woman who initially believes herself to be Catholic, and is on the verge of taking up her vows to become a nun. This process is disrupted by the arrival of her Aunt Wanda who takes her on a road trip through southeast Poland, from Łódź to Szydłów, in order to reveal Ida's past to her, namely that fellow Poles murdered her parents and Wanda's child during the occupation. Ida, who has no memory of the places that she visits on the road trip, becomes a fluid character of movement and transition. Freed from the confines of the convent which defines her identity at the start of the film, Ida spends a pivotal period of her journey in a hotel in Szydłów, before the final shots place her in uncertain space rather than a place with a stable meaning.

Ida's view of place and its divisions is historically specific to Poland, and yet it also resonates in the context of the film's release in the early twenty-first century and the increasing contestation over open borders in Europe. The Schengen Agreement (1985) abolished checks on internal borders within the European Union (EU), central to the organization's commitment to the free movement of people, a commitment made legally binding through the Charter of Fundamental Rights (European Commission 2010). This principle of openness and mobility is currently under attack, not only exemplified by the United Kingdom's vote to leave the EU, but also evident in other contemporary populist political movements (for example, Poland's Law and Justice Party, the National Front in France, and the Danish People's Party), which argue for a return to domestic control of the movement of people and the demarcation of national borders. In this context *Ida*'s message about the dangers of barriers and divisions has a contemporary as well as historical relevance in respect of how place is defined.

In this chapter, I argue that *Ida* explores the complexities of remembering national, religious, and ethnic historical trauma in the context of anxieties around the limiting nature of geographical borders. Drawing on the concepts of memory studies and approaches to defining the experience of place in modernity, I argue that the film configures the weight of the past through place – nation, towns, and buildings – as a burden which must be superseded by traveling and transition, a form of non-place. This conflict between the two states constructs a haptic response for the viewer: an understanding of the physical sensation of attempting to remember but not to be trapped by the past. In offering ways of escaping the past *Ida* questions the need for memorialization of trauma through categories of place and identity. Ida herself is a transitional figure in this movement from past to present and future, remaining in limbo at the end of the film, suggesting the difficulties as well as hopefulness of this trajectory. These positions of entrapment and movement experienced by Ida are illuminated through Gilles Deleuze's (2005) concept of the crystal-image, which suspends characters in limbo and Marc Augé's (2008) concept of non-place, a transient place without meaning or conventional definitions of identity. Augé (2008, 65) defines the differences between place and non-place as a feature of supermodernity: "If a place can be defined as relational, historical and concerned with identity, then a space which cannot be defined as relational, or historical, or concerned with identity will be a non-place." The ongoing tension in the relationship between place and non-place is echoed in Deleuze's definition of the crystal-image. In *Cinema 2* (2005), Deleuze argues that cinema's unique expression of time is due to the fact that film is inherently a crystal-image. The crystal-image is constructed through the repeated exchange of the virtual and the real; the image as it was recorded and passes becomes virtual, the present, as it is viewed, the real. Ida's character and the fluidity of her identity, suspended between the trauma of Poland's past and an unknowable future, exemplify this form of repetition and slow transformation, embracing the lack of definitive categorization of self and place.

Place and Absence in *Ida*

The use of non-place in *Ida* is imbued with a sense of loss, particularly in the representation of the life and death (by suicide) of Wanda Cruz, Ida's aunt, who represents the small number of Jews remaining in Łódź postwar. Wanda's isolated and despairing life in Łódź (signified by her reliance on alcohol and sexual relationships devoid of emotional connection) can be understood through the historical context of the city. The loss of Jewish culture is a phenomenon identified by David M. Smith (2000, 68) in his analysis of the postwar rebuilding of Łódź, as the "moral geography of absence," a process which accepts the disappearance of a group from the landscape of a country without acknowledging that absence. Smith continues,

> Its representation has to come to terms not only with the death of those quarter of a million, and the survival of so few, but also with the absence of evidence or even recollection that most of them ever lived.
>
> (69–70)

In 1939, Łódź had the second largest Jewish community outside of Warsaw, facing "the Second World War with a Jewish population of 230 000" (68). The majority of this population died in the Łódź ghetto, and the sealing of the ghetto in 1940 is a further horrifying image of separation and control. As Smith states, "with very few exceptions, those who avoided murder or starvation in the ghetto itself went to the death camps at Chelmno and Auschwitz" (68). The Jewish population at the end of the war numbered less than a thousand. In its reference to this absence, *Ida* is part of a current debate about the meaning and extent of Jewish spaces in Poland today, in cultural production as well as geographical locations. In *Jewish Space in Contemporary Poland,* Lehrer and Meng (2015, 1) argue that recent Polish cinema, such as the trilogy, *And Europe Will be Stunned* (Yael Bartana, 2007–2011), and *Aftermath* (Wladyslaw Pasikowski, 2012), has played a part in the project of restoring Jewish space in Poland, to "powerfully evoke spaces of not only past and present but also future Jewishness." Here the argument is for defined space to represent the presence of Jews in Poland, to overcome their absence. In contrast, the concept of non-place in *Ida* suggests a different way of conceiving of space, one which is positive in its lack of definitiveness. Where the themes of some Polish films and the restoration of Jewish religious sites, including the synagogue in Szydłów (the destination of the road trip in *Ida*), suggest an emerging presence and rediscovery of place as a recognition of identity, *Ida* posits a continued absence of the Jewish population.

Wanda's death in the film is configured as an image of absence, of non-place, but one which contains the traces of her presence, like a haunting.

Her death is almost mundane and every day: she puts on her coat as if to go to work, stubs out her cigarette, and then jumps from the apartment window. A long take emphasizes the empty room and the open window after she has jumped; the faint wisp of cigarette smoke and the continued soundtrack of Mozart's "Jupiter" symphony playing (a composition we associate with Wanda from an earlier scene in the film when she plays a recording of it) reinforce the lack of the woman who experienced them. Wanda's apartment becomes an empty space, which signifies tragedy and loss rather than optimism and change. Through the character of Wanda, *Ida* not only remembers the annihilation of the individual's identity in a specific time and place, the holocaust, but also imagines, through the mutable character of Ida, an existence free from definitive categories. This tension in the film, of respecting past identities while attempting to become free from them, is a fraught position in the context of memorialization and theories of identity. *Ida* makes absence within place central to a dissolution of identity categories, finding the concept of non-place ultimately more hopeful in its uncertainty, than places linked to territories and specifics of the past.

Postmemory Film as Crystal-Image

The central theme of *Ida*, whether it is possible to find a way of remembering the past but not to be trapped by it, is a particular concern of postmemory (Marianne Hirsch 2012). Postmemory explores the experience of the descendants of those directly affected by traumatic events, and the way in which memory is transmitted to later generations who did not experience the event itself. *Ida* explores one of the central dilemmas facing this group, identified by Eva Hoffman (2004, xv) as the "hinge generation," by the way in which they take on the survivor's memories with a force that may displace the latter's own memories and subjectivity. As Hirsch (2012) explains, such memories of trauma, which often precede one's own birth, raise profound questions around remembering the past while living in the present and the future. In this way, *Ida* can be understood as a product of postmemory[1], the subject matter positioned between the direct experience of a previous generation and an anxiety about the loss of remembrance within the later one. The concept of postmemory continually draws attention to the slippage of memory away from the object of remembrance. As Hirsch (2012, 22) argues, memories are shaped by fragments, imagination, and the interpretations of archival material, often photographs, which are partial and incomplete, "rather than giving information about the past, archival images function as 'points of memory' that tell us more about our own needs and desires, our own fantasies and fears, than about the past to which they supposedly bear witness." In *Ida*, this concept is explored in the attempt to return, through the road trip, to places which contain the past and the simultaneous need to escape them in order to live in the present and future.

The use of place in *Ida* can be understood as reflecting different states of the crystal-image (Deleuze 2005, 66) which is a central characteristic of the time-image. In the crystal-image, the present is defined as a form of entrapment, a kind of limbo which must be made transitory in order to escape into the real of the future. Deleuze characterizes the crystal-image as a continual splitting of the present into two images "one of which is launched toward the future while the other falls into the past. Time consists of this split, and it is … time, that we see in the crystal" (81). It is in this way Deleuze argues, that cinema explores the past and memory, configured through its inherent form as fleeting and subjective, a series of doubles and mirror images which confuse the distinction between the real and imaginary, actual and virtual images. Deleuze refers to the way in which characters can become trapped in the crystal-image, which is at times frozen and closed, with characters stuck, unable to move forward but continually dragged back into the past, or cracked, allowing for an escape into the future and freedom. The narrative of Ida and her aunt positions them as trapped within the crystal-image. For the character of Ida, this is due to her specific place in time, in limbo between childhood and adulthood, and because she is ignorant of her parentage and ethnicity. In contrast, Wanda is trapped by her own inability to come to terms with the past. These character narratives operate as a prism through which the effect of the past on an individual is explored in a narrative which is constructed through motifs of place. The characters' movement between these different types of place and the different roles that they undertake in them signifies, as with the relationship of time in the crystal-image, two different ways of constructing the past, one that may be fixed or one that is open to interpretation. In arguing this, the film emphasizes the power of the central character to change the past as well as her future, an interpretation which defines *Ida* as a time-image film which can be discussed in terms of the crystal-image and the relationship between the actual and virtual. The interplay between the actual and virtual is evident in the representation of the past, which is not fixed but can be rediscovered or reinvented. In the concept of the crystal-image, the future is also open to change, it is no longer preordained.

Definitive Categories of Place in *Ida*

The experience of the characters in the crystal-image is constructed in *Ida* in part through the esthetic of the film, which is shot in monochrome and the Academy 4:3 aspect ratio, with long takes and a frequently static camera. Matilda Mroz (2016) argues that the esthetic, particularly the framing of the characters low or at the edges of the frame, is part of the film's representation of absence: "...outside the boundaries of our field of vision. It is an apt rendering for the ways in which Polish-Jewish history and memory continually comes up against absence." The Academy ratio – particularly for spectators accustomed to viewing the 16:9 aspect ratio of widescreen – also signifies the past, constructing a feeling of restriction which entraps the characters, pinning them to their places. The use of the mobile camera which features at times of narrative transition is given meaning through its contrast to this enclosed space; it is the visual expression of Ida's conflict between staying in the confined, solid world of the convent or moving into undefined space of non-place.

Place in *Ida* is a series of contrasts which function symbolically through connotations of solidity and permanence as well as spaces of more abstract, tentative qualities. This function of place can be identified as characteristic of Pawlikowski's visual style and his interest in constructing settings, which gesture toward a realist style, such as being shot on location, but which are impossible to place. In discussing the choice of setting for his film *The Last Resort* (2000), a similar approach to that in *Ida* is evident. Regarding *The Last Resort* Pawlikowski explains, "every location was chosen because it wasn't quite real, or real but not real. I tried to stylise it to the point where it wasn't the real world at all" (Roberts 2002, 97). Within the crystal-image of *Ida*, the characters' relationships to place create a continual pushing and pulling in relation to the past and the future. They are placed in a state of limbo, caught between a desire to move forward against the weights of the past and its reliance on definitive categorization. Central to this is the role of the convent where Ida was sent as a child, an act that saved her life and which functions as both reassurance and prison as she chooses between leaving and remaining. The opening scenes of *Ida* take place in the convent, where the low framing and restricted screen ratio enhance the sense that the characters are trapped. The solid stone columns which surround the nuns are tactile, covered in indications of age through rough surfaces and cracks, and serve as a reminder of the past. The scenes recall the work of early Renaissance painters where earthly structures such as stone pillars frame and solidify angels and humans (see Duccio's *The Annunciation*, 1307–8, *Christ and the Samaritan Woman*, 1310–11). The structures' entrapment of the past is reinforced by the exaggerated, diegetic sound of the film. When Ida is called into the Mother Superior's office to be told that she must meet her aunt before she takes her orders, the echoes of Ida's footsteps accentuate the container-like quality of the office, a place which reverberates and surrounds the characters. The use of Ida's footsteps to symbolize the contrast between the closed and the open worlds she moves between is evident as she travels to her aunt's apartment from the convent. After gliding through the streets by tram, her footsteps are silenced as she approaches the apartment before being reinforced once more as she climbs the closed stairs to her aunt's.

Figure 13.1 The esthetic suggests the ways characters are trapped in their roles –
Wanda as a judge in *Ida* (Dir. Pawel Pawlikowski; Prod. Opus Film,
Phoenix Film Investments in association with Portobello Pictures,
co-produced by Canal+ Poland; 2012).

The solidity of place is also reinforced in the scenes showing Wanda
in her role as a Judge, where the *mise-en-scène* places her at the judicial
bench, but also as part of it. This setting, with its emphasis on texture
and solidity, appears to enfold Wanda so that the narrow plane of depth
frames her face as if she is part of the backdrop of sleek marbled tiles,
and the indentations of the studs of the chair are repeated in the chain
of office on her shoulders. The sturdiness of the *mise-en-scène*, and the
stillness of the shot, fix the character in place, immobile, suggesting the
static position of a person unable to move forward (Figure 13.1).

On the Road: Transitional Places

The definitive places of the narrative are contrasted with Ida's experience of other places as lighter and more mobile; places encountered on
the road trip, including bus stations, bars, transportation, and roads,
are represented by a moving camera and shifting patterns of light reflecting from car and bus windows. Images of glass in *Ida* are multi-
valent and carry different stages of meaning about place and space in
the film. Windows are both closed, such as at the convent where they
are opaque, but also transparent sites of openness, reminiscent of the
structure of the crystal-image. The reflections created by glass in the
tram windows, in bars and offices, signify actual and virtual states and
suggest alternative actions and experiences beyond the central characters' knowledge. Deleuze (2005, 66) identifies the use of reflection in

film – in glass, mirrors, and water – as the coalescence of the actual and virtual central to the crystal-image. The repeated use of reflections in film is an encapsulation of the trap of time in the crystal-image, which must be escaped, often through force. During Ida and Wanda's road trip, windows provide an opening out to the exterior world. As Wanda sits in a bar waiting for Ida to return from church, she is positioned in front of a picture window with the activity in the street outside clearly visible, which is a shift from the monumentality of the judge's chambers that previously surrounded her. When windows are covered, such as in Wanda's apartment and at the hotel where they stay on their road trip, it is with flimsy net-like material that creates patterns in the light, which quickly disappear. Wanda's resolve at the start of the film to reject her niece crumbles as she watches her through a window of an office where Ida is waiting for her. At the hotel, Ida's conversation with the young man, Lis, a jazz musician, who falls in love with her, is shot against a large window, its lightness reinforced by decorative fairy lights.

The monumentality and solidity of the material settings are also made more fragile through the representation of their age, to suggest the possibility of the dissolution of past certainties. Unlike the powerful structures of the institutions of State and Church seen in the settings of the court and convent, the buildings in Szydłów (the town where Ida's family had lived) and the surrounding countryside are marked with age. The static long take of the exterior of the block of flats, where the killer, Feliks[2], lives, focuses on the cracking concrete of the walls, the uneven surfaces revealing layers of work from different years. At the hospital where Feliks is dying, the paint is peeling off the frame of the bed and the walls behind him. The emphasis on the damage caused by age and the representation of time passing through inanimate objects suggest an inevitability to the destruction of place and, by association, categorization. This process is also evident in the first shots of the farm, which belonged to the Lebensteins before the war. As Wanda and Ida approach the farm, another long static take reveals the ages of the building in its different textures and materials from different periods. The crumbling materiality of the places associated with the past, the way in which they are both present and absent, is characteristic of the tension between places and their meaning in *Ida*. The transformation of place is another form of the interplay of the actual and the virtual, the real and the imagined within the crystal-image in which Ida exists and must escape from.

Movement and Stillness: A Haptic Experience of Place

The interplay between solidity and decay is reinforced by the formal construction of movement and stillness, whose contrasting nature configures the experience of entrapment in the crystal-image. An experience transmitted to the spectator through a haptic response creates the visceral sensation of being caught by place and time and the tension between the desire of escape and the temptation to remain. In *Atlas of Emotion* (2002, 16), Giuliana Bruno reclaims the notion of a haptic response to film. She argues that this viewing position has been displaced by the optical and that there needs to be a move from the "voyeur to voyager," making the spectator a traveler in a "haptic, emotive terrain." *Ida* provokes a haptic sensation; the emphasis on texture and surfaces appeals to the sense of touch and the possibility of an interaction with the physical objects. The viewer can feel the image and understand space in film through touch and movement. This response is reiterated in *Ida* by the emphasis placed on the textures of age, but also in the repeated patterns created by aspects of the physical setting. These include the curled wrought iron staircases at Wanda's apartment, which is repeated in the spiral staircase and the elaborate grille on the window at the hotel. These intricate patterns invite the viewer to trace the detail, feel the cold of the metal, and become familiar with the sensation. The use of ceramic tiles and marble walls as backdrops at the hospital and in Wanda's court also evoke the sensation of touch, creating a film world which is experienced through feeling as well as seeing. The types of object that transmit the haptic response are hard and unyielding, stating their presence in the material world. This is again in contrast to the fleeting nature of film itself; the stillness and solidity of the objects as felt by the viewer is opposed to the continually passing image, the tension between the actual and virtual of the crystal-image.

For Bruno (2002, 25), the haptic response is inextricably linked to film as a site of transition and mobility, but one which is in constant symbiotic relationship to stillness: "The moving image overcomes the death of 'still' photography. And just as it happens in the work of mourning, life moves on." This description of an infinite haptic overcoming of the stillness of the past, and of death, is very close to Deleuze's (2005, 89) definition of the crystal-image as "The two aspects, the present that passes and goes to death, the past which is preserved and retains the seeds of life, repeatedly interfere and cut into each other." Both transmit for the spectator the experience of characters caught in limbo, which Deleuze further conceptualizes in the form of the relationship between a ritornello and the gallop of motion, a relationship which has meaning through contrast. Deleuze (2005, 90) uses this concept to explain the experience of different temporalities:

> The gallop and the ritornello are what we hear in the crystal, as the two dimensions of musical time, the one being the hastening of the presents which are passing, the other the raising or falling back of the pasts which are preserved.

This ongoing conflict is a way of conceptualizing past, present, and future as sites of physical struggle, something painful but also exhilarating, a haptic response which transmits the characters' experience of temporality.

The esthetic of contrasting movement and stillness in *Ida* is linked to the construction of place and its symbolic meaning. For Deleuze (2005, 89), the editing of shots of differing durations is directly linked to the ritornello and gallop: "Whatever the speed or the slowness, the line, the tracking shot is a race, a cavalcade, a gallop. But safety comes from a ritornello which is placed or unrolls round a face, and extracts it from the line." A similar relationship is evident in *Ida* from the first narrative progression in place, when Ida leaves the convent to meet Wanda in Łódź. In contrast to the objective, static shots in the convent, Ida's journey is shot in point-of-view, traveling shots as she travels on the tram looking out at the street, which seems to flash by at speed. As Ida stares out of the tram, patterns of light and shade play across her face in constant movement, an image of a fluid and insubstantial world reflecting an open space in contrast to the past at the convent. This style of shot is repeated throughout the road trip, which Ida and her aunt take to reclaim the bodies of their family. The relationship between movement and stillness remains mobile, again without a definitive fixed point, as exemplified by the film's final shots.

The ending has been the source of differing interpretations, particularly as to whether it indicates that Ida is returning to the convent, which would suggest closure.[3] The disagreement is typical of the openness of the moment, but the ending withholds any definitive resolution to Ida's journey. The final shot is another long take, just over a minute in duration. The sensation of movement is created by the use of a handheld camera positioned in front of Ida and moving backwards as she walks toward the camera. Ida, dressed again in her novice's habit, walks down the country road, possibly toward the convent, but her destination is unclear. The composition of the shot emphasizes her distance from the past behind her, but provides no image of what lies in front of her; it is a place she never reaches in the duration of the film. The impossibility of arrival is emphasized by the occasional car that passes her, traveling in the opposite direction. In contrast to the movement of the composition, the camera focuses squarely on Ida's face, her eyeline steady, providing the safety of the ritornello. In this image of movement suspended, which is reinforced by the relationship between the reverse traveling shot counterpointing the forward movement of the character, Ida is an ambiguous figure, breaking out of the crystal-image of the past and its associated limitations, but nonetheless not moving into a new, defined place (Figure 13.2).

Figure 13.2 The final shot reinforces the openness and ambiguity of *Ida* (Dir. Pawel Pawlikowski; Prod. Opus Film, Phoenix Film Investments in association with Portobello Pictures, co-produced by Canal+ Poland; 2012); an image of non-place rather than place.

Non–place and the Future

Ida's position in the final moments of the film and the impossibility of knowing her decision – if she has made one – is characteristic of the ambiguity of the film. As has been discussed, the attempt to demarcate places and people is resisted in the film through the construction of the crystal-image and its relation to a haptic response. *Ida* further resists this categorization through the use of spaces of transition, places of movement, and mobility. These are sites of possibilities, of different versions of past and future, as well as suggesting absence and the unknown. The space of the possible and indefinable is expressed not just through connotations of mobility and stasis ascribed to the different places in the film, but also through the construction of the in-between place of the hotel, which is the pivotal location on the road trip. Hotels in cinema are often used to represent a non-place of transition and in-betweenness that encourages anonymity, the trying on of different personae, and the ability to rewrite oneself.[4] The space of the hotel has also been interpreted as a uniquely modern one, a place which continually slips between geographical locations, being difficult to categorize and locate.[5] The notion of non-delineated space in modernity has been conceptualized around a negative, a product or reflection of alienation, but also as a liminal place of transformation. In Augé's (2008, 83) view, the non-place such as that of the hotel is a liberating one;

> A person entering the space of non-place is relieved of his usual determinants. He becomes no more than what he does or experiences in the role of passenger, customer, or driver. . .. The space of non-place creates neither singular identity nor relations; only solitude, and similitude.

This conception is similar to Deleuze's (2005, 109) conception of "any-space-whatever," an open rather than closed space:

> It is a perfectly singular space, which has merely lost its homogeneity, that is, the principle of its metric relations or the connection of its own parts, so that the linkages can be made in an infinite number of ways.

The possibilities of indeterminate space are in contrast to the fixed nature of places linked to the past in *Ida*.

During the two nights at the hotel in Szydłów, which is celebrating its anniversary (a reference to traditional ways of commemorating the past), Ida adheres to her religion and novitiate training. She initially stays in her room and rejects her aunt's offer of a choice of party dresses to wear to the celebrations. Nevertheless, she goes on to discover the music of John Coltrane, develops her relationship with a possible romantic partner, Lis, and discusses the location of her family's graves with another visitor, Szymon, the son of Feliks. The hotel can be read as a seed in Deleuzian terms (2005, 81–82) because it reflects a series of alternative identities which Ida may try on before either staying within the crystal or "bursting forth" into life. The choices held out to Ida during the transition period of the hotel are reiterated later on in the film, reinforcing the idea of future possibilities, none of which are predetermined or concluded at the end of the film.

The hotel as liminal space in *Ida* is linked to the ritornello and the gallop, another site of constant movement and exchange, which has a particular relationship to the process of remembering the past. In this way, the hotel in *Ida* provides the backdrop for possible past and future interpretations; it is impossible to fix meaning. This setting reflects Ida's own position as a liminal figure in a stage of transition, which is symbolic of the hinge generation. Ida's transformative power is explored through her relationship to the liminal space of the hotel, her mobility between place and non-place, through to the final shot of the film which suspends her in a space of ambiguity. This ambiguity gives Ida a kind of freedom in her resistance to definitions. In doing this, the film suggests a way of negotiating the need to live with the trauma of the past while moving into the present and the future.

Conclusion

The non-place of the hotel personifies the film's movement from limiting categories represented through places and their associations with boundaries and division. Ambiguity imbues the film as a way of attempting to memorialize past losses without repeating the trap of categorization – of nations, religions, ethnicity, and gender – which led to them. The style of the film, in its movement between, and exploration of, place and non-place, the fixed and the mobile, is a response to the problems of conceiving of a replacement to memorializing the past through places and identity categories. Drawing on the concept of absence as an inherent feature of remembrance, *Ida* contributes to a process of remembering, which also allows a freedom from the past. Ultimately the film finds solace in the existence of the character of Ida in non-place rather than making claim to another divisive category of place and the associated markers of division.

Notes

1 Van Heuckelom and Van Otterdijk (2017, 11) argue that Ida experiences "accelerated experience of postmemory."
2 In a film where names carry symbolic meanings, the choice of Feliks, meaning happy or lucky, must be ironic.
3 Mroz (2016) argues that the film remains open; its homage to the ending of *The 400 Blows* (François Truffaut, 1959) reinforces this. By contrast, Elżbieta Durys (2015) places *Ida* in the tradition of a conservative form of melodrama, suggesting that Ida chooses patriarchy at the end of the film as she returns to the convent and Catholicism.
4 Many films use hotels' ability to signify places outside of everyday time and space to focus on transformation. Some recent examples include: *Somewhere* (Sofia Coppola, 2010), *Grand Budapest Hotel* (Wes Anderson, 2014), *The Lobster* (Yorgos Lanthimos, 2015), and *Youth* (Paolo Sorrentino, 2015).
5 In *Hotel* (2015, 6), Joanna Walsh refers to the way that the displacement in place created by hotels is evident in their names. They "...are named for elsewhere, each displaced by a city or two: The Hotel Bristol in Paris, the Hotel London in New York and in Berlin, the Hotel de Rome...."

Works Cited

Augé, Marc. 2008. *Non-places: An Introduction to Supermodernity*. 2nd ed. Translated by John Howe. London: Verso.

Bruno, Giuliana. 2002. *Atlas of Emotion: Journeys in Art, Architecture, and Film*. New York: Verso.

Deleuze, Gilles. 1986. *Cinema 1: The Movement Image*. Translated by Hugh Tomlinson, and Barbara Habberjam. London: Continuum.

————2005. *Cinema 2: The Time-Image.* Translated by Robert Galeta. London: Continuum.

Durys, Elżbieta. 2015. "History, Women, and Melodrama: Feminist Perspective on the Polish Cinema of National Remembrance." Paper presented at the Cinema and History conference, Università Roma Tre, November 2015.

European Commission. 2010. "Eur-Lex: Access to European Law." *Europa.* 20 April. Accessed November 3, 2017. http://eur-lex.europa.eu/legal-content/ EN/ALL/?uri=CELEX:52010DC0171.

Hirsch, Marianne. 2012. *The Generation of Postmemory: Writing and Visual Culture after the Holocaust.* New York: Columbia University Press.

Hoffman, Eva. 2004. *After Such Knowledge.* London: Vintage.

Lehrer, Erica, and Michael Meng. 2015. "Introduction." In *Jewish Space in Contemporary Poland*, by Eric Lehrer, and Michael Meng, 1–15. Indianapolis: Indiana University Press.

Mroz, Matilda. 2016. "Framing Loss and Figuring Grief in Pawel Pawlikowski's Ida." *Screening the Past.* Accessed August 22, 2017. http://www.screeningthepast. com/2016/10/framing-loss-and-figuring-grief-in-pawel-pawlikowskis-ida/.

Roberts, Les. 2002. "From Sarajevo to Didcot: An Interview with Pawel Pawlikowski." *New Cinemas: Journal of Contemporary Film* 1 (2): 91–97.

Smith, David M. 2000. *Moral Geographies: Ethics in a World of Difference.* Edinburgh: Edinburgh University Press.

Van Heuckelom, Kris, and Bram Van Otterdijk. 2017. "Pathways into the Past: Framing the Polish People's Republic in Two Recent Road Films (Ida and Ticket to the Moon)." *Studies in Eastern European Cinema.* 13 June. Accessed August 21, 2017. http://www.tandfonline.com/doi/full/10.1080/2040350X.2017.1336056.

Walsh, Joanna. 2015. *Hotel.* New York: Bloomsbury.

Filmography

Aftermath. Dir. Wladyslaw Pasikowski, Poland, 2012.

And Europe Will be Stunned. Dir. Yael Bartana, Poland, 2007–2011.

The 400 Blows. Dir. François Truffaut, France, 1959.

Grand Budapest Hotel. Dir. Wes Anderson, US, 2014.

Ida. Dir. Pawel Pawlikowski, Poland/Denmark/France/UK, 2012.

The Last Resort. Dir. Pawel Pawlikowski, UK, 2000.

The Lobster. Dir. Yorgos Lanthimos, Greece/Ireland/Netherlands/UK/France, 2015.

Somewhere. Dir. Sofia Coppola, US, 2010.

Youth. Dir. Paolo Sorrentino, Italy, France, UK, Switzerland, 2015.

14 Home and the Range

On the Concept of Home in Annie Proulx's Wyoming Stories

Kirsten Møllegaard

Introduction

As literary and cinematic landscape, the American West is one of the most hypermasculinized regions in the Euro-American geocultural imaginary, full of romantic nostalgia and hyperbole about "men with the bark on,"[1] and at the same time infused with cultural anxiety about the United States' violent past and chronic soul-searching ambiguity about culture, identity, and gender. The haunting history of white settlement and the displacement of Native American peoples, the politically entrenched philosophy of manifest destiny, and the unsustainable praxis of cattle ranching on the West's dry plains linger as three major historical forces that have formed, and continue to inform, the region's mythical realities.[2] In mainstream American culture, these three major historical processes are typically mediated by the textual and visual representations of the signifying sublimity of the vast, arid Western landscapes, tersely expressed by Louis L'Amour (1955, 15) in the novel *Heller with a Gun*: "It was a hard land, and it bred hard men to hard ways." Subversively, Proulx (2008a, 106) counters that classic line in the story "The Great Divide," a family saga about hardship and ranching, where a young wife, Helen, feels unwelcome in Wyoming and reflects, "it was a hard country with hard people." From L'Amour's and many other Western authors' narrative point of view, it is the Western landscape itself that breeds and hardens the American character. From Proulx's point of view, the character is hardened by lived experience and the deep-seated historical effects on socioeconomic everyday realities as they unfold in time and place.

Similar to visual art, literary representations of landscape constitute a "powerful mode of knowledge and discourse" (Daniels 1993, 8). Unlike any other kinds of American landscapes, the majestic mountains, deserts, canyons, mesas, and open spaces of the West have become intrinsically symbolic of a way of thinking and seeing nation and individual as forged by a topography imbued with cultural values and a national imaginary, which ultimately posits the United States as exceptional and celebrates the nomadic character of the cowboy as a culture hero, that is, a legendary ideal that embodies the very essence of the West. As depicted in countless Western films, this hypermasculine character is distinctly adverse to domesticity, marriage, husbandry, town life, small talk, and anything soft and feminine in general, and fiercely associated with individuality, silence, tough justice, stoicism, honesty, bravery, violent conflict resolution, guns, and rough social manners, not to mention the dirty, demanding job of wrestling cows, breaking horses, branding animals, and working outdoors in all sorts of weather for a meager salary. Domestic space is the very antithesis of the cowboy spirit, and classic Westerns like *Shane* (George Stevens, 1953) and *The Searchers* (John Ford, 1956) have the cowboy hero iconically ride away into the sunset rather than become bound to the homestead of the pioneers he has helped. The hard men bred in a hard land, as Louis L'Amour suggests, can only be who they are because they are not corrupted by the soft values, female dominance, and communal endeavors of domestic life.

This transference of the breeding of men from the sanctity of home to wild, open spaces is characteristic of the relegation of home and domesticity to a place of inferior importance in the grand narratives about the American West. Since the 1970s, the general trend in postmodern critique of grand narratives has seeped into the regionalism typically confining Western literature to a narrow ideological space and has inspired critical reassessment of the West as place and space. Neil Campbell (2007, 60) points out, "The American West as 'region' and 'idea' is heavily weighted with myth, national narrative, and cultural legacy and is without doubt the most real and imagined of American and global spaces." Postwestern literature emerges as hyperreal in the flow between what is real and what is imagined, for, as Krista Comer (2013, 11) states, "postwestern thought coheres in a sense of place as mobile and in a subject that can move and who is disjoined from static or singular or phenomenological spatial moorings." Postwestern writers relentlessly reexamine the past in the light of the present, tracing the fluctuations of histories over narrative spaces anchored in landscapes that evoke Old West nostalgia and clichés about righteousness, bravery, and manly men. Andy Meyer (2007, 207) observes,

> the codes and mythologies – indeed, the stock narratives – of the West on which writers and artists rely for their representations become more and more unreliable as globalization and various migrations disrupt the categories that organize the West as a conceptual space.

Postwestern writers, like their predecessors, often sketch Western landscapes as sentient characters and employ what Nancy Cook refers to as "big scenery" (2007, 228) and "postcard places" (2007, 229) for their visual rhetoric of grandeur, but they also keep a keen eye on narratives excluded or distorted by grand narratives: the multicultural West, women, dystopia, industrialization, xenophobia, and – in particular – the environmentally exhausted West.

Like many other postwestern writers, award-winning author Annie Proulx[3] is weary of the grand narratives that gloss the history of the American West in nostalgic sepia and define the region entirely by its geographical and symbolic grandeur. Rather than seeing American triumphalism springing from the frontier experience of the West, Proulx detects existential alienation, loss of history, and insecurity about identity. In *Bird Cloud: A Memoir*, where she chronicles the process of building her dream home in Wyoming, she observes, "the American experience, the focus on individual achievement, the acquisition of goods and money to prove one's social value, is built on this sense of loss, this alienation from the warmth of the home culture, isolation from genetic bonds" (2011, 20). In regard to her Wyoming stories, "home culture" clearly is a term pregnant with multiple meanings worth exploring, as it provides an extrapolating point of meaning in her literary representation of the American West, both past and present. This chapter will examine how the concept of home, a social and symbolic space deeply encoded with social, economic, and cultural gender constructions, informs the way Proulx's Wyoming stories represent the American West both historically and currently as a place in flux, constantly moved and destabilized over time by the effects of white settlement, manifest destiny, and unsustainable ranching methods.

"Story Comes from Place"[4]: Situating Wyoming Stories as a Corpus of Literature

Proulx's trilogy of Wyoming stories, *Close Range* (1999), *Bad Dirt* (2004), and *Fine Just the Way It Is* (2008), is an unruly, nonlinear, idiosyncratic corpus of short stories with rural Wyoming as the setting. Situated within the narrative traditions of the American West, Proulx's clipped prose and tough tone both mock and align with the sincere urgency of seminal male Western writers like Zane Grey and Owen Wister. The trilogy is difficult to categorize as a generic corpus of literature because the short stories range from fairy tales and magical realism over tall tales to social-realistic historical fiction; yet taken as a whole the collection is characteristic of Proulx's strong perception of the West as place in flux. She does not paint any definite portrait of Wyoming as a state in the union, but rather endeavors to portray Wyoming (and hence the mythic-historic American West as lived experience) "at the intersection of reality and the imagination" (Asquith 2014, 21). Breaking with the legacy of Wister and Grey and hence the pastoral conventions governing the more romantically inclined literature of the American West, Proulx's Wyoming stories create a grittily anti-pastoral vision of a region haunted by its own past, in particular by the excessive violence and exploitation of the natural environment and the hard luck of characters swept up in the nostalgia for myth and adventure, but stuck in the unforgiving quicksand of the historical present.

Commonly referred to as a "neo-regionalist" writer (Hunt 2009, 4),[5] Proulx is often grouped with writers of contemporary Western fiction like Thomas McGuane, Cormac McCarthy, Patrick DeWitt and the literary legacy they draw on to claim its "male territory as her own" (Showalter 2009, 508).[6] Other critics contextualize Proulx's writing stylistically with American naturalist writers like Frank Norris and Theodore Dreiser, her focus on everyday life and working-class Americans with John Dos Passos, and her predilection for macabre humor and grotesque characters with Flannery O'Connor (Rood 2001, 10–13). While such literary affiliations help to situate Proulx in relation to the American canon, the motley nature of her Wyoming stories, with their broad range of style and genre, is more akin to postmodern parody and pastiche, in particular in the way she contextualizes the past with the present by incorporating domestic and cultivated spatialities into the everyday experience of her characters. As such, Proulx writes within the generic tradition of the postwestern where her fiction explores "the cultural space and critical practice involving the crossings, flows, transnational circulations of a regionalism not-bounded" (Comer 2013, 11). The politics of non-bounded space are always already a subtext of her stories, ranging from the haunted history of the frontier to contemporary American expansionism and empire building, such as her frequent references to American soldiers deployed to Iraq.[7] In short, pigeonholing Proulx as a Western regional writer may be helpful in situating her narratives within a geocultural framework, but the regional label is only partially accurate. As a postwestern writer, she contributes an evocative point of view on the domestic and cultivated spaces of the American landscape that stirs deep-seated cultural memory about frontier history, the dislocation and genocide of native peoples, and the detrimental long-term environmental effects of ranching, agriculture, and mining.[8] Her writing always includes a keen sense of place as part of larger histories, of social spatialities that come and go, and the non-bounded, yet nostalgically bounded legacy of frontier mythology.

Proulx's Wyoming characters, often mockingly portrayed with withering sarcasm as xenophobic and narrow-minded, generally subscribe to a nostalgic vision of the past, but Proulx deftly places them within a social-realistic context where they have to cope with life in the New West where telecommuters, suitcase ranchers, and wealthy retirees buy up old ranches. Their homes are threatened to disappear under the iron heel of the urbanized New West. In "The Governors of Wyoming," the old rancher Hulse, who struggles with "the semiarid climate, the violent weather, government rules and dense bankers, alien weeds, the quixotic beef market, water problems, ornery fellow ranchers" (Proulx 1999d, 235), advises the cowboy Noyce, "last as long as you can, make things come out so's it's still your ranch when it's time to get buried. That's my take on it" (1999d, 237). Similarly, in "What Kind of Furniture Would Jesus Pick?" Gilbert Wolfscale, a hard-luck rancher whose cattle business is going south, tries to accept reality: "the old world was gone, he knew that" (Proulx 2004e, 62). He tries to hang on to the kind of life he is familiar with, but "by the end of the century Gilbert was fifty-five and caught in the downward ranching spiral of too much work, not enough money, drought" (2004e, 67). Desertification is destroying his grazing land and "the new-moneyed suitcase ranchers" encroach on what was once a community of homesteaders (2004e, 68). We understand that one day those weekend ranchers will be gone too, because nothing lasts in that "wild country" with its "dangerous and indifferent ground: against its fixed mass the tragedies of people count for nothing although the signs of misadventure are everywhere" (Proulx 1999h, 99).

The myth of the Old West as a place where men (white men primarily – only secondarily women and people of color) could forge their own destiny (that is, some form of the American Dream) lingers as a subtext to the ironic bare-bones realism with which Proulx disentangles, and re-entangles, the historical myths and social realities of the New West. In the New West Proulx portrays, the harsh sublimity of weathered landscapes is tempered by trailer parks and fences, provincialism and distrust of government, environmental changes and unsustainable ranching methods, and an ironic distance to the urban world of banks, businesses, and consumer trends that dictate the economic future of rural communities.

Home and Domestic Spaces in Wyoming Stories

To claim that home is a central motif in Wyoming stories may seem to contradict the geographical determinism often said to characterize Proulx's writing and her signature attention to landscape, not to mention the substantial amount of scholarship that contextualizes her narratives with regional Western literature with its characteristic focus on the great outdoors. However, Proulx does in fact devote a considerable amount of narrative focus to the concept of home, not only in tracing the domestic spaces, which forge and haunt her characters, but also by dismantling romantic concepts of home as an idyllic, safe, private retreat from a menacing world outside the protective walls of the house. Like the harsh weather tearing across the land, the domestic spaces featured in Wyoming stories offer neither solace nor reprieve from the storms of life; rather, they establish spatial boundaries and define characters in relation to one another and the surrounding landscape. In a tragic story about a young pioneer couple that did not make it, "Them Old Cowboy

Songs," Proulx sets up Rose and Archie's sinister destiny by swinging the purple prose brush: "There is no happiness like that of a young couple in a little house they built themselves in a place of beauty and solitude" (2008b, 50). With her signature ironic narrative twist, Proulx soon dismantles the young couple's rural idyll and exposes the dangers of a solitary abode. Archie must find work far away from home and ends up freezing to death in a line shack. Rose dies alone in childbirth, doubly trapped in the domestic confinement of the house and in the reproductive destiny of her body.

In Proulx's rural Wyoming, home is just as much a space of entrapment as she portrays marriage to be and actually often doubles as a metaphor for matrimonial space and the ghosts that loom over married life. One such ghostly haunt appears in "The Indian Wars Refought." A well-off widow, Georgina, unexpectedly marries her ranch foreman, Charlie, who not only is much younger than her, but also has been married twice before. She learns that he has a daughter, Linny, who is

> in her early twenties and apparently a pure Nevada hellcat who had already been the recipient of two unwanted pregnancies. Linny was coming to live with them, Charlie Parrott told his widow-bride. A flash of distaste crossed her features. She covered up quickly with a grand smile. "Well, it'll be nice to have another woman on the place," she said, but with some acid, as if remarking that it would be nice to have more rattlesnakes.
>
> (Proulx 2004b, 25)

As a twist on the old adage about the bad luck of having two women under one roof, Georgina soon learns that blood is thicker than water and finds herself outmaneuvered by Linny, and becomes a stranger in her own home. Proulx's bitter irony is that Georgina, being white, from a historical perspective indeed is a stranger in the West, which is the home of Charlie and Linny's ancestors, the Oglala Sioux, who two hundred years earlier had been forced away from their ancestral homelands in Minnesota due to American settlers' westward expansion. Such historical ripple effects inform Proulx's description of the West as a place always in flux, and where the concept of home consequently is fleeting and slippery.

Two aspects of home stand out in Proulx's Wyoming stories: one is the instability of home as a place of shelter, love, stability, nurture, and comfort vis-à-vis a hard world of work, an inhospitable environment, bad weather, big government, and crippling economic fluctuations. The second aspect, more abstractly, derives from the first and situates the concept of home as sociospatial catalyst for the complex relationship between humans, their geographical environment, and the social and historical conditions that govern their lives. Proulx's stories revolve around the concept of home as a Thirdspace, an elsewhere or place apart from the harsh landscape and yet a part of it. According to Edward Soja – who is inspired by Henri Lefebvre – Thirdspace straddles both perceived and imagined space. "Thirdspace is a purposefully tentative and flexible term that attempts to capture what is actually a constantly shifting and changing milieu of ideas, events, appearances, and meanings" (Soja 1996, 2). The concept of home shifts over time. As Mary Douglas (1991, 289) observes, "home is located in space, but it is not necessarily a fixed space." Whatever material structure the home has, be it a ranch house, a cabin, a bunkhouse, or a trailer, domestic space is segregated from the outside by the structure of the building and the rituals of food preparation, sleeping arrangements, sexual relations, and the hierarchies and norms for social interaction. "A home is a tangle of conventions and totally incommensurable rights and duties" (Douglas 1991, 302). In Proulx's stories, those rights and duties are more likely to teach her characters just to "stand" their problems rather than to "fix" them. This mantra is often repeated in "Brokeback Mountain": "if you can't fix it you've got to stand it" (1999a, 285), and it extends to the pessimism pervading her description of violations occurring in oppressive domestic spaces. In "Job History," for example, a young girl is sexually abused by her employer while she babysits. Her mother "advises her to keep quiet," because the man is her father's friend, and "they hunt elk and antelope together" (1999c, 88). The mother thus prioritizes the household's economic need for game to supplement their food supply above seeking justice for her daughter. In this way, Proulx's characters seldom have the courage or means to "fix" or substantially change domestic patterns of oppression. Rather, their stoicism is often a mask for "standing" it.

Proulx always places her portrayal of a home in a historical and geographical context, thus triangulating domestic space with both smooth and striated movements of culture and history through time. For example, "The Bunchgrass Edge of the World" begins with the deceptive illusion of the Western landscape as "empty ground," a "vague region" with unmarked graves and "fallen house timbers and corrals burned up in old campfires" (1999b, 121). Proulx then outlines the Touheys' ranching dynasty, starting with its founder, Old Red, and eventually getting to the core of the story, which revolves around Old Red's monstrous granddaughter Ottaline, "distinguished by a physique approaching the size of a hundred-gallon propane tank" and her yearning that someone would come for her and take her away from the ranch (1999b, 125). Like an unloved Cinderella entrapped in servitude and misery at home, Ottaline works on the ranch. Proulx underscores the corporeality of Ottaline's unhappiness as proportional to her body weight by describing a photo of her sister Shan, who had moved to Las Vegas and become a body builder. The photo shows Shan "in a black bikini, greased muscles starkly outlined, exhibiting bulging biceps and calves, spiky crewcut hair whitened with bleach" (1999b, 127–28). Shan is in control of her own body and enjoys life in the big city, while Ottaline "had eaten from a plateful of misery since childhood, suffered avoirdupois, unfeeling parents, the hard circumstances of the place" (1999b, 132). Her father will not let her drive his truck or leave the ranch. He tells her that "she had better stay on the ranch where she didn't know how good she had it" (1999b, 129). Suffering from "minstrel," that is, menstrual or gynecological, problems likely related to Old Red's sexual abuse of her when she was only four years old, Ottaline longs for romantic love and voyeuristically eavesdrops on other people's "cell-phone conversations on the scanner" (1999b, 131). "It made her jealous to hear those quarrelsome but coupled voices" (1999b, 134). Meanwhile, it suits her parents just fine that she cannot get off the ranch. It saves them from hiring labor.

In Proulx's short stories, home is never a fixed space. Rather, home is a concept fraught with anxiety about belonging. Interestingly, although home is often considered a feminine space, Proulx's stories suggest that home is a "social space that can no longer be imagined simply in terms of a territory of gender" (Gillian Rose quoted in Soja 1996, 124). It is a place of self-actualization and resistance. When Gilbert Wolfscale's mother dies, he despairs: "With his mother gone, civilization began to fall away from him as feathers from a molting hen. In a matter of weeks he was eating straight from the frying pan" (Proulx 2004e, 80). This easy association between civilization and kitchen etiquette is completely subverted in other stories. "The Wamsutter Wolf," for instance, describes in nauseating detail the interior of the Whams' trailer home kitchen, which "stank of cigarettes, garbage, and feces" (2004d, 152), and features a toddler who drinks dregs from beer cans littering the floor, "an alcoholic even before hitting kindergarten" (2004d, 156). Proulx avoids the cliché of portraying the kitchen as an exclusively feminine, civilized space. In "The Wamsutter Wolf," which is told from the point of view of a male neighbor, the drunk child's mother is as slovenly as she is promiscuous, and the chaos of the trailer home mirrors the devastation of the exhausted landscape surrounding the trailer park and its transient inhabitants, "tough as nails and restless, going where the dollars grew" (2004d, 148).

Soja (1996, 70) acknowledges the slipperiness of Thirdspace, calling it "disorderly, unruly, constantly evolving, unfixed, never presentable in permanent constructions," which at a different epistemological level are terms that may very well be applied to Proulx's unruly collection of Wyoming stories itself and the way it resists to tell a grand narrative about the West. The fragmented nature of the stories as a literary unit suggests such resistance. Thirdspace combines spatiality with sociality and historicality. Like Proulx, Soja is interested in the production of human identity (he uses the term "becoming") as formed in historical, social, and spatial environments. Proulx's West is crisscrossed by many migration tracks, from Native American to New York yuppies who drive their Infiniti across the trails of "oxcart emigrants" (Proulx 2004c, 95), and so are the homes they live and die in, built on land that was once a prehistoric sea, now stone and dirt, and where "nothing is finished" (Proulx 1999e, 203).

Philosopher Gaston Bachelard (1964, 37) famously ascribes to the family house "powers of protection against the forces that besiege it," while anthropologist Mary Douglas (1991, 287) in contrast criticizes the "tyranny of home," pointing out that "happiness is not guaranteed in a home" (1991, 289). Proulx makes this contrast of what home is perceived to be painfully clear in stories that include abandonment or abuse of children. In "Dump Junk," for example, Rose Clover's "brother Clay, eight years older than she, had sexually assaulted her from the time she was five until she left home" (Proulx 2004a, 196–97). The emotions and affective memories raised by Bachelard's and Douglas' contrasting perceptions of home point to the paradox that domestic space simultaneously occupies an elsewhere in relation to the world around it, and at the same time it is a space that produces social identity under the influence of hegemonic pressures adapted from the outside. As a case in point, in the story "Tits-Up in a Ditch," the protagonist Dakotah is abandoned by her mother and grows up in the unloving home of her grandparents. Yet, when she herself becomes a mother, she, in turn, leaves her son with her grandparents while she serves in "Eye-rack" (2008c, 203), that is, Iraq, a decision that proves fatal for her child who is killed in an avoidable accident because her grandfather believes that "not being constrained by a seat belt was the pioneer spirit of freedom" (2008c, 189). Dakotah's decision to serve in the military is based on her inability to find a full-time job in her home area that will allow her to support her child. The hard luck following Proulx's characters is obviously absurd, but also eerily realistic. Rather than being in control of their own destinies, her characters are fooled by the rhetoric of the Old West and struggle under the influence of economic and structural forces beyond their own domain.

Broken marriages and contested fatherhood dominate in several stories, typically forcing juveniles to leave home and do adult work because of absent, abusive, or incompetent parents, or simply because home entraps and suffocates rather than nurtures and enables. In "The Mud Below," aspiring rodeo rider Diamond Felts returns to his disapproving mother's house to nurse a hand injury. She is furious that he chose bronc riding instead of a college degree; he, in turn, is resentful that she – as he sees it – drove away his father, who upon departing the family home informed Diamond, "Not your father and never was" (1999f, 67). In the absence of his father, Diamond tries to assert his authority as the man of the house, but quickly learns that home is a place where time stands still. No matter his accomplishments in the hypermasculine world of bronc riding, his mother still rules the home with supreme authority and vengeful spite, saddling him with dishwashing chores, and nagging him to give up rodeo life. "It was as if he'd never left" (1999f, 56).

Their arguments take place in the kitchen, the very heart and hearth of the home, and Proulx's preferred setting for indoor scenes. It is also the very space where indoor versus outdoor behavior becomes most apparent, and where dirt is the most symbolic. Even on a ranch where dirt is everywhere outside the house, dirt becomes matter-out-of-place once it crosses the threshold to the house. Not only is the second installment in the Wyoming stories trilogy entitled *Bad Dirt*, dirt also comes to define a certain state of disengagement from acceptable norms and conventions. In "Pair a Spurs," the unsavory description of an unwashed, incontinent, widowed old rancher lays the foundation for seeing how Car Scrope's kitchen has turned into a "boar's nest" after his wife left him (1999g, 166). He "couldn't explain the lonesome gnaw a clean kitchen brought him" because a tidy, orderly kitchen reminds him of the wife who left him for another man (1999g, 166). As Mary Douglas points out, dirt in whatever actual or symbolic form (mud, dust, and excrement, or dirty language, looks, and thoughts) represents something disorderly and dangerous that can soil, contaminate, and threaten the order of the house. The abundance of dirty and messy kitchens in Wyoming stories signifies the chaos invading and distorting the characters' lives.

But dirt is not just manure-caked boots tracking mud on a clean kitchen floor. Dirty language and sexual misconduct also contaminate the sanctity of home. "You keep your dirty old prong away from my girls or I'll pour boilin water on it," Ottaline's mother threatens Old Red, when she catches him holding the squirming four-year-old Ottaline astride his lap (1999b, 124). In other stories, for example "People in Hell Just Want a Drink of Water" and "Brokeback Mountain," men castrate other men for perceived sexual misconduct; however, with a housewife approach to castigating sexual offense and cleansing her domestic space, Ottaline's mother threatens to sterilize the dirty old man with a domestic means of disinfection: boiling water. In "The Mud Below," Diamond uses foul language and his little brother Pearl is "excited by the forbidden words and the low-down grammar spoken in their mother's kitchen. He expected to see the floor tiles curl and smoke" (1999f, 57). This image of the kitchen floor catching hellfire because of Diamond's disrespect for his mother's rules brings to mind the frigid kitchen scene in Ang Lee's 2006 film adaptation of "Brokeback Mountain," where Ennis asks Jack's parents for permission to spread Jack's ashes on Brokeback Mountain. The kitchen's naked, shabby, white-washed walls, where Jack's nervous mother hovers by the sink while his rigid, hostile father is seated at the table, make this scene a powerful metaphor for the dynamics of Jack's home and upbringing. In the novella, the coldness of the kitchen scene reminds Ennis of a story Jack told him of how his father beat him as a child. Hidden in the closet in Jack's childhood room, Ennis discovers his own old shirt from Brokeback Mountain tucked into Jack's shirt, "the pair like two skins, one inside the other, two in one" (1999a, 283). The forbidden erotic imagery evoked by the two shirts is of course accentuated by the fact that Jack hid them in the closet, meaning the domestic hiding place for his true identity as a gay man, which his father did not accept.

There is no fixity of home in Wyoming stories. Like the weather-beaten Wyoming landscapes – "indigo jags of mountain, grassy plain everlasting, tumbled stones like fallen cities, the flaring roll of the sky" (Proulx 1999h, 99) – characterizing the story collection, the concept of home is weighted with a highly gendered discourse on the social production of feminine and masculine spaces, hopes and dreams thwarted by reality, public versus private interests, settlement versus migration. Like the homes they build, Proulx's characters are transient existences under the vast movement of weather and landscapes over time. Proulx's concept of home nestles between the real and the imaginary and hangs suspended in her narratives as an indicator of her characters' existential fragmentation and sense of loss.

Conclusion

The trilogy of Wyoming stories forms a meandering collection of gritty, occasionally quirky and humorous, but often vitriolic and uncannily violent short stories that demythologize the romantic aura of the Old West and Western masculinity through the leitmotifs of identity (especially gender and sexual identity) and spaces of belonging amidst the tough, unforgiving landscapes of Wyoming.

Wyoming stories operate with the Old and New American West as geocultural imaginaries richly imbedded with cultural symbols and perceptions about borders, spaces, territoriality, sovereignty, settlement, and the ways in which humans establish individual and collective identity in relationship to Western landscapes. As Simon Schama (1996, 61) points out, landscapes are "culture before they are nature, constructs of the imagination projected unto wood and water and rock." Seen this way, Proulx's Wyoming stories can be read as postwestern narratives, a term which according to Krista Comer (2013, 11) invokes "the cultural space and critical practice involving the crossings, flows, transnational circulations, of a regionalism not-bounded." Critics generally agree that Proulx escapes the dearth of the "regional writer trap" (Asquith 2014, 31) because her narratives portray the hyperreal New West that is continuously in cultural flux between past and present. Margaret E. Johnson (2009, 26) argues that "the hyperreality that is present in the dramatically realistic landscape and natural environment of the West exposes the fragmentation and ethical uncertainly that underlie [Proulx's] work and characterize it as distinctly postmodern." As a corpus of postwestern narratives, Proulx's Wyoming stories go beyond the limitations of the binaries of home versus open landscape and female domestic space versus male public space, and instead posit Western places (including the concept of home) as changing and evolving textual spaces, both striated and nomadic as Gilles Deleuze and Félix Guattari (1987, 474–500) have argued, both real and imagined as Soja (1996) claims, and both regional and transnational as theorists of postwestern culture (Krista Comer 2013; Neil Campbell 2007) believe. Proulx's trilogy posits home as a loaded cultural signifier for the social spaces and structures that forge her characters' identities. It is home that enables or disables her characters' ability to either "fix" or "stand" whatever life throws at them.[9] The predominance in her short stories of abusive, tension-filled home environments delivers a scorching portrait of the emotional and economic ruin of the rural household under the weight of what Proulx posits as the manifest destiny of patriarchal institutions and late capitalism in Western landscapes of failure.

Notes

1 *Men with the Bark On* (1900) is the title of famed Western illustrator and sculptor Frederic Remington's memoir. Proulx's novel, *Barkskins* (2016), plays on the association between rough bark and masculinity.

2 In *Myth and Meaning*, Claude Lévi-Strauss (1979, 43) famously argues that "history has replaced mythology and fulfills the same function," namely to create order and hence meaning in the world. Marshall Sahlins (1981), from whose book title *Historical Metaphors and Mythical Realities: Structure in the Early History of the Sandwich Islands Kingdom* I borrow the term "mythical realities," essentially agrees. The dichotomy between myth and history masks the overlap between the two and erroneously constructs myth as false and history as true, a logical either-or fallacy of wide-ranging epistemological impact on the way the American West is represented in cinema and literature.

3 Annie Proulx's many literary awards include the PEN/Faulkner Award (1993), the National Book Award (1993), the Pulitzer Prize (1994), and the 2002 WILLA Literary Award for Women Writing the West.

4 In an interview with the *Paris Review*, Christopher Cox (2009, n.p.) asks Proulx, "Do you start writing a story with the setting in mind?" Proulx replies, "Always, yea. It's the place that interests me, and the social and economic situation in a place – how people live, how they make their living, the culture – but the story comes from place."

5 Proulx herself resists getting labeled as writing within that tradition. In the *Paris Review* interview, Christopher Cox (2009, n.p.) asks her, "When you started writing the Wyoming Stories, did you feel any need to get acquainted with the tradition of writing about the American West?" Proulx scuffs, "Why the hell would I do that? That's not a tradition. [. . .] Writing about the American West is just like writing about the American East or wherever." With this remark Proulx may indicate that her writing about the West does not differ in style or technique compared to her writings about Newfoundland and the American North East.

6 Elizabeth Abele (2009, 114) categorizes Proulx with Rick Bass, Richard Ford, Jim Harrison, and Ron Hansen.

7 The war in Iraq, or the Second Persian Gulf War, 2003–2011.

8 Proulx's literary works range from the New England and Newfoundland settings of *Heart Songs and Other Stories* (1988) and *The Shipping News* (1993) to the accidental and irrational journeys across the continent in

Postcards (1992) and *Accordion Crimes* (1996) to the Texas panhandle in
That Old Ace in the Hole (2002). *Barkskins* (2016) is a sweeping saga of the
transformation of North America's wilderness by logging.
9 "But if you can't fix it you got a stand it," says Ennis to Jack in "Brokeback
Mountain" (1999a, 271).

Works Cited

Abele, Elizabeth. 2009. "Westward Proulx: The Resistant Landscapes of *Close Range: Wyoming Stories* and *That Old Ace in the Hole.*" In *The Geographical Imagination of Annie Proulx,* edited by Alex Hunt, 113–25. Lanham, MD: Lexington Books.

Asquith, Mark. 2014. *The Lost Frontier: Reading Annie Proulx's Wyoming Stories.* New York: Bloomsbury.

Bachelard, Gaston. 1964. *The Poetics of Space.* Translated by Maria Jolas. New York: Orion Press.

Campbell, Neil. 2007. "Critical Regionalism, Thirdspace, and John Brinckerhoff Jackson's Western Cultural Landscapes." In *Postwestern Cultures: Literature, Theory, Space,* edited by Susan Kollin, 59–81. Lincoln, NE: University of Nebraska Press.

Comer, Krista. 2013. "Introduction: Assessing the Postwestern." *Western American Literature* 48 (1 & 2): 3–15.

Cook, Nancy. 2007. "The Romance of Ranching; or, Selling Place-Based Fantasies in and of the West." In *Postwestern Cultures: Literature, Theory, Space,* edited by Susan Kollin, 223–43. Lincoln, NE: University of Nebraska Press.

Cox, Christopher. 2009. "Annie Proulx. The Art of Fiction No. 199." *Paris Review* 188 (Spring).

Daniels, Stephen. 1993. *Fields of Vision: Landscape Imagery and National Identity in England and the United States.* London: Polity.

Deleuze, Gilles and Félix Guattari. 1987. *A Thousand Plateaus: Capitalism and Schizophrenia.* Translated by Brian Massumi. Minneapolis, MN: University of Minnesota Press.

Douglas, Mary. 1991. "The Idea of Home: A Kind of Space." *Social Research* 58 (1): 287–307.

Hunt, Alex. 2009. "Introduction: The Insistence of Geography in the Writing of Annie Proulx." In *The Geographical Imagination of Annie Proulx*, edited by Alex Hunt, 1–11. Lanham, MD: Lexington Books.

Johnson, Margaret E. 2009. "Proulx and the Postmodern Hyperreal." In *The Geographical Imagination of Annie Proulx*, edited by Alex Hunt, 25–38. Lanham, MD: Lexington Books.

L'Amour, Louis. 1955. *Heller with a Gun.* Greenwich, CN: Fawcett.

Lévi-Strauss, Claude. 1979. *Myth and Meaning. Cracking the Code of Culture.* New York: Schocken Books.

Meyer, Andy. 2007. "'Might be Going to Have Lived': The West in the Subjunctive Mood." In *Postwestern Cultures: Literature, Theory, Space*, edited by San Kollin, 201–22. Lincoln, NE: University of Nebraska Press.

Proulx, Annie. 1999. *Close Range: Wyoming Stories.* New York: Scribner.

——— 1999a. "Brokeback Mountain." In *Close Range: Wyoming Stories*, 253–85. New York: Scribner.

———— 1999b. "The Bunchgrass Edge of the World." In *Close Range: Wyoming Stories*, 119–48. New York: Scribner.

———— 1999c. "Job History." In *Close Range: Wyoming Stories*, 83–89. New York: Scribner.

———— 1999d. "The Governors of Wyoming." In *Close Range: Wyoming Stories*, 211–47. New York: Scribner.

———— 1999e. "A Lonely Coast." In *Close Range: Wyoming Stories*, 189–207. New York: Scribner.

———— 1999f. "The Mud Below." In *Close Range: Wyoming Stories*, 41–80. New York: Scribner.

———— 1999g. "Pair a Spurs." In *Close Range: Wyoming Stories*, 149–86. New York: Scribner.

———— 1999h. "People in Hell Just want a Drink of Water." In *Close Range: Wyoming Stories,* 99–117. New York: Scribner.

———— 2004. *Bad Dirt: Wyoming Stories 2*. New York: Scribner.

———— 2004a. "Dump Junk." In *Bad Dirt: Wyoming Stories 2*, 187–206. New York: Scribner.

———— 2004b. "The Indian Wars Refought." In *Bad Dirt: Wyoming Stories 2*, 15–46. New York: Scribner.

———— 2004c. "Man Crawling Out of Trees." In *Bad Dirt: Wyoming Stories 2,* 93–124. New York: Scribner.

———— 2004d. "The Wamsutter Wolf." In *Bad Dirt: Wyoming Stories 2*, 143–76. New York: Scribner.

———— 2004e. "What Kind of Furniture Would Jesus Pick?" In *Bad Dirt: Wyoming Stories 2*, 59–86. New York: Scribner.

———— 2008. *Fine Just the Way It Is: Wyoming Stories 3*. New York: Scribner.

———— 2008a. "The Great Divide." In *Fine Just the Way It Is: Wyoming Stories 3*, 93–120. New York: Scribner.

———— 2008b. "Them Old Cowboy Songs." In *Fine Just the Way It Is: Wyoming Stories 3*, 45–78. New York: Scribner.

———— 2008c. "Tits Up in a Ditch." In *Fine Just the Way It Is: Wyoming Stories 3*, 177–221. New York: Scribner.

———— 2011. *Bird Cloud: A Memoir*. New York: Scribner.

Rood, Karen L. 2001. *Understanding Annie Proulx*. Columbia, SC: University of South Carolina Press.

Schama, Simon. 1996. *Landscape and Memory*. New York: Knopf.

Showalter, Elaine. 2009. *A Jury of Her Peers: American Women Writers from Anne Bradstreet to Annie Proulx*. New York: Knopf.

Soja, Edward. 1996. *Thirdspace: Journeys to Los Angeles and Other Real-and-Imagined Places*. Malden, MA: Blackwell.

Filmography

Brokeback Mountain. Dir. Ang Lee, USA, 2006.

Shane. Dir. George Stevens, USA, 1953.

The Searchers. Dir. John Ford, USA, 1956.

15 Narratives of Water

Changing Places and Contested Spaces in Swedish Literature

Joanna Wilson-Scott

Introduction

In recent years, Scandinavian crime novels have garnered tremendous international success, particularly so since the 1990s. Beyond their commercial accomplishments, narrative mysteries, and textual intrigue, such works are also of cultural significance, existing as compelling narratives of place that represent their respective countries, both culturally and topographically, to the wider international audience. In the context of Scandinavian crime fiction, place is a "semantically rich site of representation and contestation" (Nestingen and Arvas 2011, 13), and novels produced by Swedish authors are no exception. Through their "frequent expressive use of [Sweden's] wide open terrain, and its crowded cities, dotted amidst vast woodlands" (Peacock 2014, 99), Swedish crime authors use space and place to provide insights into their society and its continual evolution in an increasingly globalized world.

Writer and journalist Barry Forshaw has written compellingly on the general topic of Scandinavian crime fiction, seeing it as a form of "death in a cold climate," to borrow the title of his 2012 study. Beyond temperature, however, is the issue of topography, and a common element that characterizes the landscape of Swedish crime fiction is the presence of water. After all, as Steven Peacock points out, there are endless possibilities in Swedish crime novels to use "the vast open spaces of the country and countryside as voids into which people can vanish" (2014, 105), and lakes, rivers, and the sea provide fertile opportunities to juxtapose the scenic with the brutal. This chapter retains a focus on the geographical nature of Swedish crime fiction by exploring examples of death by water in a selection of novels, and by taking a literal approach to Jakob Stougaard-Nielsen's description of the "liquid" nature of Scandinavian crime fiction, in which "the very landmarks [...] take liquid form" (2017, 114). In doing so, the work takes an ecocritical approach to the use of water symbolism and its ability to narrativize change, looking specifically at literal examples of liquidity: rivers, lakes, and the sea. As an element of real and literary landscapes, water has the ability to signify change through its fluidity, narrativizing both sociocultural spaces and idealized places. When flowing and fresh, literary depictions of water can serve to exemplify change, although not necessarily stability, but when stagnant or frozen there is the implication of a resistance to change. Water can thus represent unity or disunity, as well as openness or insularity, which is particularly relevant since the geography of Sweden is "informed by an isolationism complicated by borderline closeness to others" (Peacock 2014, 102). Water can be both bridge and barrier, connecting places via ferry and shipping routes, but also separating or cutting through bodies of land. Water symbolism is additionally caught up in dialogues about life and death, making it a particularly useful lens to explore contemporary Swedish crime novels.

Murders occurring in or near water in Swedish crime fiction pre-date the voracious international appetite for Scandinavian crime novels that has arisen since the 1990s, with earlier examples including Maj Sjöwall and Per Wahlöö's first novel in their Martin Beck series, *Roseanna* (1965), in which the body of a young American tourist is found in the Göta Canal. Since then, novels by internationally recognized authors such as Mari Jungstedt, Camilla Läckberg, Stieg Larsson, Henning Mankell, Liza Marklund, Håkan Nesser, and Johan Theorin have featured deaths by water, often in quiet seaside, island, or lake towns. The focus of this chapter is on the use of water and death in Swedish crime novels to represent change, including both ecological and sociological transitions. There is, for Peacock, "the aura of a Scandinavian mood traced through the relationship between landscape, characters, and national sensibility" (2014, 102), and this is clearly realized in the juxtaposition of nature and violence in Swedish crime fiction. The "rich and atmospheric" essence of Swedish crime novels (Forshaw 2012, 1) allows for an ecocritical exploration of literary representations of water, one that uses nature to consider the way in which liquid places have the capacity to provoke consideration of both change and permanence within a national and cultural context, and how they challenge and even deconstruct, when presented as the site of death, notions of a rural, utopian ideal. Sweden is a country arguably as much defined by water as it is by the land, with centuries of nautical prowess and exploration expanding its actual and imaginary borders, and topographically characterized by lakes and its extensive coastline. Thus, this chapter explores what such a connection between water and death means in this specific context, and how the combination of the two is used metaphorically to represent social change in Sweden around the turn of the millennium, with the country increasingly becoming what Mary Louise Pratt (1992) termed the "contact zone."

In order to explore violence and death by water in Swedish crime fiction, a selection of novels by Henning Mankell, Kerstin Ekman, Camilla Läckberg, and Stieg Larsson, published in the years leading up to, including, and immediately following the turn of the millennium, are used as lenses through which to explore water symbolism and its ability to convey a sense of the Swedish landscape while probing into pertinent issues of social change around the turn of the century. The first is Mankell's *Faceless Killers* (1991), the initial novel in what was to become his popular Kurt Wallander series. In the text, violence begets violence in close proximity to the sea, and the crimes are the result of the meeting of disparate peoples, reminiscent of Pratt's contact zone, and a clash between nostalgic notions of the old, idealized Sweden, and the new, multicultural Sweden. Two years later, Kerstin Ekman published her novel *Blackwater*, an example of ecofiction that is more commonly discussed in academic circles in relation to its focus on the forest and the effects that systematic deforestation has had on the Swedish landscape. However, it is also a novel in which water plays an integral role, in the description of place and as a site of violence, as both the English title and original Swedish title *Händelser vid vatten* ("Events by water") suggest.

Whereas Ekman stages her story in the fictional town of Blackwater, located in the forested landscape of the northern province of Jämtland, Mankell's novel is set in Skåne, in and around the far southern, provincial, and coastal town of Ystad, a busy port bordered by the Baltic Sea, and thus both places are heavily shaped by their close proximity to water. This theme of death by water is also found in novels written in the twenty-first century, including Camilla Läckberg's *The Ice Princess* (2003), set in the fishing village of Fjällbacka and involving the discovery of a corpse in a frozen bathtub of water, and Stieg Larsson's *The Girl with the Dragon Tattoo* (2005), in which murder and the concealment of corpses take place in the waters around the fictional Hedeby Island in Norrland.

Collectively, these four novels form the analytical basis of this chapter, as they explicitly involve violent death in the vicinity of water. However, before exploring them in more detail, it is useful to consider an example outside of the crime genre in order to think about the ways in which water can be used by Swedish writers to establish their novels as narratives of place that comment upon both the Swedish landscape and Swedish society. As such, this chapter begins by looking at Mikael Niemi's *Popular Music from Vittula* (2000), in which water is personified in a manner that intricately connects it with Swedish society, fusing the people and the landscape as one. This chapter will then consider Larsson's *The Girl with the Dragon Tattoo* in order to introduce the link between death and water in Swedish crime novels. Following this, an analysis of Läckberg's *The Ice Princess*, Ekman's *Blackwater*, and Mankell's *Faceless Killers* will allow for an examination of the fusion of water, death, and change in Swedish literature, providing the basis for the argument that the combination of these three elements allows for an exploration of changing places and contested spaces in Sweden, and the existence of contact zones. Finally, this chapter will consider how water can also be used to signify resistance to change, as in some instances death in Swedish crime fiction occurs in or around stagnant water, suggestive of a reticence in the face of cultural and social progression.

Transforming and Uniting People and Place

Mikael Niemi's *Popular Music from Vittula* is a *Bildungsroman* set in the far northern municipality of Pajala, close to the Finnish border, and it is simultaneously a narrative of place and of adolescence. Matti, the young protagonist at the center of the narrative, is intricately connected to the landscape in which he lives, as both undergo change and transformation. The description Matti provides of a melting river of ice in spring serves as a particularly useful example when considering water's ability to signify change in Swedish literature, both ecologically in the transformation of the wintery and frozen landscape, and sociologically, as the icy river is presented as a metaphor for Swedish society. Not only is the change witnessed by the local community, who rush to observe the melting ice, but the river itself is presented as a living organism, and described in a distinctly personified manner:

> And now, at this very moment, the river breathes in and its ribcage expands, pressing up against its three-feet-thick case, filling lungs and blood vessels like an escape artist intent on breaking out, digging in its heels, swelling up, slowly forcing up thousands upon thousands of icy tons, inch by inch.
>
> (Niemi 2000, 109)

The explicit corporeal depiction and personification of a frozen river beginning to melt, complete with anatomical metaphors, emphasizes a change that is inherently social and inextricably bound with the fate of humanity, one that fuses the Swedish landscape with the Swedish people who, as we shall see, are present when the ice begins to melt. Furthermore, change is implied as violent, filled with force and effort, indicated by the connotation of escape and freedom, with the icy past a heavy weight that needs to be lifted in order for the river to be released. The violence of this change is made all the more explicit through imagery that depicts a thunderous fracturing of the wintery landscape:

> Then it happens. Two terse crackling sounds. And then the snow-white surface splits asunder, crackling and splintering. A torrent of black water. A rumbling, new cracks, shattering axe-blows all over the mass of ice. Swelling blisters split open. Movement everywhere, everything starts moving. The whole of this incredible marble floor.
>
> (Niemi 2000, 109)

The breaking of the solid surface of ice to reveal the moving and fluid water beneath is not depicted as a smooth transition, but instead is harsh, abrupt, and violent, enhanced through fragmented sharp sentences and vivid onomatopoeias, as well as through graphic images of "shattering axe-blows" and "blisters splitting open." The water, as the "escape artist," has been trapped beneath the ice, but in breaking free of it the purity of the "snow-white [...] marble floor" is replaced by a "torrent of black water," something that is new and different: the rush of water and the fragmentation of the ice indicate that spring has arrived, and with it both opportunity and uncertainty.

Yet aside from being arduous, difficult, and initially violent, such change is not depicted as negative, as despite the force of the event, winter has simply ended and spring has begun, and with it "everything starts moving." The fragmentation and total destruction of the static and unmoving ice create a powerful force that cannot be held back, and one that affects and unites the whole of society:

> Then the locals arrive. Park at the end of the bridge and come running out to join us, lining up along the iron railings; old men and old women, young lads and young lasses and little girls and tiny tots held tightly onto. Cousins and neighbours and old pals and even solitaries, as if the river had gone around the village and bade them all to attend, as if they'd all gotten the urge at the same time.
>
> (Niemi 2000, 110)

So, despite the natural occurrence of a river breaking free from winter's grip, the change being described is one of anthropological or sociological rather than ecological interest. Change is depicted as social, violent, and unstoppable, and affecting the whole of society, from the oldest to the youngest members, and regardless of the passivity of individuals. The river has "bade them all to attend," forced them to acknowledge and witness the change, even the so-called "solitaries," swept along in the rush of movement and the sense of community. Change is not something exclusive or privileged, but rather it unites the local community in its inevitability.

These excerpts from Niemi's novel exemplify how water, under the influence of seasonal transformations, can metaphorically be used to represent cyclical changes, uniting the people who come to witness the event. But beyond this, the observers are inextricably connected with the Swedish landscape, one that is personified in order to establish it metaphorically as an element of society. The link between the residents of Pajala and the melting river indicates a wider coming together that extends beyond the confines of this specific locale, suggesting an intimate fusion of the Swedish land and the Swedish people. And given that the novel is a *Bildungsroman*, despite the melting river being an annual event, this particular scene carries more weight due to its connection with the protagonist's own personal changes, steps into the adult world, and progression toward an awareness of what it means to be part of Swedish society.

The breaking of the ice and the breathing in of the river imply a rebirth, a return to life that simultaneously necessitates the death of winter and the past, and ushers in something new, both topographically and culturally. In the context of the novel, young protagonist Matti witnesses Pajala, his small, isolated, and extremely peripheral northern town, swept into an increasingly globalized world, where rock and roll music enriches the lives of the younger residents and where dirt roads "disappear under a layer of oily black asphalt" (2000, 12) that connects Pajala's inhabitants to the Swedish welfare network. Thus, both Matti and Pajala come of age together, entering the wider Swedish society alongside each other. In its temporary liquid form, the asphalt itself is like the "black water" of the ruptured river, connecting, opening, and expanding the town.

Yet while they move and flow with a sense of progression and the thrill of the future, the blackness of the asphalt and the water indicates an opacity, a sense of uncertainty, which while certainly not presented as prescriptively pejorative can nevertheless indicate an element of fear of the unknown, and a sense of societal trepidation. It is this aspect of water, this uncertainty and unstoppability with the suggestion of danger, which fits so well within narratives of death and violence.

Death by Water in Swedish Crime Fiction

Taking Swedish crime novels as narratives of place, the central concern of this study is how death by water, a double meaning intended to express both proximity and (in some instances) cause, is used as a lens through which to explore change. Swedish crime fiction has seen an increase in the thematic representation of "the clash between traditional and national identities and the process of Europeanization and globalization" since the start of the twenty-first century (Bergman 2012, 57). Both Ekman's *Blackwater* and Mankell's *Faceless Killers* indicate that this preoccupation was in fact present toward the end of the twentieth century, as they tackle issues of social change through narratives that center around violent murder in seemingly gentle and rural places, where atrocity is not expected, and in which traditional Sweden comes face-to-face with modern Europe and the wider, globalized world. Ekman's and Mankell's explorations of death by water are akin to popular crime novels such as Camilla Läckberg's Fjällbacka series, set in the coastal village of the same name, and the first novel of Stieg Larsson's Millennium Trilogy, *The Girl with the Dragon Tattoo*, to which we now turn in order to consider how death by water can be linked with themes of concealment and escape, and by extension, change.

In Larsson's *The Girl with the Dragon Tattoo*, the dysfunctional and at times abhorrent Vanger family and their island home are central to the crime element of the novel. Of relevance is the use of water as the site of death, as it is off the shore of Hedeby Island where the serial killer Gottfried Vanger drowns, and it is the water where his son, Martin, disposes of the bodies of his female victims. As such, both Gottfried and Martin, the eponymous "men who hate women" (in the case of the Swedish title, *Män som hatar kvinnor*), intricately link death with water. In this sense, there is an element of purification, in both the drowning of the iniquitous and depraved Gottfried, as well as Martin's disposal of the murdered women, which could arguably be interpreted as washing away his crimes. Yet this is perhaps according Martin an undeserved sense of shame and guilt, which is not particularly manifest in Larsson's descriptions. A more appropriate analysis may be the link between water and concealment, with Martin taking advantage of its capacity to obscure and its ability to serve as an oblivion, hiding his crimes and enabling him to continue undetected: water, as Larsson's protagonist Mikael Blomkvist prophetically states, "can hide most things" (2005, 74), returning us to Peacock's assertion that the Swedish landscape is replete with "voids into which people can vanish" (2014, 105).

But water is also a means to freedom, as Niemi's novel suggested. It is by drowning her father and escaping from her brother across the bridge and over the water that the abused and traumatized Harriet Vanger is able to escape the past and flee toward the future. Like the black torrent of water in Pajala and the asphalt road, water can be a route to both change and progression, even when linked with death. Yet within Swedish crime novels, sites near water are also frequently presented as contact zones, where people not only meet but clash, often with violent consequences.

Changing Places and Contested Spaces

Death in *The Girl with the Dragon Tattoo* is an intimately familial matter, involving hereditary violence passed from father to son, with water providing a means of escape for Harriet. But change, water, and death can extend beyond the confines of violent families in Swedish crime fiction, being used instead to probe into wider sociological issues of changing places and contested spaces.

In Läckberg's novels, for instance, change occurs dramatically by the sea partially as a result of the shifting tide of people, with the steady transformation of the protagonist's familiar traditional fishing village into an unfamiliar tourist hotspot:

> Fishing has been Fjällbacka's livelihood for centuries. The unforgiving environment and the constant struggle to survive, when

everything depended on whether the herring came streaming back or not, had made the people of the town strong and rugged. Then Fjällbacka had become picturesque and began to attract tourists with fat wallets. [...] A many-headed monster that slowly, year by year, swallowed the old fishing village by buying up houses near the water, which created a ghost town for nine months of the year.

(Läckberg 2003, 7)

Fjällbacka is thus an example of not only a changing place but also, to a limited extent, a contested space. It is, to borrow again from Pratt, a contact zone, one in which the traditional and the modern, the locals and the outsiders, and the rural and the urban clash, with water representing different values, both economic and recreational. It is the presence of the sea, while unchanging itself, that heralds the transformation of the Swedish provincial landscape, a change prompted by its picturesque attraction to outsiders who buy up houses only to use them as holiday homes, turning Fjällbacka into a ghost town, one more related to death than life. This is reiterated by the presence of actual death, which serves as a metaphor for the demise of traditional Fjällbacka. As the setting for a crime series, the town not only becomes an architecturally and demographically altered place through the arrival of newcomers, but it is also the site where death occurs by water, with the use of murder coming to represent figuratively the death of traditional Swedish society. It is, after all, the protagonist's childhood friend who dies, a woman who is associated with the past, and thus her loss mirrors a nostalgia for times gone by, and for something that is irrevocably gone. Perhaps it also suggests what Jenny Andersson refers to as "a kind of nostalgia for a future lost" (2009, 238), with change not only serving to sever the past, but also more idyllic and even utopic notions of the future. Together, these combine to form a more pervasive sense of both transformation and, subsequently, loss, especially in the 1990s, when "depression and crisis" (2009, 229) came to characterize Sweden, and novels such as Kerstin Ekman's *Blackwater* arrived to explore the interstices of nostalgia, violence, and place.

Blackwater, as Jan Sjåvik asserts, is a successful postmodern integration of mystery and literary practice (2006, 56), but it is also an example of ecofiction (Dwyer 2010, 92) that transgresses genre boundaries (Forsås-Scott 1995, 78) and in which the wilderness is a "powerful presence" (Paterson 2010, 4). The novel is set in the fictional (and eponymous in the case of the English title) town of Blackwater, and begins with Annie Raft seeing her daughter with the man she erroneously believes committed a violent double murder on the banks of the river eighteen years earlier. This sight triggers an analepsis, through which the reader is transported back to the period just before the initial double murder, when Annie and her daughter Mia first arrive in Blackwater. The novel is permeated with a rich description of the landscape and also its transient nature, interlinked with notions of memory. Helena Forsås-Scott describes Ekman's literary landscape as one of "perpetual transformation [where] memories acquire a unique weight" (1995, 75). Memory is exemplified in the paths that cut through the forest, yet for Christopher Oscarson this is "not a simple romantic nostalgia or reactionary longing for an essentialized, lost, Edenic nature" (2010, 9), but is instead one that is collectively possessed, and which emerges from physical contact with an ever-changing landscape (2010, 9). This, as we shall see, is in contrast to Mankell's *Faceless Killers*, which consciously explores romanticization, nostalgia, and idyllic notions of the Sweden of yesteryear.

Although much emphasis has been placed on Ekman's preoccupation with the forest (Forsås-Scott 1995; Paterson 2008; Paterson and Ekman 2008), in *Blackwater* one of the central environmental features is the river, which bears witness to all three murders in the novel: the initial double murder of the tourists, and the eventual murder of Annie, all of whom, it should be noted, are outsiders, which raises questions of belonging. Ekman's river is both a site of permanence and transience, and while the river stays the same, as a primordial witness to the changing landscape and the communities that inhabit it, the people who visit it change. Forsås-Scott discusses Ekman's use of water as "forever transforming this landscape, undermining any familiar bearings" and in particular the ability of flowing water to "untiringly" modify and remodel (1995, 75). So, despite its permanence, here we find water explicitly linked with change and destabilization, characterizing the Swedish landscape and also a Nordic model of modernity that is inherently liquid (Stougaard-Nielsen 2017). The river attests to transformations to both the environment and society, the flow of life, and the progression into modernity and an increasingly globalized world where there are no longer any completely isolated and untouched places. This reaffirms the river's symbolic social nature and unstoppable capacity, which affects all people as discussed in relation to Niemi's *Popular Music from Vittula*, as change is inevitable.

The use of water as a site of death attests to the destruction inherent in change, as well as water's existing link with death, as discussed in relation to Larsson and Läckberg. Yet, as with Larsson's use of water in dealing with death, there is also an element of purification and iconoclasm in Ekman's novel: "The water kept bubbling under the ground, seeping through it and flowing over it in the spring light, dissolving everything done by human beings" (Ekman 1993, 251). Water thus has the ability to cleanse and remove any traces of human actions, a regeneration further compounded by the allusion to spring, the season of rebirth, regrowth, and rejuvenation. Through its role as an agent of change, the river has the dual capacity to wash away previous actions while symbolizing the ushering in of new times. Around the turn of the millennium, this wave of change involved increasing multiculturalism and globalization, and Sweden's response to these transitions is explored in Mankell's work.

In *Faceless Killers*, Mankell's readers are introduced to Kurt Wallander, an anxious and ambivalent senior police inspector who, despite his appeal, readers are not encouraged to admire (Nestingen 2008, 236), in large part due to his xenophobia and other flaws, such as alcoholism. The novel, and thus the series, begins when a farmer discovers that his elderly neighbors have been brutally tortured, one of them violently murdered and the other near death. Later, the dying elderly lady, who through her age, ethnicity, connection to the land, and rural lifestyle is symbolic of traditional Sweden, provides the clue that the perpetrators may be "foreign," and thus symbolic of the new and globalized Sweden, one that, in this case, has threatened the traditional way of life. This results in the attack becoming the catalyst for a novel that explores the effects of racism and contested spaces. The elderly lady does not provide any suggestion as to where her attackers were from, but simply indicates their otherness. While it transpires that they were in fact immigrants from Eastern Europe, they become through the collective category of "foreign" the eponymous "faceless killers," in that they are invisible in their alterity. Simultaneously, however, they are highly conspicuous in that they come to be found, to the fearful and xenophobic characters in the novel, in the faces of every immigrant, which results in a Somalian man who is completely unrelated to the original crime being killed in retaliation.

Faceless Killers is set in a place where different cultures encounter one another, similar to Pratt's contact zone, a "social space where disparate cultures meet, clash, and grapple with each other" (1992, 7). Unlike Ekman's *Blackwater*, where the grappling cultures are generational and regional, or in Läckberg's *The Ice Princess*, where they are urban or rural, in Mankell's novel the emphasis is shifted to a globalized Sweden, with immigration and racism playing key roles. The belief that the murderers are foreign ultimately leads to more racially motivated murder, creating a cycle of violence as a response to and rejection of change. As such, the novel explores globalized change in Sweden since, as Andrew Nestingen asserts, Mankell has gone to great lengths to "impute to Wallander antisocial and racist attitudes" (2008, 249–50). Thus, the protagonist is not the voice of reason, but rather a reflection of Sweden's ambivalence to and uncertainty about immigration and change; in this sense, Wallander personifies a more conservative, traditionalist Sweden.

As with *Blackwater*, Mankell's novel is permeated by nostalgia, although the author chooses to illuminate the romanticization of an idyllic Swedish past, "a lost paradise" (Mankell 1991, 246) and an imaginary utopia, one where things were simple, especially in relation to notions of who belongs and who does not. Stougaard-Nielsen reminds us that a fixation in Swedish crime fiction on the threat to a sense of the rural idyll can be found as early as the 1950s in the work of Maria Lang, whose novels shaped the genre's "preoccupation with the idyllic spatio-temporal (dis)location" of traditional and rural Swedish spaces (2017, 120). The Swedish landscape and nature in general have long been linked in Sweden with a sense of national identity, with Mikael Ahlund observing that the "method of turning nature into an instrument for a national self-assertion" was a recurrent theme in the topographical literature of the last few decades of the eighteenth century (2016, n.p.). Wallander, as an unreliable and out-of-touch narrator, is preoccupied with this lost ideal, and muses that even crime was better in the past, reminiscing about "car thieves and safe crackers of the old days, who doffed their caps and behaved like gentlemen when we came to take them in. But those days have irretrievably vanished" (Mankell 1991, 246–47). Yet even Wallander, while ruminating about such courteous and gentlemanly criminals, is aware that perhaps such memory is unreliable, and acknowledges that he is uncertain whether those days "were as idyllic as we remember them" (1991, 247).

As with Ekman and Läckberg's novels, water is the agent of change in Wallander's world. In *Faceless Killers*, the focus is on the Baltic Sea that borders the coastal town of Ystad in which the novel is set. It is the sea and its port that provide a route for immigration and globalization, opening up Sweden's borders and serving as a link with the outside world rather than as a barrier. In this sense, the water of the Baltic Sea is not only symbolic of change, but also contributes to its facilitation. Mankell keeps the concept of change close to the surface in the text, presenting it as a frequent consideration and concern of his protagonist. The narrator states that "it again occurred to Wallander that a change was taking place in Sweden" (1991, 268). Kerstin Bergman discusses the effect that the European Union's expansion has had on many nation-states' sense of stability, with many feeling threatened and suffering from identity crises (2012, 57). Sweden joined the Union in 1995, resulting in concerns during that decade and into the twenty-first century surrounding immigration from other member states, with increased multiculturalism deemed by some to be a threat to Swedish cultural uniqueness and "the values of Nordic modernity" (Andersson 2009, 240). This is largely the result of Sweden's long held notion of a racial homogeneity, and despite this "purity" being unlikely even in the early years of the twentieth century (Mattson 2014, 322), it has and continues to hold currency.

Read in this light, the violent deaths in *Faceless Killers* can be seen as representative of xenophobia and fear in the face of inevitable change. While reminiscent of Niemi's unstoppable river and the powerful emotions that change brings to the surface in people and society, in Mankell's novel the uncertainty surrounding change is taken to an extreme. Literary violence is thus a hyperbolic expression of cultural anxieties. Motivated by a fear of change, xenophobic responses also prompt transformations, as when racism and fear of the other become societal rather than individual problems, spaces are given new meaning and become places where atrocities happen.

Stagnant Water and Resisted Transitions

Throughout some of the novels discussed in this chapter, dark, black, or muddy waters are frequently found. Niemi refers to the melting river as a "torrent of black water" (2000, 109), perhaps attesting to the inability of knowing what such change will yield. Black water implies depth as well as opacity, and it is this obscurity that suggests, particularly in relation to the town of Blackwater in Ekman's novel, a hidden, sinister, and dark side to humanity, with multiple instances of violence occurring. Yet in *Faceless Killers*, Mankell takes the notion of opacity even further by using mud as the site of death.

After it is made public that "foreigners" may be responsible for the death of the elderly farming couple, an uninvolved Somalian refugee becomes the victim of a revenge crime. The fact that he is shot in the head at point-blank range in retaliation for the original murder is arguably a commentary designed to highlight not only the atrocity of racially motivated violence, but also the erroneous assumption of the homogeneous status of the putative other, in that a Somalian man comes to stand for all that is "foreign." Yet what is of interest to this analysis is that after being murdered while out for a walk, the man is found face down in the mud. The positioning of the body in what is essentially dirty water, stagnant in its motionlessness, invites a Douglasian reading: the dirt and impurity in which the Somalian man lies indicate that he is seen as exterior to Swedish notions of homogeneity, positioned as what Mary Douglas termed "matter out of place" (1966, 44).

Further, rather than being symbolic of change, mud as dirty water represents a lack of clarity and thus a myopic perspective, one in keeping with xenophobic responses to immigration. The mud is symbolically linked with a racist and right-wing aspect of Swedish culture, one that fears globalization and immigration and which has deep roots in the rhetoric of neo-Nazism (Bergmann 2017, 23). It is of note that Mankell's first novel was published in 1991, the same year that the New Democrats became the first right-wing populist party to find success and "pass the threshold into the Swedish parliament" (Bergmann 2017, 171). In *Faceless Killers*, such xenophobia results in the senseless and brutal murder of a man who comes to signify for the murderer everything that is foreign and thus not Swedish. The shotgun blast obliterates most of the Somalian man's head, removing his identity and making him, like the killers of the elderly farming couple, simply a faceless other. He is no longer a man but is rather a foreigner, face down and obscured by both the violence of the shot and the stagnant shroud of mud in which he lies.

Thus, when immobile and lacking clarity, water can be interpreted as a metaphor for a resistance to change. Whereas opaque water itself does not imply this resistance, instead alluding to uncertainty, when coupled with stagnation it presents a very interesting opposite to the flowing river of change described by Niemi. Further, the fusion of earth and water into something entirely new brings us back to the contact zone and a sense of contestation over space, further highlighting perceptions of who belongs and who does not.

Conclusion

Swedish crime novels provide the valuable opportunity to explore narratives of place, ones in which the settings of the texts enrich the work through an atmospheric and evocative portrayal of watery landscapes. They have the ability to provide a topographical depiction of Sweden, evoking an environment that has long been associated with a sense of national identity. Yet beyond reading such novels as examples of, to varying extents, ecofiction, water also has the capacity, especially when the site of death, to reveal pressing sociological concerns and issues to do with immigration and globalization.

Such concerns, as novels like *Faceless Killers*, *Blackwater*, and *The Ice Princess* reveal, are often intimately linked with a nostalgia, not only for the past but also for the future, a utopian ideal that is perceived to have been a natural progression from the romanticized and traditional past but that has, as a result of modernity, been lost. All change, inevitably and by its very definition, comes with a price: the old way is gone, and something new and uncertain arrives. Watery places such as rivers and the sea can be witness to such transformative events, remaining natural and physical presences despite the socioeconomic fluctuations that occur around them, but can also serve as the agents of change, bridging the land and uniting disparate peoples. In this sense, water creates contact zones, places where people meet and negotiate their shared space, often with a reactionary hostility and aggression at the perceived threat to national identity. Yet such contested spaces also provide opportunities, something that crime novels do not overlook, as the implication is that violence is not the inevitable outcome of contact zones. Instead, water's liquid nature attests to the "fluid, fast-paced globalizing world" (Stougaard-Nielsen 2017, 16) in which we live, and reveals metaphorically that society is a moving, shifting entity.

Works Cited

Ahlund, Mikael. 2016. "Topography, Iron-Making and National Identity in the 18th Century – A British-Swedish Comparison." Accessed January 15, 2018. www.bl.uk/picturing-places/articles/topography-iron-making-and-national-identity-in-the-18th-century-a-british-swedish-comparison.

Andersson, Jenny. 2009. "Nordic Nostalgia and Nordic Light: The Swedish Model as Utopia 1930–2007." *Scandinavian Journal of History* 34 (3): 229–45.

Bergman, Kerstin. 2012. "Initiating a European Turn in Swedish Crime Fiction: Negotiation of European and National Identities in Mankell's *The Troubled Man*." *Scandinavica* 51 (1): 56–78.

Bergmann, Eirikur. 2017. *Nordic Nationalism and Right-Wing Populist Politics: Imperial Relationships and National Sentiments*. London: Palgrave Macmillan.

Douglas, Mary. 1966. *Purity and Danger: An Analysis of Concepts of Pollution and Taboo*. Abingdon: Routledge.

Dwyer, Jim. 2010. *Where the Wild Books Are: A Field Guide to Ecofiction*. Reno, NV: University of Nevada Press.

Ekman, Kerstin. 1993. *Blackwater*. London: Vintage.

Forshaw, Barry. 2012. *Death in a Cold Climate: A Guide to Scandinavian Crime Fiction*. Basingstoke: Palgrave Macmillan.

Forsås-Scott, Helena. 1995. "Stories in a Changing Landscape: Kerstin Ekman's Latest Novel." *Swedish Book Review* Suppl.: 74–78.

Läckberg, Camilla. 2003. *The Ice Princess*. London: Harper Collins.

Larsson, Stieg. 2005. *The Girl with the Dragon Tattoo*. London: Quercus.

Mankell, Henning. 1991. *Faceless Killers*. London: Vintage.

Mattson, Greggor. 2014. "Nation-State Science: Lappology and Sweden's Ethnoracial Purity." *Comparative Studies in Society and History* 56 (2): 320–50.

Nestingen, Andrew. 2008. "The Burned Out Policeman: Henning Mankell's Transnational Police Procedural." *Crime and Fantasy in Scandinavia: Fiction, Film and Social Change*. Seattle: University of Washington Press, 233–64.

Nestingen, Andrew, and Paula Arvas (eds.). 2011. *Scandinavian Crime Fiction*. Cardiff: University of Wales Press.

Niemi, Mikael. 2000. *Popular Music from Vittula*. London: Flamingo.

Oscarson, Christopher. 2010. "Where the Ground Answers the Foot: Kerstin Ekman, Ecology, and the Sense of Place in a Globalized World." *Ecozone* 1 (2): 8–21.

Paterson, Anna. 2008. "Landscapes Remembered: Kerstin Ekman and Nature." *World Literature Today* 82 (4): 40–42.

——— 2010. "Kerstin Ekman and Swedish crime." *Swedish Book Review* 1: 3–9.

Paterson, Anna, and Kerstin Ekman. 2008. "Mistress of the forest: An interview with Kerstin Ekman." *World Literature Today* 82 (4): 43–46.

Peacock, Steven. 2014. *Swedish Crime Fiction: Novel, Film, Television*. Manchester: Manchester University Press.

Pratt, Mary Louise. 1992. *Imperial Eyes: Travel Writing and Transculturation*. Abingdon and New York: Routledge.

Sjåvik, Jan. 2006. *Historical Dictionary of Scandinavian Literature and Theater*. Lanham and Oxford: Scarecrow Press.

Sjöwall, Maj, and Per Wahlöö. 1965. *Roseanna*. London: Fourth Estate.

Stougaard-Nielsen, Jakob. 2017. *Scandinavian Crime Fiction*. London: Bloomsbury.

Index